Kenneth Strickfaden,
Dr. Frankenstein's Electrician

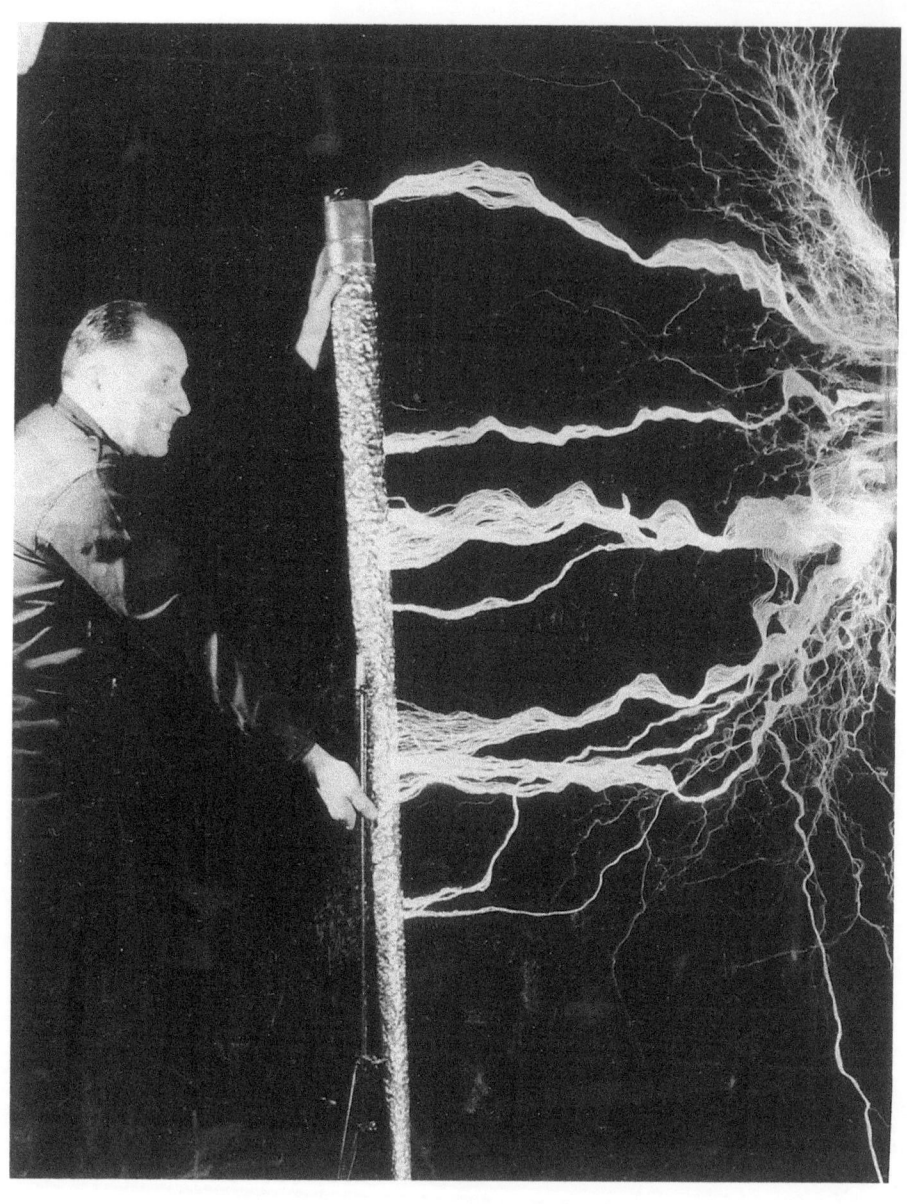

Kenneth J. Strickfaden performing a high voltage feat
with the "Megavolt Senior" Tesla coil,
as he had demonstrated in numerous lectures.
He is believed to have been involved
with more than 100 film and television productions.

Kenneth Strickfaden, Dr. Frankenstein's Electrician

HARRY GOLDMAN
Foreword by Ed Angell

McFarland & Company, Inc., Publishers
Jefferson, North Carolina, and London

LIBRARY OF CONGRESS CATALOGUING-IN-PUBLICATION DATA

Goldman, Harry, 1923–
    Kenneth Strickfaden, Dr. Frankenstein's electrician / Harry Goldman ; foreword by Ed Angell.
        p.   cm.
    Includes bibliographical references and index.

    ISBN-13: 978-0-7864-2064-3
    softcover : 50# alkaline paper ∞

    1. Strickfaden, Kenneth. 2. Cinematographers — United States — Biography. 3. Cinematography — Special effects. I. Title.
    TR849.S87G65   2005
    778.5'345 — dc22   2005022636

British Library cataloguing data are available

©2005 Harry Goldman. All rights reserved

No part of this book may be reproduced or transmitted in any form or by any means, electronic or mechanical, including photocopying or recording, or by any information storage and retrieval system, without permission in writing from the publisher.

On the cover: Kenneth Strickfaden in the 1960s; background ©2005 Photodisc

Manufactured in the United States of America

McFarland & Company, Inc., Publishers
   Box 611, Jefferson, North Carolina 28640
   www.mcfarlandpub.com

Dedication

This book is dedicated to the memory of John O. Foster and Richard G. Aurandt.

John O. Foster was a high school student when he first experienced a Kenneth Strickfaden lecture. Young Foster was so overwhelmed that he developed a burning desire to meet Strickfaden. John and Ken developed a friendship that continued unabated until Strickfaden's passing in 1984.

After attending El Camino College, John went to work for the Los Angeles school system. When his 30-year career had come to an end, Foster had been serving as Director of Maintenance while overseeing 80 of the district's schools. He also taught classes at Los Angeles City College.

Throughout the years, John assisted friend Ken Strickfaden in numerous lecture demonstrations. After his retirement from the L.A. school system, John and Ken became a permanent duo of fun-loving lecturers.

Foster was a skilled technician with an expertise in electricity and mechanics. He displayed an affection for precision scientific instruments and high voltage apparatus. John and Lois Foster became attentive to Ken Strickfaden's welfare during the latter's critical and final years.

John O. Foster (1919–1993).

Richard Aurandt was also a high school student when he attended his first Strickfaden lecture. Dick was so affected by the experience that he decided to pursue a career in the electrical sciences. It was the striking performance of Strickfaden's high voltage electrical apparatus that influenced young Aurandt to delve into what was to become a lifelong investigation into the mysteries of the Tesla coil. Dick formed a close friendship with Ken and often assisted the master electrician during lecture tours. Richard later found similar employment with the Moody Institute of Science under the direction of Dr. Irwin Moon. Both experiences gave the young experimenter ample opportunities for investigating high voltage apparatus.

Richard Aurandt, John Foster, Ed Angell and others fortunate enough to be counted among Strickfaden's friends established a small but cohesive group of electrical wizards. Several had later gone on to provide special electrical effects for the motion picture industry. One of the films for which Dick provided electrical effects was *The Entity* (1983).

Richard G. Aurandt
(1934–1991).

Friends of Aurandt who were familiar with his life's activities often referred to him as the "ultimate collector." Dick's cache of artifacts included player pianos, Hamilton-Beech blenders, Hoover vacuum cleaners, Singer sewing machines, mechanical writing and calculating machines, motors and a variety of high voltage devices. Dick loved cats and had been caring for 20 felines prior to his passing.

Richard served in the aerospace industry for more than 25 years. He had been a Senior Assistant Technician with the Aerospace Corporation in El Segundo, California. He earned a U.S. patent for a process to bond thermocouples in a vacuum using the high frequency discharge of a Tesla coil.

Acknowledgments

In the writing of this book, I relied heavily upon the assistance of the following (listed in alphabetical order):

Edward and Janice Angell, close friends to Kenneth Strickfaden, who supplied materials and information regarding Ken's career and their own personal relationship with him. I am also grateful to Ed and Jan for reviewing the original manuscript.

Mrs. John (Lois) Foster, without whose cooperation this book would not have materialized. I am greatly indebted to Lois for allowing me the privilege of examining Ken Strickfaden's notes, photos, and personal papers and using several materials in this book. Mrs. Foster's reminiscences of the special friendship between Ken and the Foster family were especially enlightening.

Mrs. Marilyn S. Throssel, Ken Strickfaden's surviving daughter. I am beholden to Mrs. Throssel for providing information relating to the Strickfaden family history and for the loan of photos and family papers. I am also indebted to Mrs. Throssel for her critical review of the original manuscript.

Others who provided valuable assistance are Elayne Alexander, President of the Venice Historical Society; Leland I. Anderson; Gene Arntzen; Edward Aronson; Peter Barvoets of the Begley Library, Schenectady County Community College, New York; Margaret Cheney; *Classic Images*; Steve Cole; Crandall Library, Glens Falls, New York; Facets Multimedia; George Fogelson; Lawrence Geddie; Ray Harryhausen; Ralph E. Hedges; Sharon Al Jarrah; Steve Karkus, Lightning Effects, Inc.; JoAnne F. Keller; Kathryn Kornaus; Ellen R. Kufeld, Curator, the Bakken

Museum, Minneapolis, Minnesota; Gary Landis; Cynni Murphy, Archivist, the Santa Monica Public Library, California; The Museum of Modern Art, New York; Doug Norwine; Jennifer Oyama, the Santa Monica Public Library, California; Kenneth Perry; Susan S. Salancy; John Schultz, Chico (California) VFW Post #1555; Jeffery Stanton; Betty B. Stoutenberg; Pamela Strickfaden; Mary F. Taylor; Dee F. Vandercook; and William C. Wysock.

I am also obligated to the following for supplying information and materials relating to Ken Strickfaden's birthplace: Colleen Ferguson of the Hearst Free Library, Anaconda, Montana; Carol Gilluly, Clerk of the Commission Deer Lodge County, Montana; Jerry Hansen, Curator, Anaconda Deer Lodge County Historical Society.

Those who assisted in my search for information and photos relating to the Paul Whiteman Orchestra are Ray Avery; Sylvia Brown, Special Collections Library, Williams College, Williamstown, Massachusetts; Robert Grafton; Linda Hall, Archives Assistant, Williams College, Massachusetts; Mark Rosenblum; and Duncan Scheidt.

I am particularly indebted to my wife, Ruth, for her painstaking examination of dusty and dimly lit bookshelves in various libraries and book shops while searching for information pertinent to this book. I also owe a debt of gratitude to Ruth's supervisors at the Genpak Corporation in Glens Falls, New York, for allowing her to surf the Internet during non-business hours.

Table of Contents

Acknowledgments vii
Foreword by Ed Angell 1
Preface 3

1. Where Have We Met Before? 7
2. For Unto Us a Wizard Is Born 12
3. The Road Taken 22
4. From the Halls of Montezuma... 29
5. California, Here I Come! 36
6. Dr. Frankenstein's Electrician 42
7. The Man Who Doubled for Boris Karloff 53
8. On the, Road Again — and Again 61
9. The Tesla Coil Connection 74
10. "I Could Have Retired a Millionaire..." 84
11. The Last Frankenstein Picture Show 89
12. "We Had a Ball!" 96
13. No Ordinary Man! 109
14. Notes from Charles, the "Littler" One 121
15. "Re-Memories" (of Early Santa Monica) 132
16. Saying Goodbye to Mr. Electric 138
17. A Sampling of Mad Scientist Films 142
18. The Strickfaden Legacy 150
19. A Final Word 154

Appendix A. Photographica   158
Appendix B. Technical Notes and Sketches   168
Appendix C. Miscellaneous Illustrations   184
Appendix D. Film and Television Chronology   199
Selected Bibliography   205
Index   209

Foreword by Ed Angell

This book is a tribute to two passions. The first is Ken Strickfaden's lifelong romance with electricity. The second is the author's quest to honor Ken for his importance to both the film industry and to his fellow electrical experimenters. It is dismaying that individuals such as Nikola Tesla and Ken Strickfaden would fall into relative obscurity if it were not for the efforts of people like Harry Goldman. Having been involved in a failed attempt to get an oral history from Ken in the early 1980s, I applaud Harry for all the information that he was able to assemble on such a personally private individual.

Had the author and Ken not met some 50 years ago during a school assembly, we might not have been afforded this look into the life and development of a truly creative genius. I like to think the initial spark that inspired the author to form the Tesla Coil Builders' Association was born at one of Ken's early science demonstrations.

Like so many artists, Ken Strickfaden contributed more to the film industry than he was ever credited for. Many of Ken's ideas are the basis for many visual and audio effects that we enjoy today. As contemporary electrical experimenters, we have both learned and prospered from the Strickfaden legacy. I am very certain that fame and fortune were the last things on Ken's mind over the long span of his career. And I am just as sure that he was having the time of his life while doing what he enjoyed the most.

I was privileged to be part of Ken's group of friends. I fondly remember how he held court and with great joy and enthusiasm discussed his early film projects. Among the highlights of any meeting at Ken's house were the live demonstrations conducted by the master showman. If you are interested in this book, I'm sure that you have seen a number of the film productions attributed to Ken and can imagine what the cast and crew must have thought at seeing his special effects for the first time.

Ken's legacy is the excitement he brought to literally millions of people over the course of his career. That legacy extends well into the future. I sincerely hope that Ken Strickfaden will be remembered by future generations. After all, he was the beginning of the spectacular special effects of today.

Preface

Electrical Illusionations
— The Kenneth Strickfaden notebook

Special effects in motion pictures and television, both dangerously real and illusionary, have reached a peak of perfection. So talented are today's special effects technicians that when viewing their work, it becomes difficult to separate the real from the unreal. However, the present miracles seen in motion pictures and television are not the result of spontaneous generation. That is, they did not suddenly appear out of the blue but resulted from a long and protracted evolvement. Illusionary effects can be traced back to the early magicians and court performers who perfected their craft first in the streets and later on the stage. It is only natural that special illusionary effects would move to the screen when motion pictures arrived.

Every era of motion picture and television history has had its innovative geniuses. During the transition years when silents were being replaced by sound films, there appeared on the scene a fabulously talented character by the name of Kenneth Joseph Strickfaden. It was Strickfaden who created the mad scientist and science fiction apparatus that entertained, thrilled and frightened us in more than 100 motion picture films and television programs such as *Frankenstein* (1931), *The Wizard of Oz* (1939) and the television series *The Munsters*. In addition to his behind-the-scenes movie work, Strickfaden presented some 1,500 traveling lectures on the physical sciences which proved to be both highly educational and hilariously entertaining.

Admittedly, the text of this story is far from complete. The primary reason for this is due to the fact that Kenny Strickfaden left us little information about his personal and professional life. But even if he were still alive, there are no guarantees that he would cooperate in an undertaking such as this. Strickfaden's surviving friends can tell you that getting the man to talk about himself was far more difficult than pulling an impacted wisdom tooth. As an example of his unassuming character, Ken politely declined an offer from Ed and Janice Angell, two very close friends, to record an oral history of his life and career. On the other hand, the wizard would be more than accommodating when anyone showed an interest in his electrical paraphernalia. Strickfaden was a born teacher who loved to explain and demonstrate the scientific principles upon which his machines functioned.

Another explanation for the brevity of this text is that those who knew Kenny, and might have been able to supply personal information about the man, had either passed on, could not be located, or were unknown to me. Of the Strickfaden friends I managed to locate, only a small number agreed to participate. Lastly, there is very little reference material available on Ken's life. Most of the published data on the electrician is limited to his special effects work. But even that information is narrow and repetitious.

This was not the first book intended on Strickfaden's behalf. The master electrician was once approached by an author who proposed writing his biography. Strickfaden loaned the would-be biographer a substantial quantity of personal material. Unfortunately, the project never materialized and Strickfaden's attempts to retrieve his property were without success. After Strickfaden's passing, friends and associates made similar attempts to reclaim the collection. Their passionate pleas fell upon inattentive ears.

I regret that a book of this nature has been so long overdue. But a book that is both short and late is better than no book at all. Nevertheless, lost to us are the many anecdotes that might have been revealed regarding Strickfaden's experiences with Hollywood and its personnel. Think of the effect created by Strickfaden's lightning when unleashed in the presence of unsuspecting participants filming a scene.

What the reader will find here is the result of sifting through Strickfaden's personal notes, news clippings and photos, and valuable information obtained from his few surviving friends and family members.

What the reader will not find is a tell-all Hollywood exposé. Readers of this book should look elsewhere if anticipating such Tinseltown stories as adultery, alcoholism, homosexuality, murder, betrayal, and other immoral activities so closely tied to Hollywood history. This writer is not a Hollywood historian or film analyst. But even if such traits were part-and-parcel of the author's expertise, Hollywood would not be the theme of this book. The subject, you see, was not a Hollywood figure nor did he live a Hollywood lifestyle. Kenneth Strickfaden embraced Methodism and dedicated his life to God, family, country and fellow man.

1

Where Have We Met Before?

Electrescence and Auratronics
— The Kenneth Strickfaden notebook

Back in the autumn of 1950, Ken Strickfaden and I were in the same auditorium for a period of 60 minutes. He had been hired by the New York State Department of Education to present a series of science lectures at the local schools. Strickfaden's program was not only fascinating to watch but also an experience of humorous delight. That, however, was long before I learned of his illustrious affiliation with the motion picture industry. Not until several years had passed was I able to grasp the significance of the occasion as well as the opportunity lost.

When this writer began publishing the Tesla Coil Builders' Association newsletter *TCBA News*, Ken Strickfaden was selected to be our first honorary member. Ken demonstrated a keen interest in the publication and often contributed valuable tips for the benefit of our subscribers. When he received requests for information about Tesla coils from junior electro-scientists, Ken would recommend that they contact "Harry Goldman at the TCBA." One of my fondest possessions is a flyer advertising a Strickfaden lecture program on which he had written the memo "Harry Goldman — success to you in your TCBA project — Ken Strickfaden."

As a matter of fact, Ken Strickfaden affected my life even earlier, in the '30s, when my baby-sitting teen-aged sister dragged me along to see a film called *Frankenstein* (1931). I was but eight years of age at the time.

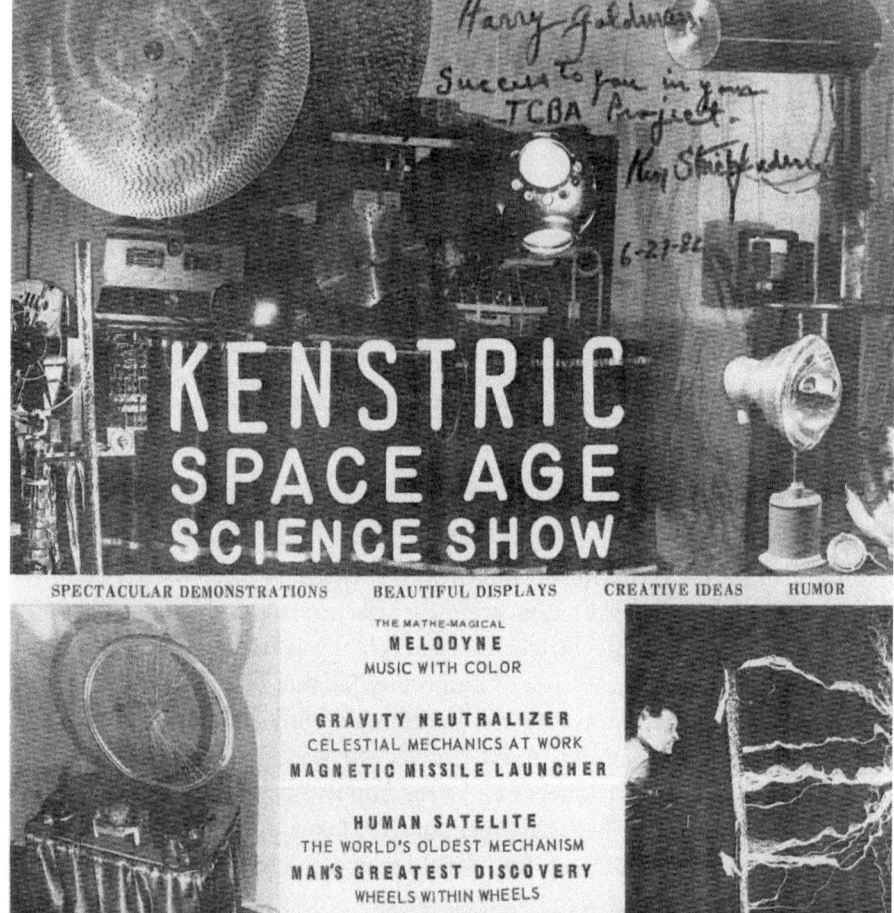

One of the many flyers advertising Strickfaden's lectures. This remains one of the possessions the author is most fond of.

The theater was only a ten-minute walk from home, less when we kids dared to take the shortcut through the back wood lot. Taking that route, however, required running a gantlet of hoboes who used the area as a campsite. The wood lot was within a stone's throw of our backyard so it was not uncommon to find a weary traveler at the rear door begging for a handout. Those were the years of the Great Depression, an era during which food in our home was rarely abundant. Nevertheless, sandwiches of bread and butter or mother's raspberry jam were appreciatively accepted by the hoboes.

Watching *Frankenstein* was a terrifying experience. The thunder and lightning created by the mad doctor's electrical apparatus were more than I could bear. I recall crouching down with eyes closed and ears covered while anxiously waiting for Henry Frankenstein's astonishing experiment to end. To my dismay, I prematurely raised my head in time to see the Monster move and hear Frankenstein make the declaration with which the film will be forever associated: "*It's alive!*" At that moment I came to the realization that my urinary bladder had released its contents. I suspect my sister was similarly victimized but she would never admit to it. Although the event occurred some seven decades ago, I am unable to view the 1931 classic without recalling that traumatic childhood experience.

Darkness was approaching when we left the theater so my sister and I began a slow trot toward home. The reader will be correct in assuming that we did not take the shortcut through the woods. From time to time we would glance back to make sure the Frankenstein Monster was not on our trail. Our trot accelerated to a full-fledged sprint as we approached the poorly lighted section of town. I hardly slept that night, fully expecting the Monster to appear at my upstairs bedroom window. Of the many thoughts racing through my mind, writing this tribute to the man whose machines brought life to Frankenstein's creation was not one of them. Life often presents strange twists and turns.

The above detailed scenario was once described in a TCBA newsletter. Strickfaden saw it and conveyed an appraisal to friend John Foster. I was later informed that Ken looked upon my childhood memory with "utmost affection."

The Frankenstein experience was 18 years in the distant past when I began teaching school in upstate New York. The first assembly program was scheduled for the third week of school. On stage was an array of electrical apparatus reminiscent of the mad scientist machines seen in

A configuration of electrical apparatus in readiness for a performance. The scene is reminiscent of a Ken Strickfaden lecture delivered before the author's students during the autumn of 1950.

the science fiction and horror movies of the 1930s. The narrator, a Mr. Strickfaden, retained a firm grip on our attention throughout the lecture. The program consisted of such demonstrations as musical wheels, roaring lightning-like bolts of electricity, strange lights that oscillated from dim to bright and then back again to dim, and eerie sparks that ascended into the air—all of which were accompanied by the pungent odor of ozone gas. The scene presented an atmosphere of impending doom.

One of the most captivating demonstrations occurred when Mr. Strickfaden held an unconnected light bulb in his hand and brought it to full brilliance. That we were mesmerized by the magical feat was plainly evident in the sighs and gasps emanating from the student audience. But the real show-stopper took place as the wizard held arms overhead while sparks 20–24 inches in length leaped from the performer's fingertips. The shrieks pouring forth from the hysterical audience were deafening.

It was not until years later, when watching a 1930s mad scientist movie on television, did I come to the realization that the Mr. Strickfaden seen during my early teaching years turned out to be the same person whose name appeared among the film's credits. At long last, I had finally come to recognize the man about whom this book is written.

Commentary

I have often wondered how *Frankenstein* affected the young people who later watched it on a small television screen in the comfort of a well-lighted living room among family, friends and the family pet; with refreshments in hand and the option of changing channels or retreating to a more comfortable environment in the home (bedroom, playroom, etc.)?

I, on the other hand, at the age of eight (nearly nine), watched the film on a bigger than life screen in a large dark room and surrounded by strangers. The only alternative available to me was to run from the theater to the darkened street where the Monster might be hiding behind trees, alleys, etc. I was sure that the Monster would do to me what he did to that nice little girl. Yes, dear readers, there *are* varying degrees of fear.

2

For Unto Us a Wizard Is Born

Teacher: Unsung hero
— The Kenneth Strickfaden Notebook

George Peter Strickfaden of Bavaria did not approve of his country's continuous military involvements. A pacifist, George chose not to answer the call to arms. In 1849, Strickfaden left his native land and emigrated to the United States of America. He settled in the Indiana town of Saint Leon, an area inhabited by fellow German immigrants. It was in Saint Leon where George was able to successfully continue his trade as a harness maker. Strickfaden married a kindly woman who, in 1855, delivered a son christened Francis (Frank) Joseph Strickfaden. Frank's mother passed away during his twelfth year. George Strickfaden remarried but there was much friction between Frank and his stepmother. The rebellious youngster found the situation intolerable and left home. Frank was but 14 years of age at the time of departure.

Young Strickfaden had been impressed by the narratives describing the lives and adventures of the "forty-niners," a title given to the participants in the great California gold rush of 1849. He determined that there was a future for him in mining precious metals. Frank made his way to Colorado where he secured a job in the gold and silver mining industry. However, he soon came to the realization that digging for gold was not only physically exhausting but that the mine owners, not the mine employees, were the ones getting rich. Frank left the mines and obtained a job driving a team of horses as a hauler of merchandise and wares. It

2 — For Unto Us a Wizard Is Born

appears that he possessed a good sense of business. When traveling to town for supplies, Frank would cash the miner's checks and fill their shopping needs. A small fee was charged for the service. He made enough money at this, and other business ventures, to afford the purchase of real property. Young Strickfaden foresaw the financial opportunities in buying and selling land so he decided to establish a commercial realty and insurance enterprise. Frank J. Strickfaden had, at last, found his niche in life and would continue as a realty and insurance broker until his passing.

In 1889, Frank moved the business to Butte, Montana. While pursuing business matters in Butte and nearby Anaconda, Frank met a charming young lady by the name of Nancy Creek. The courtship led to a Catholic church wedding in Anaconda that same year.

Anaconda was founded by Marcus Daly in 1883. In the days of the forty-niners, the area had been a paradise for Native Americans, buffalo, hunters, trappers, traders and so on. The discovery of gold brought a stampede of miners, doctors, lawyers, teachers and adventure seekers from all walks of life. The Anaconda Company was formed for the purpose of reducing the ores being hauled in from nearby Butte. Copper smelting was the dominant industry while zinc, lead, silver and gold were byproducts of the operations. In addition to Anaconda's overwhelming scenery, the area offered an abundance of wildlife and fertile soils, as well as endless open spaces. There were also great quantities of fresh water, timber and other precious metals. The Butte, Anaconda & Pacific Railway (BA&P) and other lines served the area's diverse transportation requirements.

Although small in population, Anaconda was a community bustling with activity. In addition to the commercial opportunities offered, the community boasted fine hotels (some lighted by electricity), excellent library resources, an innovative school system, rail transportation and other conveniences. The low rate of unemployment and the abundance of land available for development enticed Frank and Nan to choose Anaconda to be the new site for home and commerce. He and Nan established a residence in a large dwelling located at 502 Cherry Street.

On August 14, 1891, Nancy Strickfaden gave birth to a baby girl. The infant did not survive the first day of her life. The Strickfadens suffered a similar tragedy on July 20, 1892. Their second child was a boy. The mental suffering caused by these family events did not deter the

The Strickfaden home at 502 Cherry Street in Anaconda, Montana, as it appears today. The external dimensions have changed little since the family occupied the building as a residence in the 1890s (courtesy of Marilyn S. Throssel).

Strickfadens' resolve to raise a family. On May 26, 1894, Nancy Strickfaden presented her husband a boy to be named Frank Louis Strickfaden. And on May 23, 1896, just three days shy of Frank Louis' second birthday, Kenneth Joseph Strickfaden became a member of the family. A third son, Charles Grayson Strickfaden, was born on June 1, 1900. All three of the Strickfaden boys received their early education in Anaconda's Public School District #10. In 1902, the family moved into a smaller dwelling located just around the corner at 209 East 5th Street.

In 1908, the Strickfadens moved from Anaconda to Ashland, Oregon. The new setting was located on a large tract of land which included a fruit orchard. In addition to the responsibility of cultivating and harvesting crops, the boys shared the duty of overseeing the needs of a small stock of farm animals. This introduction to the rigors of country living greatly broadened Kenny's appreciation for the natural environment. The boy made frequent trips afield and became convinced that he could hear the everpresent forest breezes whispering his name. Young Strickfaden's

2 — For Unto Us a Wizard Is Born

In 1902, the Strickfadens moved to a dwelling located behind the Cherry Street residence at 209 East 5th Street. Both homes continue to be occupied as private residences (courtesy of Marilyn S. Throssel).

encounters with wild animal species offered a perspective as to the beauty of nature that no school text or nature magazine could provide. He gained notoriety among the locals as a boy who kept a menagerie of creatures under care. Owls were among Ken's favorite wild animal pets. He once had raised six owlets that he and friends had scooped out of a cliff-mounted nest. Other critters with whom Kenny had made friends were raccoons, rodents, amphibians and reptiles. Some of the clientele at Strickfaden's wildlife hotel had been found in an injured state as a result of both natural forces and man's inhumane acts. Unfortunately, Ken's files contained no photographic records of his zoological experiences.

Because Kenny was now living a fully involved daily routine, it seems that he would have had little time for taking on new interests. Be that as it may, it is a fact that his infatuation with electricity emerged during this period of life. The following entry in Ken's childhood notes (ca. 1909) reveal the moment: "My first electric shop in dad's apple cellar." It is unclear as to what environmental force steered the lad in this direction. Perhaps it was a schoolteacher who prompted him to read about the lives of great inventors such as Thomas Edison, Nikola Tesla, Guglielmo Marconi and similar heroes of science. Technical books of the period which might have accelerated young Kenny's interest in the electrical sciences were *The ABC of Wireless* (Trevert), *Induction Coils* (Norrie), *How to Make Things Electrical* (multiple contributors), *Wireless Telegraphy and High Frequency Electricity* (Twining) and Morgan's *The Boy Electrician*. It is also probable that Ken gained additional inspiration from reading periodicals of the day such as *Popular Electricity*, *Electrician & Mechanic* and *Modern Electrics*.

Ken's older brother Frank also took an interest in the electrical sciences. The boys were able to obtain components for replicating science textbook experiments with funds acquired through the sale of orchard fruit and by carrying out errands for local business firms. Their cache of technical paraphernalia included wire, batteries, insulators, glass plates, incandescent bulbs, glass jars, switches and an induction coil. The first subjects to attract their attention were electrostatics and electromagnetism. The young

An early Strickfaden laboratory (ca. 1915). A revolver can be seen hanging within a coil of wire. Is this the same revolver with which Ken's younger brother, Charles, was accidentally wounded in the rump by friend Harry Hoag? See Chapter 14, "Notes from Charles" (courtesy of Marilyn S. Throssel).

2 — For Unto Us a Wizard Is Born

scientists continued on to skillfully construct rheostats, a clever system of converting house currents by employing banks of incandescent lamps, and self-designed measuring devices such as volt and ampere meters. Other experiments included investigations into chemistry, electric motor construction and a harmless but effective electric chair scheme for surprising neighborhood friends. It worked!

Brother Charles demonstrated no interest in becoming an electrical wizard. While Frank and Ken were busy making with the sparks, Charles could be found in his room practicing on the saxophone, clarinet and other instruments. One can only speculate upon his decision to enter a field of study so markedly dissimilar than that pursued by brothers Frank and Ken.

Upon graduating from high school, Charles entered the University of California at Berkeley. His fondness for outdoor activities (hunting and fishing) were influential in his choice of majoring in forestry and agriculture rather than music. After one year, Charles left to follow a career as a freelance musician. In 1924, he auditioned with the Paul Whiteman orchestra. Apparently Charles' dedication to practicing finally paid off. In the biography *Pops: Paul Whiteman, King of Jazz*, author Thomas A. Delong stated, "Reed player Charles Strickfaden brought an unusual talent and dedication to the band ... Paul called Strickfaden his quadruple threat

Charles Grayson Strickfaden as he appeared while playing with the Paul Whiteman Orchestra in the 1920s. Whiteman called Charles a "quadruple threat" because of his having mastered four instruments.

PAUL WHITEMAN and HIS ORCHESTRA

PAUL WHITEMAN, Conductor

HENRY BUSSE, *Assistant Conductor*

KURT DIETERLE, *Concert Master*   JAMES McKILLOP, *Librarian*

FERDIE GROFE, *Arranger*

Personnel

KURT DIETERLE—Violin
JAMES McKILLOP—Violin
IRVING ACHTEL—Violin
PAUL DAVEN—Violin
CHARLES GAYLORD—Violin
MARIO PERRY—
    Violin
    Accordion
JOHN BOWMAN—Viola
JULIUS MINDEL—Viola
FRANK LEON CAVALLO—Cello
WILLIAM SCHUMAN—Cello
WALTER BELL—
    String Bass
    Bassoon
    Contra Bassoon
JOHN SPERZEL—
    Tuba
    String Bass
HARRY PERRELLA—Piano
RAYMOND TURNER—
    Piano
    Celeste
MICHAEL PINGITORE—Banjo
AUSTIN (SKIN) YOUNG—
    Banjo
    Guitar
WILBUR HALL—Trombone
ROY MAXON—
    Trombone
    Bass Trumpet

BOYCE CULLEN—
    Trombone
    Baritone
HENRY BUSSE—Trumpet
FRANK SIEGRIST—Trumpet
THEODORE BARTELL—Trumpet
CHESTER HAZLETT—
    B Flat Soprano Saxophone
    E Flat Soprano Saxophone
    E Flat Alto Saxophone
    E Flat Clarinet
    B Flat Clarinet
    Bass Clarinet
HAROLD McLEAN—
    B Flat Soprano Saxophone
    E Flat Alto Saxophone
    E Flat Baritone Saxophone
    1st Oboe
    English Horn
    Bass Clarinet
CHARLES STRICKFADDEN—
    B Flat Soprano Saxophone
    B Flat Tenor Saxophone
    E Flat Baritone Saxophone
    2nd Oboe
    B Flat Clarinet
E. LYLE SHARPE—
    B Flat Soprano Saxophone
    E Flat Alto Saxophone
    E Flat Baritone Saxophone
    B Flat Clarinet
    Bass Clarinet
    English Horn
GEORGE MARSH
    Drums
    Tympani
    Traps

General Manager: F. C. COPPICUS, Aeolian Hall, New York City

For Mr. Coppicus on tour: F. C. HAAS

Personnel making up the 1925-26 Paul Whiteman orchestra. Arranger Ferde Grofé, an excellent pianist and violinist, would later gain fame as a composer and leader of his own orchestra. Notice misspelling of Strickfaden. Souvenir Program, 1925.

2 — For Unto Us a Wizard Is Born

because of his ability to master the clarinet, saxophone, oboe, and English horn. But music was not his sole occupation. In later years he built a fortune through real estate, investments, a restaurant business, and airline operations. He was also an accomplished writer, skilled photographer, and all-round sportsman." Richard M. Sudhalter, author of *Lost Chords*, quoted a source describing Charles as a man "with few peers among orchestral players."

The Whiteman ensemble emerged as one of the most popular radio and recording groups of the jazz era. Many aspiring jazz and pop artists owed much of their success to Whiteman's leadership. Among the more familiar personalities who benefited from his influence were Jimmy and Tommy Dorsey, Jack and Charlie Teagarden, Bix Beiderbecke and Eddie Lang and singing stars Bing Crosby, Johnny Mercer, Mildred Bailey and Morton Downey.

Charles attained the reputation of a reliable and steady performer. In addition to his work with the Whiteman band, he also participated

A section of the Paul Whiteman orchestra ca. 1930s. Charles Strickfaden is seated at the center of the front row dressed in a light-colored suit (Williams College Archives and Special Collections [by permission]).

with groups under the leadership of Bix Beiderbecke, Jack Teagarden, Frank Trumbauer, Eddie Lang and the Joe Venuti-Eddie Lang combo.

Strickfaden's 12 years with the Whiteman orchestra, although financially rewarding, turned out to be a nomadic and hectic lifestyle. Musicians had to literally live out of a trunk due to the necessity of constant road travel. Theater performances, weekly radio programs, recording schedules, motion picture commitments and seemingly endless preparatory sessions left little time for relaxation or attention to personal matters. Charles took on additional duties such as managing the orchestra's schedules, assisting with the band's financial affairs and acting as librarian for the orchestra's musical scores. He also contributed articles to several musical publications such as *Metronome, Orchestra World* and others.

After 12 years with the Whiteman organization, Charles decided it was time to seek new horizons. In 1937, he took a leave of absence and journeyed to Los Angeles for a rest and to focus attention on business and family interests. Except for his participation in the 1945 film *Rhapsody in Blue*, Charles never again played with the Whiteman group. Instead, he enjoyed the less demanding schedule of an instrumentalist with the Hollywood studio orchestras, recording soundtracks for motion pictures. He also drew wide attention for his skills in performing classical music with symphony orchestras. Charles spent his golden years on the island of Maui, Hawaii. His death in 1981 resulted from a losing battle with leukemia. Charles left a wife, Sally (Richardson), and a daughter, Pamela. A previous marriage to Marion Bruyere ended with a divorce.

Little is known of Frank Strickfaden's life. He left home at an early age and in 1915 joined the U.S. Navy. Frank served as an electrician aboard the cruiser U.S.S. *Buffalo*. During World War I, the ship transported the Special Diplomatic Mission to Russia and later was stationed at Gibraltar where it operated as a repair ship to destroyers and sub chasers. Frank left the ship on December 31, 1918. He was honorably discharged in April 1919 with the rank of Chief Electrician.

Upon returning to civilian life, Frank was employed by the Union Oil Company in Sacramento. He served as supervising electrician in charge of installing gasoline and fuel stations throughout California. Because his work schedule kept him away from home most of the year, Strickfaden traveled from assignment to assignment in a fully equipped trailer. Years later, Ken Strickfaden's daughters would look forward to visits from Uncle Frank. They enjoyed romping through the home-on-wheels as though it was their own private playhouse. Frank's last place of employment was with Phillips Petroleum. He carried out business matters under the professional name of Frank L. Strick.

In 1971, Frank's health took a sharp downward turn due to a cancerous condition of the colon. Unable to withstand the pain brought on by the ravaging disease, he ended the suffering with a self-inflicted gunshot wound to the head. Although there had been several marriages, Frank had no children. The body was interred in the Glen Oaks Memorial Park in Chico, California.

But back in 1908, 12-year-old Kenneth Strickfaden did not spend much of his time worrying about the future. He was too busy with school and domestic chores to be concerned with the unforeseeable.

Frank L. Strickfaden served with the U.S. Navy aboard the U.S.S. *Buffalo* during World War I. He attained the rank of Chief Electrician (g) (courtesy of Marilyn S. Throssel).

What little time he had for himself was occupied with electrical experimentation and nature trips. Wireless telegraphy was the hot topic of the day and it became his passion to establish a transmitting and receiving radio station. Another goal was to construct a Tesla coil. Kenny's immediate plans, however, were thwarted by a traumatic family circumstance — an event that would cause a major upheaval in his life.

3

The Road Taken

Wizard of Gauze — Mummy
—The Kenneth Strickfaden Notebook

The Strickfadens remained in Ashland for nearly two years. Sometime between 1909 and 1911, the marital fabric binding Frank and Nan began to unravel. The reasons for the decline in their marriage, and how long the problematic embers had been glowing, have been lost with time. The fact that their betrothal had been a May-September union may have had something to do with it. By 1912, the couple had divorced and gone their separate ways. Brothers Frank and Charles stayed with Nan. Ken and his father hopped into a 1908 Model T Ford and headed for Santa Monica, California. In those days, restaurants and motels were few and far between so the trip provided little opportunity for food and rest. The two travelers did their best to find nourishment and used the Model T's folding-down front seat for a bed. Father and son successfully weathered the hardships of the long and dusty ordeal and settled in a house situated on the corner of 5th and California streets.

Kenneth entered the Santa Monica school system and immediately began developing new friendships. One of the first students with whom he teamed was Paul Walter. The two youngsters would remain loyal friends throughout their entire lives. Carl Spangenberger was another new acquaintance. Carl and Ken would years later open the S&S Auto and Airplane Repair Shop. But the student who most captivated Ken's attention was a petite young lady by the name of Gladys Ward. Their childhood infatuation with one another would eventually flower into a more serious and permanent relationship. The making of new friends combined with the opportunities offered by a larger school system brought much joy to Ken. His school chums affectionately addressed him as "Strick" or "Stricky." These abbreviated modifications (nicknames) for Strickfaden would be linked to Ken for the remainder of his life. For young Kenneth Strickfaden, life, it seemed, couldn't be better. But better it became when brother Charles returned to Santa Monica to live with him. All three of the Strickfaden boys kept in close contact throughout their lives and rarely missed a Christmas family gathering.

Ken excelled in high school physics, chemistry and mechanics. He enjoyed making chemical explosives and once blasted a short section of railroad track high into the air. Unfortunately, the science of trajectory was ignored and the heavy piece of airborne metal crashed down through the roof of the Strickfaden home. A Strickfaden prank in physics class raised the ire of his teacher, a heavyset Pennsylvania Dutchman. "Schtrickfodden," he roared, "you do dot vonce again undt I trow you oudt der vindow." Young Strickfaden participated in extracurricular activities such as photography, athletics and drama. His impish sense of humor made him a natural for the part of Bottom (the weaver) in *A Midsummer Night's Dream*. Ken played the part magnificently.

Young Ken also demonstrated a talent for music by playing the double bass in the orchestra and tuba for the band. He also had an affection for the violin and organ. Ken made his first violin from a cigar box, and personally picked the hair for the bow from the tail of a friend's pet horse.

By 1913, Ken had his very own workshop in which he would spend many hours designing wireless telegraphy apparatuses. A downward trend in the economy required that he contribute to the family's financial needs. Ken's first experience as a parttime employee was with the Santa Monica Company's electric shop. In 1914, he got a similar after-school job with the Tom Rider Electric Company in Los Angeles. While at Rider, young Strickfaden developed skills in the manufacture and use of X-ray equipment and also participated in Rider's electrical show at Venice Pier. Ken recalled that year as a milestone in his career. He successfully completed construction of his first Tesla coil. This device would later become one of Strickfaden's favorite "mad scientist" special effects accoutrements.

Several significant events occurred in 1915. For one, Ken took on a new part-time job at the Braun Corporation's machine shop. It paid a dollar a day. Secondly, he finished one step behind the winner of the mile event at the California State High School Track and Field Championships. And in that same year, Strickfaden replicated a historical radio transmission. On Christmas Eve 1906, inventor Reginald Fessenden utilized a modulated spark gap wireless oscillator to make the world's first radio broadcast of the human voice. The skilled inventor also transmitted the sounds of "O Holy Night" on the violin. His radio transmission created a sensation among those fortunate enough to own a receiving instrument. Nine years later, Strickfaden repeated Fessenden's experiment by transmitting modulated radio signals using a tuned rotary spark gap. But unlike Fessenden's violin transmission, Ken broadcast military bugle calls. Whether or not his radio feat qualifies as an important event in wireless history is for others to judge. However it does make for a good radio trivia question. Who was the first to broadcast military bugle calls over the radio?

Upon graduating from high school, Ken left home and traveled to nearby Venice where he got a job with "Professor Willard's Temple of Music," a touring sideshow playing the vaudeville circuits under the entrepreneurship of Charles and Laura Willard. Local papers publicized the show as "A Trip to Melodia." A sign decorating the entrance spelled out the word M-E-L-O-D-I-A. Ken had been a frequent visitor to the amusement park zones of Venice Pier, Ocean Park Pier and Santa Monica Pier. Apparently he possessed a natural fascination for the carnival-like ambience of the areas. Young Strickfaden enjoyed mingling with the traveling performers who continually provoked his imagination with stories of faraway places and events. This is the kind of environment to which Ken was attuned and Willard's "Temple of Music" would pave a road for him to follow.

Ken served as electrician and mechanic to Willard's operations. The young employee turned out to be a valuable source of new ideas and innovations. One novel and entertaining act to which Strickfaden added improvements was a musical saw demonstration. Scantily clad women, whose most noticeable clothing apparel consisted of welding glasses, played melodies on chimes which were electrically connected to a row of circular saws. Each saw would create writhing electrical sparks when a corresponding chime was struck. The sparking "sawmill" proved to be one of the most successful drawing cards among the performing acts.

Another of Strickfaden's contributions to Willard's excitatory apparatus was an instrument he named "Melodyne." It consisted of a perforated

3 — The Road Taken

A multiple exposed print (circa 1917) of Kenneth Strickfaden testing Willard's sparking saws at Coney Island. In performance, the saws were energized by chimes played by scantily clad women whose most noticeable apparel consisted of welding glasses (courtesy of Marilyn S. Throssel).

metal disc which is made to spin at a high speed. A musical note can be heard when a column of air is directed through the openings. In the hands of a skilled operator, the disc is capable of producing a melodic song.

Ken also added a musical lightning device. This high voltage apparatus, probably a Tesla coil, drew record numbers of visitors. The electrician planned on building a similar, larger unit capable of emitting musical lightning many feet in length. But Strickfaden's involvement in multiple undertakings left little time for accomplishing the feat.

In 1917, the Willards moved their Temple of Music to Coney Island, New York. Originally, the Island was nothing more than a five-mile stretch of sand located at the foot of Brooklyn. From the very first inhabitants, Coney is said to have drawn "the odd, the bizarre, the far flung, and the ridiculous." Because of the unsavory atmosphere permeating the area, Coney became known as "Sodom by the Sea." During its finest years, however, Coney Island was both fascinating and frightening, and could rightfully claim to be the mother of all expositions. The entertainment areas consisted of several parks, the largest and most important of which were Steeple Chase, Luna and Dreamland. The facilities included just about every conceivable ride, from the Loop-the-Loop to the Shoot-the-Chute to the Parachute. If there is anything for which Coney can, or should, be remembered, it is the rollercoaster and the hot dog.

Other forms of entertainment included 450 motion picture houses, all of which operated simultaneously each day. Coney housed herds of elephants, some 300 little people (then called midgets), hundreds of monkeys and a building dedicated to incubating premature (human) babies. Coney Island was no stranger to calamities, the most serious of which was fire. One of the worst tragedies occurred on May 27, 1911, when Dreamland burned to the ground. Among the terrible and appalling sights witnessed was the demise of numerous caged animals. Another

Perhaps the rarest of all Coney Island photographs is this (circa 1917) internal view of Willard's Melodia establishment. Notice the calliope (center rear) and the sparking saws and chimes at the left. Strickfaden eventually inherited 84 pieces of Willard's equipment.

3 — The Road Taken

One of the many photographs with which Kenneth Strickfaden recorded the visual history of Coney Island (ca. 1917). Several have appeared in books on America's amusement centers (courtesy of Marilyn S. Throssel).

distasteful event was the painful death by electrocution of an elephant that had gone berserk. The service and equipment needed to complete the task was provided by men working for inventor Thomas Edison.

For the most part, however, Coney presented visitors with a circus-carnival atmosphere with all the trimmings including naked women, magicians, sword swallowers, freaks of nature and so on. Attendees in the mood for natural disasters could take in the gigantic re-creations of the Galveston and Jamestown floods as well as an eruption of the Mount Vesuvius volcano. Another form of entertainment was the opportunity to descend into the bowels of a Pennsylvania coal mine. It can be stated without reservation that if you didn't find it at Coney Island, you wouldn't find it anywhere.

Willard's Melodia establishment settled in Luna Park, "The Heart of Coney Island." Luna Park also earned the titles of "Electric Eden" and "City of Lights" because of the manner in which its 250,000 bulbs lighted up the night sky (Dreamland boasted 1,000,000 lamps). Although Ken

When not engaged with work or taking photographs, Strickfaden (shown above) churned up the dust at local race tracks in a hot rod he called "Cootie" (ca. 1917) (courtesy of Marilyn S. Throssel).

was impressed by the spectacle, he was not altogether unfamiliar with large entertainment enterprises. He had, after all, received his "baptism under fire" at the Venice and Ocean Park amusement piers. "The Venice/Ocean Park area had become the finest amusement center on the west coast and was achieving fame as the 'Coney Island of the Pacific'" (Stanton, 1993, p. 75).

With camera in hand, Strickfaden photographed the entertainment establishments just as he had done at the California amusement piers. Three of his Coney photos, plus several from the West Coast parks, appeared years later in *The Great American Amusement Parks* (Kyrazi, 1976, pp. 63–64, 98, 147–53). When not engaged with work or taking photographs, the versatile electrician turned to automobile racing. He churned up the dust at local race tracks in a hot rod called "Cootie" (named for an insect parasite).

Life at Coney Island appeared to be one grand and glorious party without any indication of ending. But no life experience, good or bad, lasts forever and Kenneth J. Strickfaden would soon find himself confronted by an irresistible calling.

4

From the Halls of Montezuma...

Vagaries of Vulcan's Valley
— The Kenneth Strickfaden Notebook

Since 1914, Europe had been embroiled in a military conflict unlike any in the history of mankind. Mechanized warfare far more advanced than used in any past international breach of the peace was being applied to death and destruction. The American citizenry was itself at variance over the situation. One side took the position that the war was Europe's problem and that Uncle Sam should keep his nose out of it. The opposition perceived a victorious Germany as a threat to world democracy and clamored for intervention. Of course, there were the neutrals who sat on the fence and enjoyed the debate as though watching two out-of-town baseball teams slugging it out.

The dispute remained somewhat unchanged until May 7, 1915, when the British passenger ship *Lusitania* was torpedoed by a German submarine. One hundred twenty-eight of the 1198 innocents who lost their lives were Americans (mostly women and children). As shocking as the incident may have been, the argument over which stand America should take shifted only slightly in favor of intervention. Three vital events forced America's hand: (1) the sinking of three American ships by German submarines; (2) the sabotage of a New Jersey munitions depot by German agents; (3) efforts by the German government to convince Mexico to attack the United States. On April 6, 1917, the United States Congress declared war on Germany. Shortly thereafter, recruiting posters became prominently displayed at U.S. government buildings and enlistment centers.

Capitalizing on the nation's patriotic mood, music publishers and recording companies flooded their respective markets with flag-waving melodies. George M. Cohan's "Over There" proved to be the most popular song of the war, selling two million copies of sheet music and one million phonograph recordings. As an indication of the change in the public's position regarding the war, the pre-war song "I Didn't Raise My Boy to Be a Soldier" was replaced with "I Didn't Raise My Boy to Be a Coward." The fledgling motion picture industry moved into high gear in exploiting America's crusade for making the world safe for democracy. Among the films destined to provoke the public's fear of German spies and saboteurs, as well as its hatred for the enemy, were *The Border Wireless* (1918),* *Claws of the Hun* (1918), *I'm a Man* (1918), *The Prussian Cur* (1918) and *The Hun Within* (1919). Chapterplays such as *A Daughter of Uncle Sam* and *The Eagle's Eye* (both 1918) were intensely popular productions.

By mid–1917, young men and women from all parts of the nation began showing up at recruitment stations. Ken Strickfaden spent the remainder of 1917 clearing up personal and business obligations and enlisted in the spring of 1918. During the journey to a New York City enlistment location, Ken's patriotic fervor was further aroused by the sight and sounds of a military band leading a parade of uniformed personnel marching in full battle dress. They were being trailed by a large contingent of flag-waving Boy Scouts. He became emotionally overcome by the spectacle and was unable to hold back the tears. Another sight to catch his attention was a United States Marine recruiting poster. The die had been cast.

Strickfaden's military training officially began at the Philadelphia Marine Barracks in May 1918. He was assigned to a crew of machine-gunners. Ken successfully met all challenges including the barrage of ethnic slurs hurled in his direction by a bigoted Marine. The war had created an intense prejudice against Germans and too many Americans were unwilling, or unable, to draw a line between loyal Americans of German descent and the Germans with whom we were at war. Ken did not take

---

*William S. Hart, one of the most celebrated stars of silent era Westerns, played the leading role in *The Border Wireless*.

the verbal assaults lightly and gave a good account of himself. The incident served to remove any doubts, had there been any, regarding Strickfaden's competence in meeting Marine toughness standards. Unknown to the Marine involved in the fracas, Ken was German on his father's side. His mother, Nancy Creek, was of English stock. Kenny never revealed his family lineage to the narrow-minded Marine.

Since its inception, America had been infected by the microbes of racial and religious bigotry. The military, sad to say, served as an incubator for such diseases. Strickfaden was well aware of the separation of

Marine Private Kenneth J. Strickfaden prior to embarking for Europe where the war to end all wars was being waged (ca. 1918) (courtesy of Marilyn S. Throssel).

the races and had witnessed several violations of U.S. Constitutional guarantees. On one of those occasions, a Jewish Marine was the victim of a physical attack by several thugs dressed in military uniforms. Ken fully embraced the principles upon which America was founded and believed that a person's worthiness was not dependent upon ethnicity, race or religious affiliation.

The 11th Marines left for Europe aboard the U.S.S. *Henderson* in October 1918. Except for a tense moment instigated by the sight of a submarine's periscope, the crossing was without incident. The Americans landed in England where the war-weary British welcomed them as heroes. Shortly after setting foot on British soil, the Marines were crammed into railroad boxcars and transported to a staging area. They next climbed aboard a ship and sailed for France. The travel-weary Marines disembarked at the port of Saint Nazaire. Servicemen passing through the area tagged the town with the epithet "Stench Nazaire" because of its numerous houses of prostitution. Venereal diseases had become endemic to the region and officials were forced to wage a "war within a war" in an attempt to stem the spread of infections. A prominently displayed poster declaring "A German bullet is cleaner than a whore" served as a warning to the consequences of careless liaisons.

After being assigned lodging (in places like barns, cellars, tar paper huts and leaky pup tents), the men were given further simulated battlefield training (in rain-soaked muddy terrain, uncomfortable cold night temperatures, etc.). By the time Strickfaden's company received its orders to take up an advanced field position, the war had come to a close. Except for being nicked by shrapnel from an errantly thrown hand grenade, Ken had come through the war uninjured. Eighty thousand Americans were not so lucky. Furthermore, thousands of servicemen not killed in battle lost their lives to the great influenza epidemic of 1917–18. Ken survived

A peaceful scene in Belleau Wood, France, where some of the war's fiercest battles had taken place. This is one of many scenes photographed by Kenneth Strickfaden during his European tour of duty (courtesy of Mariyn S. Throssel).

both the war and the disease. But even those who came through the war unscratched did not return untouched by the horrible experience.

Strickfaden was appalled by the devastation that war had wrought and felt compelled to make a personal photographic record of the scene. He processed the photos in a self-designed mobile darkroom. Another sight that made a deep impression was the work of the Red Cross. He never forgot the experience and years later made a significant financial contribution to the organization. Strickfaden also cherished the work of the YMCA volunteers who offered respite and entertainment for the troops. Even the friendliness of the French citizenry was greatly appreciated. His European tour of duty continued until August 6, 1919, after which time he sailed for home aboard the U.S.S. *Orizaba*.

The Marine veteran spent several days in New York City enjoying the hustle and bustle of big city life. He could not avoid noticing the stark contrast between war-ravaged Europe and the untouched American landscape. One of the first items on his itinerary was a close-up view of the Statue of Liberty.

Another item on Strickfaden's agenda was a visit to the Electro Importing Company. The firm was known for supplying the latest innovations in radio and electrical equipment. Also well-known was Hugo Gernsback, the force behind Electro Importing. Strickfaden had long admired Gernsback, who was also an inventor and publisher of technical and science fiction magazines. Both men shared an interest in electrotechnology and held a mutual admiration for inventor Nikola Tesla. Tesla had developed the system of alternating current electricity presently in use throughout the world, and had also discovered the principles which made wireless (radio) communications possible. Of particular interest to Strickfaden, however, was Tesla's high voltage transformer (Tesla coil). Gernsback's publications had carried numerous articles on the Tesla coil and biographical articles on its inventor.

Strickfaden was in Marine uniform when visiting the Electro Importing Company. Electro's office personnel was impressed by the neat appearance of the handsome Marine and presented him with a welcome reserved solely for war heroes — a standing ovation. Gernsback, who had emigrated from Luxembourg, was fervently patriotic and promptly ushered the blushing Marine into his office. Although it was inevitable that their discussion would focus on the recently ended war, the two men soon directed their attention to the latest developments in the fields of radio and electricity. Gernsback was impressed with the Marine's understanding of electrotechnology and urged the veteran to enter the monthly "Amateur Electrical Laboratory Contest" being sponsored by *Electrical Experimenter* magazine. Strickfaden took seriously the publisher's suggestion and the November 1919 issue featured Ken's portrait along with two photos of his laboratory equipment. Kenneth Strickfaden had won first prize!

Although fascinated with big city life, Strickfaden's heart and mind were elsewhere — Santa Monica. A Marine private's salary, however, fell far short of covering the cost of a coast-to-coast excursion. Strickfaden launched a brief business venture selling war photos to the public. The $150 earned, combined with his Marine Corps separation pay of $255.08,

A clipping from the November 1919 issue of *Electrical Experimenter* announcing Kenneth Strickfaden as first prize winner in the "Amateur Electrical Laboratory" contest. A large Tesla coil stands at the left.

The electrical lab with which Ken Strickfaden won first prize in a contest held by *Electrical Experimenter* magazine. It was featured in the November 1919 issue.

provided Ken with enough funds for the purchase of a dilapidated 1912 Model T Ford and enough cash remaining for covering the expense of repairs, fuel, food and other necessities. With spirits high, the happy-go-lucky Marine declared, "I have a Ford car specially fixt up and decorated in which 'Yours truly' and all the 'junk' will attempt to fly across the continent to sunny California, my old home town — Santa Monica" (*Electrical Experimenter,* November 1919, p. 668).

With repairs completed and supplies aboard, Kenneth Strickfaden and his "co-pilots" (Marine buddies Evan Allen and Tobias Weston) headed westward. The next several years of Strickfaden's life would have qualified for a series of articles in a 1920s dime adventure magazine.

5

California, Here I Come!

When you try the impossible, you have no competition.
— The Kenneth Strickfaden Notebook

Although federal and state government programs had been underway for providing the nation with a continuously paved highway system, any tourist brave (or foolish) enough to attempt a cross-country automobile trip in 1919 was required to traverse territories with yet unpaved paths and areas lacking facilities for food, rest and automobile repair services. Consequently, a coast-to-coast journey required not only the skills for driving a vehicle but also the expertise for servicing it. A complete set of tools and automobile spare parts were essential components of every traveler's arsenal. Furthermore, tourists faced the challenge of such diverse hardships as desert temperatures, freezing mountain snow and ice storms, floods, deep-rutted roads, highway criminals and so on. Considering the many hazards to be faced, it is reasonable to assume that more than a few of the well-intended (though unprepared) vagabonds undertaking a cross-country drive not only failed to reach their destination but were never again heard from.

On September 27, 1919, Kenneth Strickfaden and two friends began a trip from New York to California in a rehabilitated 1912 Model T Ford. According to commentaries in Ken's notes, it appears that passengers Evan Allen and Tobias Weston disembarked when the trio arrived in Detroit. From that point onward, Strickfaden faced the challenge of crossing the semi-tamed west on his own. The following chronicles represent

5 — California, Here I Come!

excerpts from Ken's notebook with commentaries on the trials and tribulations of the experience.

SEPTEMBER 27, 1919 — The happy trio of travelers put $1.35 worth of gas and $.20 of oil in the car and cross the State of New Jersey. They sleep at a "roadside bed outside of Philadelphia."

SEPTEMBER 28, 1919 — While traveling through Pennsylvania, Ken takes a "bad detour through the mountains." He finds the sharp curves and dips to be "great roads for the loop-the-loop." The car develops a broken spring and tire trouble. They again spend the night on a "roadside bed."

SEPTEMBER 29, 1919 — They reach Pittsburgh and find a service station. Expenditures are $4 for a spring; $.10 for an oil cap; gas, $.90 and $1.68 (one of the gas purchases may have been an extra supply for emergency purposes); oil, $1; and $15 for a breather(?). Ken visits Bob Hoffman, a promoter of health and strength programs. "Roadside bed."

SEPTEMBER 30, 1919 — The Model T Ford transports the adventuring Marines to Akron, Ohio, where they experience a blowout. Gas expenses are $.90. They sleep in a field.

OCTOBER 1, 1919 — Everything going okay as the trio travels through Cleveland and other Ohio cities. Rest is taken at the roadside.

OCTOBER 2, 1919 — The next stop is Toledo, Ohio, where they purchase gas for $1.50 and obtain "plugs from the Champ. Co." Strick makes a detour north to Detroit, and gets a room at the YMCA. (The reason for the stop at Detroit is unexplained. It is believed that passengers Allen and Weston had reached their destination and disembarked).

OCTOBER 3, 1919 — Ken spends $1.25 on gas, $.20 on oil and meets "E. W." ("E.W." may refer to Tobias Weston's father, who "worked at the Mather Spring Co.") Ken replaces a rear spring.

OCTOBER 4, 1919 — Strickfaden backtracks to Toledo, Ohio, where he spends the night. "Slept in a garage."

OCTOBER 5, 1919 — Ken goes through such Ohio towns as Swanton, Archbold, Bryan and Edgerton. He stops for gas ($1.50) and parts ($1.95). The tired traveler "slept on corn stalks."

OCTOBER 6, 1919 — Ken is rudely awakened by police officers who question him in regard to identification and motives. Released, he returns to the road and passes such Indiana communities as Kendalville, Ligonier, Goshen and South Bend. Expenditures for gas and oil are (respectively) $2.00 and $.20. He buys 24 pounds of bananas!

Ken visits someone called "Fitch." The night is spent sleeping on a haystack.

OCTOBER 7, 1919 — The lonely traveler stops to replenish his supply of gasoline ($1.15) and replace two tires. He drives through the Indiana towns of La Porte and Valparaiso, and goes on to Chicago. He slept at a service station.

OCTOBER 8, 1919 — Strickfaden rises early and pays $1.12 for gas and oil. He continues the trip through the Illinois communities of Geneva, De Kalb and Rochelle, where he stops to repair two tire punctures. Ken spent the night on a porch.

OCTOBER 9, 1919 — Illinois roads taken on this date pass through Dixon, Sterling and Morrison. Strickfaden crosses state lines and visits the Iowa towns of Clinton and Wheatland, where he spends the night in a barn.

OCTOBER 10, 1919 — Ken reaches Cedar Rapids.

OCTOBER 11, 1919 — The lone traveler continues the trip through Iowa and passes the community of Marshalltown. He reaches the city of Colo and sleeps in a barn.

OCTOBER 12, 1919 — Strickfaden arrives at the Iowa town of Nevada. After a short breather, he continues on to Boone, where he finds a haystack on the outskirts of town.

OCTOBER 13, 1919 — Traveling along what is today's U.S. Route 30, the adventurous ex–Marine passes the communities of Jefferson, Carroll and Denison. He then heads in a southerly direction toward Council Bluffs and locates a brush pile on which to sleep.

OCTOBER 14, 1919 — Leaving Council Bluffs, Iowa, Ken heads for the Nebraska border. The exhausted traveler takes rest in the "YMCA Eng. Room" in Omaha.

OCTOBER 15–21, 1919 — Strickfaden pauses for major repairs which include valve grinding, wheel bearing replacement, a new oil pan and some minor parts. He takes a temporary job with the Page Tree Service to help pay for repairs and traveling expenses.

OCTOBER 22, 1919 — Ken passes through the Nebraska towns of Freemont, Columbia and Central City. The Ford develops ignition trouble. He slept by the roadside.

OCTOBER 23, 1919 — Continuing through the great state of Nebraska, Strickfaden passes through Grand Island, Kearney, Lexington and Gothenberg. He makes a bed at the roadside.

OCTOBER 24, 1919 — The daring traveler steers his Ford through the

5 — California, Here I Come!

Nebraska towns of Brady, North Platte and Sutherland. He records the word "Mack'naws" in his notes. A corn field is his new rest stop.

OCTOBER 25, 1919 — Now three-quarters through Nebraska, Ken heads in the direction of Ogallala, Big Springs, Chappell and Sidney. The trip is delayed by a frozen radiator. Strickfaden is adopted by a stray dog. He and the animal rest in a haystack.

OCTOBER 26, 1919 — Strickfaden enters Wyoming. He passes through Cheyenne and rests on the ground for the night.

OCTOBER 27, 1919 — The only entry for this date is "lost dog under platform."

OCTOBER 28, 1919 — There is a malfunction of the Ford's universal joint as Strickfaden enters the Wyoming city of Laramie. Rest is taken in a woodshed at the University of Wyoming.

OCTOBER 29, 1919 — The tired traveler reaches Rock River and takes refuge in a "bank vault."

OCTOBER 30, 1919 — Ken runs into severe winter weather at Wyoming's Medicine Bow. He becomes stalled in a snowstorm. The radiator and gasoline lines freeze up. To make matters worse, the handle of the engine crank breaks off. (The Model T Ford had no self starter. The engine had to be hand-turned to get it started.) Ken finds rest in a "guard house" in the town of Hanna.

OCTOBER 31, 1919 — Strickfaden passes through Fort Fred Steele and goes on to the city of Rawlins. He stays at the Ferris Hotel "thru the kindness of Mr. Stephenson."

NOVEMBER 1, 1919 — While traveling through Wyoming, Ken passes Red Desert and heads in the direction of Rock Springs. He takes refuge in a "grocery store."

NOVEMBER 2, 1919 — The weary traveler steers the Model T through Green River and spends the night in a "new building" in Evanston.

NOVEMBER 3, 1919 — It is raining heavily as Ken crosses the Wyoming-Utah border. The Ford becomes stuck in the mud. An attempt to free the automobile causes a breakdown of the differential. The frustrated traveler sleeps in a "telephone station."

NOVEMBER 4, 1919 — After making temporary repairs, our hero continues the journey through Coalville and in the direction of Salt Lake City. He spends the night in a "desert gym."

NOVEMBER 5–15, 1919 — Strickfaden has been on the road for nearly two months. The hardships and misfortunes have taken their toll on his patience and enthusiasm. He stays in Salt Lake City for rest and revitalization. The Ford is given the necessary repairs for continuing the trip.

NOVEMBER 16, 1919 — With renewed determination and resolve, the rested traveler resumes the journey to California. He takes the route that leads to Grantsville, Utah. After passing several hamlets, Ken stops at an "old house" to spend the night.

NOVEMBER 17, 1919 — While crossing the desert, the Ford suffers a tire puncture. Notes for this date mention Fish Springs, Kearney's Ranch and Gold Hill. Ken sleeps in a "new garage."

NOVEMBER 18, 1919 — A serious mechanical breakdown occurs when the Ford's flywheel is damaged. The disheartened motorist sleeps on the desert floor on a bed of sagebrush.

NOVEMBER 19, 1919 — Strickfaden is now without transportation. He walks a distance of ten miles in the direction of Gold Hill where he stops at a house owned by the Sheridans. The night is spent "with Indians."

NOVEMBER 20, 1919 — The day is spent working for room and board at the Sheridan home. Ken chops wood for their stoves and stays the night in their "cabin."

NOVEMBER 21–DECEMBER 4, 1919 — There are no entries to account for the dates of November 21 through December 4. It is reasonable to conclude that the time was spent retrieving and servicing the disabled Ford.

DECEMBER 5, 1919 — Strickfaden anxiously resumes the trip to California. He turns south into the state of Nevada and finds rest at "old man Brewer's" place.

DECEMBER 6, 1919 — The new route takes the traveler through Shellbourne Pass. Because of its dangerous turns and hazardous terrain, he calls it "Hellbourne Pass."

DECEMBER 7, 1919 — Strickfaden reaches McGill, Nevada. On the way to Ely, he runs into a blinding snowstorm. The conditions for travel become intolerable, if not impossible, so Ken stops at an old barn.

DECEMBER 8, 1919 — The Model T Ford is driven through the city of Curran to a place called Nyala. The tired traveler sleeps on "Mrs. Alared's dining room floor."

DECEMBER 9, 1919 — Although the driving conditions remain dangerous and difficult, the veteran race track driver continues through Twin Springs, Warm Springs and Tonopah. Ken beds down in an old cabin.

5 — California, Here I Come!

DECEMBER 10, 1919 — Better weather conditions allow Strickfaden to reach the cities of Gold Field, Palmetto and Oasis. He stays the night at an "old Indian camp."

DECEMBER 11, 1919 — Our noble and courageous traveler crosses the California border and reaches Big Pine. He stops to visit with "Edna and Mrs. Hall." The night is spent in a garage.

December 12, 1919 — Strickfaden passes through Independence and continues on to Indian Wells. He takes refuge in a "cave."

DECEMBER 13, 1919 — With spirits high, Kenny drives through Mojave and heads for Bakersfield. The Model T Ford breaks down. Repairs are made to bearings, radiator, and tire tubes. The exhausted driver sleeps in a woodshed.

DECEMBER 14, 1919 — Nearing his destination, the traveler takes an unexplained detour north to Delano and stops at Merced. He spends the night in a "new house."

The final page of Strickfaden's New York–to–California diary. The small stick figures represent Ken and brother Charles (Chas.) Strickfaden.

DECEMBER 15, 1919 — Ken continues on to Tracy and then turns west to Livermore. He sleeps in a culvert.

DECEMBER 16, 1919 — Strickfaden travels north through Oakland and then to Berkeley, where he visits with brother Charles. His notes feature a sketch of two figures representing himself and Charles in a happy reunion.

DECEMBER 17, 1919 — No entries appear under this date. Presumably the final leg of the long and arduous journey from New York to Santa Monica has been completed.

6

Dr. Frankenstein's Electrician

Success has many friends.
— The Kenneth Strickfaden Notebook

Servicemen returning from the war were forced to make social and economic adjustments. Many had difficulty finding a source of income. Ken Strickfaden had no such problems. He was able to keep financially afloat by repairing electrical and mechanical devices featured at local amusement centers. This source of funds enabled him to resume a project begun as early as 1914 — photographing the Santa Monica area sights. Strickfaden's photographs gained recognition for their value as a historical record and were later to be placed on permanent display at Santa Monica's cultural institutions.

Ken and Carl Spangenberger opened the S&S repair shop in Venice in 1920. The partnership was dissolved in 1922. It was during this period that Strickfaden became associated with Santa Monica's Metropolitan Studios. The firm later merged with other entertainment interests to become Metro-Goldwyn-Mayer (MGM).

Not much is known as to how Ken became affiliated with Metro or how long he stayed with the company. It appears that his servitude at any one place of employment was rarely lengthy and that he took jobs as dictated by his pocketbook assets. Apparently Strickfaden was happier doing his own thing and disliked being bridled by the restrictions of formal employment.

Strickfaden's father remarried in 1920, taking Clara M. Dunston as

Top: The midway at California's Venice Pier. The Giant Dipper roller coaster rides appear at the left. *Bottom:* Another view of the Venice Pier amusement area from a different perspective. Photographs by Ken Strickfaden during the early 1920s (courtesy of the Santa Monica Public Library Image Archives).

his wife. The couple established a residence at 1217 Eleventh Street in Santa Monica. Ken found Clara to be a pleasant person and a good stepmother and called her "Mom." Clara later faithfully served as "grandma" to Ken's children.

Pressed by a compulsion to settle down, Strickfaden asked Gladys Ward, his high school sweetheart, for her hand in marriage. Gladys' heritage can be traced back to the early settlers of New England. She was born in Somerville, New Jersey. In 1901, the Ward family moved to Ocean Park, California, where her father opened a grocery store. Ken and Gladys embraced Methodism in early life and became active in church affairs. The couple exchanged marital vows in 1921 at the Bible Institute in Los Angeles.

Ken and Gladys Strickfaden (circa 1928). Ken constructed the corrugated metal workshop seen in the background (courtesy of Marilyn S. Throssel).

With the pressure of marital obligations now resting upon his shoulders, it became essential for Ken to find steady employment. He was hired as an assembly line worker at the H&H Ford Motor Company plant ($2 per car, four per day). The job lasted until there occurred a downturn in automobile sales. In his never-ending search for employment, Strickfaden took work at the Armacost Tree Nursery, the Oleson Lumber Company and as a "cement jockey" with a construction firm building the University High School in West Los Angeles. One of the school's most distinguished graduates would be a lad by the name of Roddy McDowall, who later gained fame for his performances in such films as *How Green Was My Valley* (1941), *Lassie Come Home* (1943) and *Cleopatra* (1963) and many television programs. He was among the thousands of children brought to the United States from Great Britain during World War II. McDowall was an avid photographer and authored several books. His acting career began in the late 1930s and continued as a leading character star into the 1990s. McDowall passed away at the age of 70 on October 3, 1998.

In 1923, Strickfaden obtained employment at the Douglas Aircraft plant in Santa Monica. He was assigned to assembling one of several planes being prepared for an around-the-world journey. The historical event began on March 17. Even though their departure signaled an end to his employment with Douglas, Ken was unhesitant in demonstrating his pride and joy as the planes lifted into the air. But Ken's exodus from the aeronautics firm did not discourage his enthusiasm for flying. He signed on as a mechanic with the 478th Pursuit Squadron, 3rd Army Reserve.

Apparently the nature of Strickfaden's service with the 478th did not interfere with his finding steady employment elsewhere. "In the '20s, I was working at Universal Studios in the electrical department. The president, Carl Laemmle, Sr., personally showed me the ropes. I had the run of the lot and my work brought me on every set at some point or other" (Ackerman, *Lon of 1000 Faces*, 1983, p. 213). Ken did not make clear as to whether he had any involvement with the filming of *The Hunchback of Notre Dame* (1923) but he did get to see silent film star Lon Chaney on several occasions.

Strickfaden's outlook on life took a sharp upturn on August 14, 1923, when Gladys presented him a daughter. The couple's first child was named Carolyn.

Employment in 1924 included a temporary stay with the Globe Electric Company. Ken also picked up extra pocket money servicing amusement park machines. He was again at Universal when the firm was filming *The Phantom of the Opera* (1925). The capable electrician was assigned to maintenance of the large lamps illuminating the sets. One of the problems that occurred during the filming of *Phantom* involved a large chandelier. The script required that it come crashing to the opera house floor. Director Rupert Julian and staff were confronted with the challenge of accomplishing the task without causing serious injury or death to the actors and extras upon whom the chandelier would fall. Ken presented a brief description of how the problem was resolved. "We rigged the chandelier so that it was lifted from the floor to the ceiling and photographed the sequence in reverse!" (Ackerman, *Lon of 1000 Faces*, 1983, pp. 213–14).

After completing his stint with the 478th, Ken indulged his love for flying by joining the 322nd Pursuit Squadron. This activity lasted until the early part of 1926. Never one to sit around while others were doing exciting things, Strickfaden became involved with building and racing speedboats at Venice Pier. These hazardous adventures continued until the birth of daughter Marilyn in May of that year.

Strickfaden's love for children is amply displayed through his work with youth groups such as the Boy Scouts, the YMCA and a club called the Pioneers. Activities included classes in astronomy and crafts, picnics and trips to sporting events and cultural centers. Strickfaden also taught Sunday school classes and held youth meetings at his home. One of the astronomy outings coincided with an eclipse of the moon. The event occurred much later in the evening than anticipated, which required the chaperone to answer to the complaints of several irate parents. Ken "sweet-talked" his way out of the situation and continued to chaperone young people in various activities such as hiking and photography. He especially enjoyed taking the family to the Big Sur and Big Basin State Parks where daughters Carolyn and Marilyn found great pleasure communing with nature.

Kenny's notes mention motion picture work at Lasky (1926) and Fox (1927). His duties at Fox included keeping electrical circuits intact as well as maintenance and operation of the giant 36-inch search lights seen at grand Hollywood events. In 1927, the electrician was inducted into the International Brotherhood of Electrical Workers. Undoubtedly, the IBEW was instrumental in opening doors of opportunity for Ken. One of the films recorded in his notebook is Paramount's war drama *Wings* (1927), winner of the first Best Picture Academy Award. Ken was assigned to the crew responsible for operation of the special sound effects apparatus which Paramount purchased from the General Electric Company. The machines recreated the sounds of roaring airplane engines and the rat-a-tat of machine guns.

Strangely, Strickfaden's records for 1927 also include the earlier *The*

Hunchback of Notre Dame (1923) and *The Phantom of the Opera* (1925). This entry caused a bit of confusion in regard to chronicling Ken's film work. Further investigation revealed that Universal had undertaken a program of adding sound effects to some of its silent films. No record was found regarding the distribution of a sound version of *Hunchback* but *Phantom* was reissued in 1929 augmented with talking sequences, musical score and special sound effects.

Years later, when an interviewer mentioned that Ken had rarely received a screen credit, the technician replied, "but I did receive credit on many pictures as a sound engineer!" ("Kenneth Strickfaden" by Scott MacQueen, *Gore Creatures* #24, October 1975, pp. 24–26).

Hoot Gibson, a real cowboy who starred in numerous Westerns, is mentioned in Ken's notes for 1927. Although the cowboy hero was featured in seven Westerns that year, not any of the titles appear in Strickfaden's records.

In 1928, Ken came into possession of Willard's complete inventory of entertainment devices. The collection consisted of 84 trunks — enough equipment to fill a railroad baggage car. Strickfaden later applied some of this equipment to his public lectures. Among the many interesting Willard entertainment properties was a broken-down calliope. Ken fully restored this fascinating "cousin to the organ" and rented it out to Universal for its production of *Showboat* (1929). The calliope was eventually sold to the Disney Corporation. Years later, the instrument became a familiar sight at Disneyland.

Other films with which Strickfaden was associated were *Romance of the Rio Grande* (1929), *Cockeyed World* (1929), *Words and Music* (1929), *Pleasure Crazed* (1929), *Follies of 1929* (1929), *Harmony at Home* (1930) and *Just Imagine* (1930). The latter film featured such futuristic elements as a unique medical laboratory, VTOL aircraft, television and a rocket ship trip to Mars.

The Return of Sherlock Holmes (1929) is believed to be the first sound film to employ a Strickfaden special electrical effect. A search for a home video version of this film proved unsuccessful. Some of the initial special electrical effects Ken was called upon to produce include the sizzling hum of an electric chair (by directing a high voltage discharge into a block of wood) and lightning destroying a tree.

During the 1920s and 1930s, scientists began taking serious interest in the phenomenon of death rays. Experiments in Great Britain by

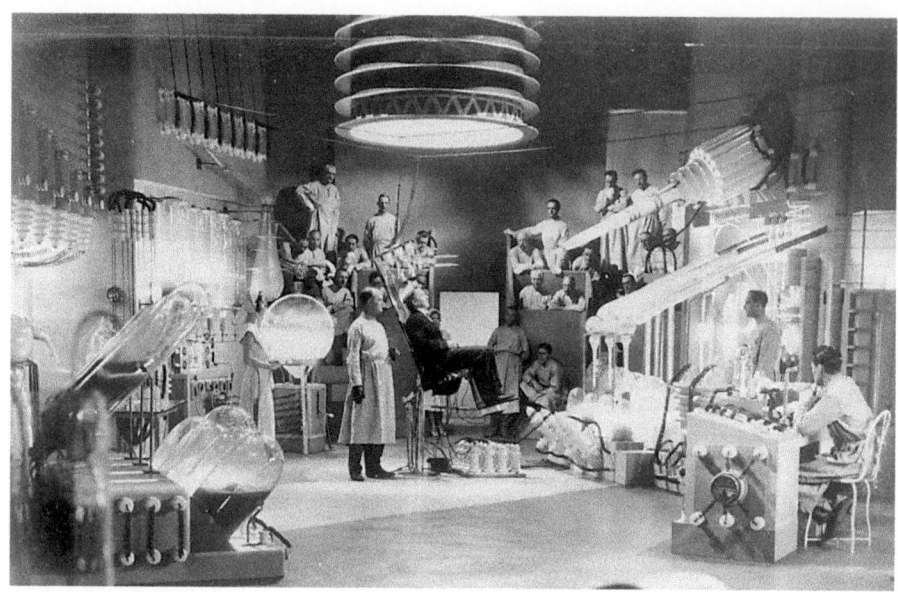

Just Imagine (1930), a science fiction musical, predicted futuristic achievements such as modern medical laboratories, VTOL aircraft, television and a rocket trip to Mars (courtesy of The Museum of Modern Art/Film Stills Archive).

Grindell H. Matthews captured newspaper headlines throughout Europe and America. Other scientists followed suit with claims for similar inventions. The Pathé Company gave emphasis to Matthews' work through a film appropriately titled *The Death Ray* (1924). In the 1930s, Nikola Tesla had proposed a particle beam weapon capable of destroying 10,000 aircraft at a distance of 250 miles. Great Britain, faced with the threat of Germany's rearmament program, saw Tesla's invention as an electric wall for thwarting Hitler's high-flying bombers. Negotiations for Tesla's services were halted when elections brought a change in the country's ruling party.

For many years, science fiction writers had been saturating pulp magazines with stories of death rays. The public's unending appetite for science fiction literature did not go unnoticed by Hollywood. During the 1930s, science fiction adaptations to film graced movie screens in increasing numbers. An early Strickfaden-contrived death ray invention appeared briefly in *Sherlock Holmes* (1932). The device was designed to fry an automobile's ignition system. In the opening laboratory scene, Holmes (Clive Brook) is seen dabbling with an electrical gadget. Off to the left of the screen, a Strickfaden spark wheel is whining and whirling at a high speed. Alice Faulkner (Miriam Jordan), Holmes' female companion, enters the room and shuts down the spark wheel. After an exchange of greetings, Holmes brings attention to his latest anti-crime weapon. It is a prototype of a ray gun which will enable the police to prevent criminals from making an escape in a speeding automobile. The clever detective gives Faulkner a demonstration of his latest creation by pushing downward on a handle (of a dynamite plunger); a powerful beam of light is emitted by an attached light-projector device. The beam of light strikes a toy-sized automobile and, puff, the engine goes up in smoke. I looked forward to seeing Holmes apply the instrument in his war with arch-enemy Moriarty (Ernest Torrence) but the ray gun plays no further part in the plot.

Other films featuring Strickfaden's death-ray inventions are *Behind the Mask* (1932), *Chandu the Magician* (1932), *The Mask of Fu Manchu*

Sherlock Holmes (Clive Brook) and female companion Alice Faulkner (Miriam Jordan) appear to be contemplating the next move in their battle against the evil Moriarty. Ken Strickfaden's whirling spark-spitter device provided a science fiction element in *Sherlock Holmes* (1932) (courtesy of Jerry Ohlinger's Movie Material Store, Inc.).

(1932), *Air Hawks* (1935), *Flash Gordon* (1936), *The Invisible Ray* (1936), *Buck Rogers* (1939) and *The Shadow* (1940). The death ray weapon used in *Murder at Dawn* (1932) was a device Ken defined as a "DXL Accumulator."

In 1931, Universal achieved a much-needed financial boost and a considerable prestige through the success of the film *Dracula*. Encouraged by the public's reception of the horror film, Carl Laemmle, Jr., and director James Whale teamed up for an adaptation of Mary Shelley's *Frankenstein: or the Modern Prometheus*. In retrospect, it seems appropriate to assume the scriptwriters had Kenneth Strickfaden in mind when incorporating special electrical effects into the screenplay. The collaboration might best be characterized as "a marriage made in cinematic heaven."

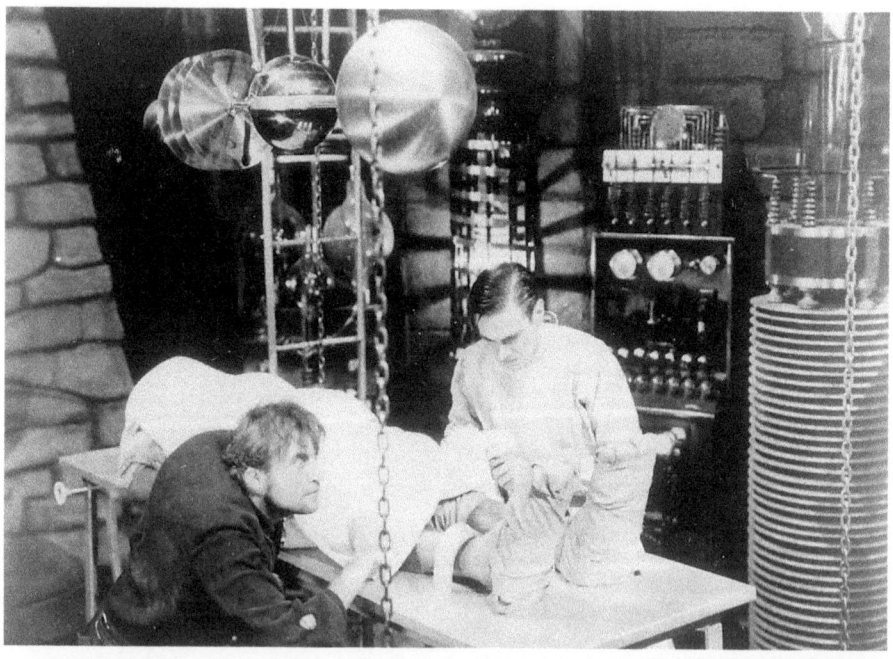

Henry Frankenstein (Colin Clive) and assistant (Dwight Frye) in preparation for one of the most astonishing scenes in the history of filmdom. The addition of Ken Strickfaden's high voltage props might best be characterized as a marriage made in cinematic heaven. The laboratory apparatus used in *Frankenstein* subsequently appeared in numerous science fiction and horror films (courtesy of The Museum of Modern Art/Film Stills Archive).

Ken proceeded to prepare a sketch of the laboratory in which Henry Frankenstein would carry out his creation experiments. Strickfaden's rendition of the laboratory is one of a number of important papers missing from his files. Be that as it may, several authors have managed to incorporate the Strickfaden plan in their own publications. One of the many interesting electrical apparati proposed for the Frankenstein laboratory was a large Tesla coil named "Megavolt Senior." This device was capable of hurling lightning-like discharges beyond ten feet. Sparks of those dimensions represent an actual electrical potential of 1,000,000 volts (with breakout voltages of 1,500,000). For reasons unknown to this author, "Meg Senior" was replaced with a Tesla coil of different design. Other Strickfaden constructed inventions making up Frankenstein's laboratory were a "Vacuum Electrolyzer," "Baritron Generator," "Lightning Bridge," "Neutron Analyzer," "Resonarium" and a "Cosmic Ray Diffuser." The

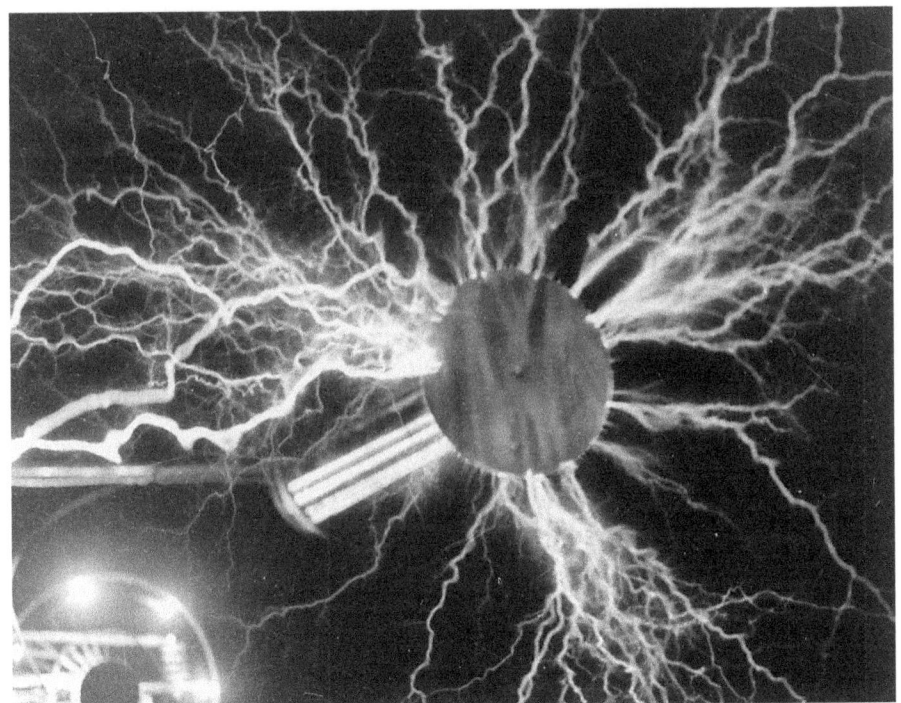

Strickfaden designed the Frankenstein laboratory around his "Megavolt Senior" Tesla coil. For some unexplained reason, a Tesla coil of different design appeared in the film.

figurative titles Ken gave to his various gadgets show the man's imaginative talents.

Once filming of *Frankenstein* began, word of the spectacular electrical displays traveled throughout the film community faster than a fire in a tinder-dry forest on a windy day. Mae Clarke, the romantic interest in the plot, later recalled, "Everybody from miles around came to watch when they pulled the switch" (Ackerman, *Famous Monsters* #100, p. 66).

Strickfaden's arrangement of electrical properties required several operators to handle the machinery. Ken, Frank Graves, Raymond Lindsay, Danny Hall and a host of studio employees made up the special electrical effects crew. Ken was kept occupied replacing over-heated and short circuited components that failed due to their need for large amounts of current. The ozone gas, and the resulting veil of smoke caused by the man made lightning, irritated the eyes and nose passages of the actors and set attendants.

> The awesome electrical paraphernalia which sparked, buzzed, and crackled so magnificently was the creation of Kenneth Strickfaden who had masterminded the laboratory for Fox's 1930 *Just Imagine*, and would later contribute his bizarre electrical effects to such films as *The Mask of Fu Manchu*, *The Wizard of Oz*, and *War of the Worlds*, as well as Universal's Frankenstein series [*Frankenstein*, MagicImage Filmbooks, 1989, p. 37].

As a measure of *Frankenstein*'s success, and the impact it had on the film industry, the 1931 production was listed among the 100 Best American Films by the American Film Institute, the British Film Institute and the National Registry of the Library of Congress. No other film of the Frankenstein category, including the highly praised *Bride of Frankenstein* (1935), made all three listings. Strickfaden's homemade electrical contraptions contributed as much to the success of the film as did the highly talented cast acting out the photoplay. The film's memorable visuals set a precedent for all genre movies and earned Kenneth Strickfaden the title of "Mr. Electric."

Frankenstein hit theaters at a time when this nation was in the throes of a serious economic nightmare. The Great Depression brought about a social collapse such as the United States had never before experienced. Bread lines and soup kitchens became a way of life. Considering the scarcity of currency then in circulation, Universal's payment of $3,000 for Strickfaden's services and lease of equipment was no small amount of change.

7

The Man Who Doubled for Boris Karloff

> *A tall tale gains momentum when repeated.*
> — The Ken Strickfaden Notebook

The stock market crash of 1929 propelled this nation into the depths of a devastating financial crisis. For nearly a decade, the citizenry of the United States struggled through an era known as the Great Depression. Unlike many corporations and business firms whose doors were locked shut, the motion picture industry suffered only a minor "miscarriage." Motion picture houses soon reopened their doors when the public began looking to movies as a temporary escape from their domestic problems.

In 1931, Ken Strickfaden was fortunate enough not to be among this nation's 12,000,000 unemployed. Having established a reputation as a special electrical effects wizard, he became a popular figure at both major and independent studios. Ken's days of job-hopping were over. By the time his career had come to a close, Strick had been involved with more than 100 film and television productions.

Another feature film of 1931 for which Ken provided electrical effects is *A Connecticut Yankee* starring Will Rogers, Maureen O'Sullivan and Myrna Loy (look for Kenny's "Retrogressive Wave Charger"). Other films of 1932 displaying Strickfaden's high voltage devices were *Doctor X*, *The Mask of Fu Manchu* and *Six Hours to Live*. Generally his equipment was under the control of a mad scientist intent on committing evil deeds. *White Zombie* (1932) is another title to which the electrician contributed his talents.

In 1931, Strickfaden journeyed to the Grand Canyon as part of the sound crew filming *The Rainbow Trail* (1932) starring George O'Brien and Cecilia Parker. He again worked with O'Brien and Parker in *Mystery Ranch* (1932). Ken claimed that those films were among the first sound features filmed in the Grand Canyon. Upon cessation of filming, Strickfaden cut several Yucca plant stalks and had them autographed. It is clear that O'Brien had been impressed with Ken's work. "Here's to you Strick, a good scout and what a man for hard work! Hope we are together again."

Camera and sound crew preparing a scene for *The Rainbow Trail* (1932) starring George O'Brien and Cecilia Parker. Ken Strickfaden (center) claimed it to be the first sound feature filmed in Arizona's Grand Canyon. Ken assisted with operation of the sound equipment (courtesy of Marilyn S. Throssel).

In 1934, Ken divided his time working for such employers as Universal, Monogram, Harold Lloyd and Monarch. *Mystery Liner* (1934) featured visuals typical of a Strickfaden-designed electrical lab. As with many of the science fiction films of the time, the plot revolved around a mysterious invention whose owner would possess great power and riches. In 1935, Universal again sought out Ken for special electrical effects. This time it was for *Bride of Frankenstein*. This sequel to the 1931 production presented him with an opportunity for pulling out all the stops.

Elaborate electrical apparatus crowded the floor of the laboratory, and when all was ready for the experiment the fantastic machinery literally sprung to life. Spurts of flame leaped from strange appliances ranged along the walls, and loops of fire floating upward. Sparks, well everywhere, and a great cosmic diffuser, lowered to a position above the still figure, boomed and flared into brilliance. Puffs of white smoke exploded as contacts were made, and rolled toward the roof. Outside a terrific storm raged and thundered, and flashes of lightning still further illuminated the laboratory. The din was almost overwhelming... [*Bride of Frankenstein*, MagicImage Filmbooks, 1989, unpaged].

Universal, Columbia, Mascot, Republic and other studios found serials to be a good source of income. Each Saturday, children of all ages flocked to theaters to witness the latest 20–30-minute chapter of an ongoing series of episodes. Chapterplays in which Ken had a hand are *The Vanishing Shadow* (1934), *The Lost City* (1935), *Phantom Empire* (1935), *The Clutching Hand* (1936), *Flash Gordon* (1936), *Undersea Kingdom* (1936), *The Fighting Devil Dogs* (1938), *Flash Gordon's Trip to Mars* (1938), *Buck Rogers* (1939), *Flash Gordon Conquers the Universe* (1940), *Mysterious Doctor Satan* (1940) and *Manhunt of Mystery Island* (1945).

Kenny's first serial, *The Vanishing Shadow*, starring Onslow Stevens, displayed numerous high voltage devices. The introduction to each chapter was sandwiched with scenes of long writhing high voltage discharges, weird pulsing bulbs and crackling displays of man-made lightning created by Ken's "Megavolt Senior" Tesla coil.

Another Strickfaden serial in which spectacular electrical displays occur is *The Monster and the Ape* (1945). Several of the lightning-like bolts span a point-to-point distance of eight feet. Discharges of those lengths represent electrical potentials of three-quarter million volts! It could not be determined whether the electrical displays had been done in miniature and then combined with the scene or if the spark distances were real. "Photography can stretch a spark of a few inches into laboratory length," said Strickfaden. Regardless of the method employed, the electrical displays in *The Monster and the Ape* were awesome.

Anyone conversing with Strickfaden would hardly suspect that he was somehow connected with the motion picture industry. The electrical wizard rarely discussed his affiliation with films. But just mention high voltage electricity and you might be the beneficiary of a detailed lecture on the physics of man-made lightning. No one interviewed for this book was able to say whether Kenny held a particular film close to heart. However, I can think of two films significant in his career, *Frankenstein* (1931) and *The Mask of Fu Manchu* (1932). The former film established Ken's reputation as a special electrical effects technician; the latter marked Strickfaden's first (and only) appearance in a feature film.

In *The Mask of Fu Manchu*, Boris Karloff plays the role of a barbarous Oriental ruler bent upon exterminating the white race. By achieving such a goal, he would become master of the world (sound familiar?). To execute his plan, Fu Manchu must first obtain possession of a ceremonial mask and scimitar, made of pure gold and once owned by the mighty Genghis Khan. The criterion for determining the sword's purity is its ability to withstand a high voltage electrical current. The instrument chosen for supplying the cascading lightning was Strickfaden's conical Tesla coil. However, it appears the special electrical effects were further enhanced with Ken's "Megavolt Senior" apparatus (hidden in the background). The script called for the high voltage sparks to fall upon the long copper fingernails of Fu Manchu's hand; the current is then

The spectacular electrical discharge spanning a distance of eight or nine feet, as seen in this rare photo from *The Monster and the Ape* (1945), represents a potential of three-quarter million volts. It could not be determined if the electrical displays had been done in miniature and then cut into the scene or if the spark distances were real. "Photography can stretch a spark of a few inches into laboratory length," said Strickfaden.

7 — The Man Who Doubled for Boris Karloff

Fu Manchu (Boris Karloff) appears to be casting out evil powers in this scene from *The Mask of Fu Manchu* (1932) as Fu Manchu's daughter Fah Lo See (Myrna Loy) and captive Terry Granville (Charles Starrett) look on. Strickfaden's "Multistributor" spark wheel stands behind Fu Manchu. A conical Tesla coil is in the foreground. This device also appeared in *Frankenstein* (1931) (courtesy of The Museum of Modern Art/Film Stills Archive).

transferred to the scimitar. When Fu Manchu obtains the sword, the high voltage melts it. Fu Manchu has been deceived. But by the use of a cunning deception, the Oriental leader is able to obtain the genuine Genghis Khan scimitar. He then prepares a second test.

Karloff was inordinately voltage-shy and begged out of playing that particular scene even though extra precautions had been taken to protect him from electric shock. The purpose of the copper fingernails was to prevent a direct lightning strike upon the skin. Otherwise, the spark would be not only painful but induce serious blistering due to the heat of the electric currents. A wire attached to the copper fingernails was threaded up Fu Manchu's sleeve and then down a pant leg. The remaining loose end was attached to a ground connection (water pipe, power panel conduit, etc.). This procedure of rendering stray electric currents harmless by grounding is common in the electrical industry. Be that as it may, Boris' fear of electricity remained undiminished. He rejected Ken's assurances that the feat could be accomplished with complete safety.

Karloff had been plagued by a vivid memory of a nightmare he was forced to endure when acting out the creation scene in Universal's *Frankenstein*. While strapped to Frankenstein's experimental table, Boris was able to look directly above and see the prop men dueling with electrically charged carbon rods. Bright flashes of lightning and descending particles of hot-glowing carbon were dispersed each time the rods came into contact. Karloff later remarked, "I hoped that no one up there had butterfingers" (Eisenberg, "Memoirs of a Monster," *Saturday Evening Post*, 11/3/62, pp. 77–80).

Considering the quantity of literature published on this film, it is puzzling that not one explains why it was Strickfaden and not a professional stuntman who ended up as Karloff's temporary replacement. The

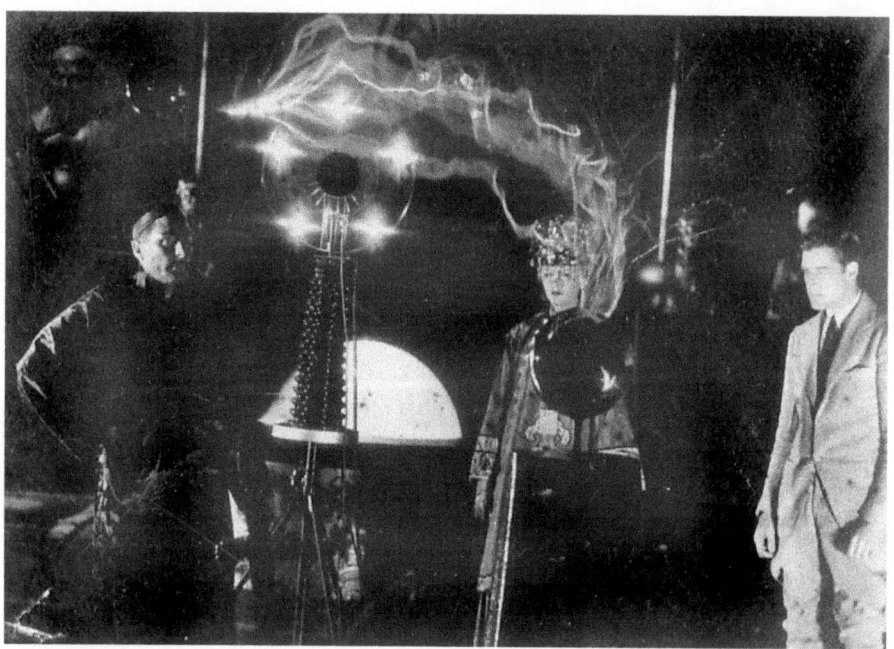

A rare and previously unpublished photograph of a rehearsal for a scene in which Kenneth Strickfaden substituted for voltage-shy Boris Karloff. Charles Starrett looks on with some trepidation as high voltage discharges pass overhead. The first take was a disaster. Strickfaden received a painful shock that knocked him to the floor.

makeup crew did a remarkable job of transforming the electrical wizard into a Fu Manchu double.

The first take of the scene in which Kenny doubled for Karloff resulted in near disaster. The following narrative describing the cinematic event is taken from Strickfaden's personal account of the incident. It was presented before the Los Angeles Bellerophon Society at Ed Angell's Hollywood Set Shop. Approximately 100 of Kenny's admirers were in attendance. During the first portion of the event, the arthritic-hampered octogenarian stood on a stage where a dozen Strickfaden-constructed props awaited their master's commands. Ken proceeded to demonstrate the effects each device was designed to produce. A question-and-answer period followed Ken's presentation. The audience response appears in parenthesis.

The actual scene from *The Mask of Fu Manchu* in which Kenneth Strickfaden played the leading role. The script required that he come in direct contact with 1,000,000 volts. Few theatergoers watching the scene were aware of the switch.

    Request from the audience:
      Tell us about the stunt you did for Boris Karloff in *The Mask of Fu Manchu* (chuckles and laughter).
    Strickfaden:
      I thought you'd never ask (laughter). We were filming *The Mask of Fu Manchu*, many man smoke but fu man chu (laughter). And Boris said, "There's nothing in my contract that says I have to do that," which was to take the big spark on copper fingernails and lead it over to a sword, that's s-w-o-r-d, which would melt when the juice hits it. And he says, "No, I'm not going to do that. You do it."

I didn't mind because Myrna Loy was there to catch me (chuckles). I had wires on my back so that I wouldn't feel any shock. The juice was supposed to go through those wires instead of me. But one of my hind feet didn't have a wire on it and a spark jumped through that to a conduit in the floor. And great was the wrath thereof weeping and gnashing its teeth (chuckles). They said I did a back flip but I don't remember that.

Anyway, I lit on a buckle right on my back. I think the hole is still in my back. And the director — how many of you people know Theda Bara? (several affirmative replies) Oh, you know her. Well, her husband, Mr. Brabin, was the director. He says, "Now that's fine Ken, let's do it again" (hysterical laughter). And we did. I didn't feel a thing that time.

It would be interesting to know what thoughts were racing through Boris Karloff's mind when witnessing the spectacle.

Another version going around claimed that Ken executed a perfect aerial somersault when receiving the electric shock. This account of the incident goes on to reveal that Ken was lying flat on his back and in a semi-conscious state when Mr. Brabin noticed a slight flickering of Strickfaden' s eyelids. It was at that moment when the director made the declaration to repeat the take.

Shortly after the filming of *The Mask of Fu Manchu*, Ken was interviewed for an article to be published in a West Coast newspaper. He was questioned about the near-electrocution event. "I thought I was a goner," explained Ken. "I've taken shocks before ... but never one like that. The only outward effect I suffered was a badly blistered big toe, but believe me, boy, I was lucky" ("Movie Edison — Diabolic Genius" by John Scott, publication undetermined, ca. 1932, pp. 13, 19). At the time, Strickfaden was a member of the sound crew filming *Cavalcade* (Fox, 1933). It won the Academy Award for Best Picture, Best Director and Interior Decoration.

8

On the Road Again — and Again

> *Science, not monsters, is my interest.*
> — Ken Strickfaden

The stock market crash occurred in 1929, but the nation's economy did not hit rock bottom until 1932–33. The growing numbers of bread lines and soup kitchens were grim reminders of the realities of the times. Bankers, corporate heads, etc., accustomed to handling millions of dollars, were now going door to door selling brushes, magazines, Christmas cards, etc. Railroad companies faced the problem of contending with thousands of down-and-outers who were illegally using freight lines for their transportation. The fragile economy, with its social implications, furnished substance for authors of both fiction and non-fiction literature. One of the most notable publications of the period was John Steinbeck's *The Grapes of Wrath*.

In 1933, the Kenneth Strickfadens moved into a newly constructed Santa Monica house located at 853 Twenty-Sixth Street. It is the home which Ken designed and paid for from earnings made through his work in *Frankenstein*. It is also the property on which Ken constructed his laboratory and storage facilities. Neighbors viewed the barn-like structure as a violation of the serene residential environment. Furthermore, the Twenty-Sixth Street community was mystified by the occasional failure of their electrical appliances to function according to the manufacturer's specifications. Whenever Ken fired up the lab's exotic high voltage apparatus, their motors labored, lights dimmed and radios buzzed. Gladys learned it was better to be out shopping during those days.

Much if not all of the published material on Ken Strickfaden has focused on his work in motion pictures. While it is true that he made a living in the film industry, it was the lure of science and not Hollywood which held Ken's interest. He publicly declared, "Science, not monsters, is my interest," and expressed disappointment in being better known for creating Frankenstein effects than as a teacher of science. Few people were aware of the fact that Ken did not like monster pictures.

> You know ... I've designed and built a lot of apparatus for these horror pictures and made quite a bit of pin money out of it, but I don't like that type of film at all. Seems to me the people who go to theaters are fed up on it. I saw a picture the other night — all about a poor Italian man who adopted a little crippled child — it was a swell show and people came out of the theater satisfied.

In the 1930s, science and mathematics were considered subjects better understood by the mentally gifted. Students of lesser intellect shunned the highly technical subjects as though they were deadly plagues. In some cases, their attitudes may have been justified. The problem, of course, had been the manner in which the subjects were presented. Ken wanted to correct the situation, not only for the children but also for their taxpaying parents who voted on school budgets. If anyone could have altered the prevailing negativism toward the physical sciences, it was Kenny Strickfaden. His command of the subject matter and skills for presenting it made science enjoyably fascinating. My take on Strickfaden is that of a man composed of an unusually complex DNA: part teacher, preacher, musician, mechanic, cartoonist, physicist, stage entertainer, inventor, stand-up comedian, electrical wizard and a mix of not yet fully understood amino acid configurations. Although Ken never entered the mainstream educational process, it is just as well that he did not obtain a formal teaching degree. He would have found the rigid educational structure too limiting for his free-spirited personality.

On May 20, 1933, Strickfaden, a.k.a. "Elecstrick" or "Kenstric," presented the first of a lifetime 1,500 "Science on Parade" demonstration lectures. It was given before the Schoolmasters Club at the John C. Freemont High School in Los Angeles. Ken provided the educational program at no charge. Lectures were also presented without remuneration before Boy and

8 — On the Road Again — and Again

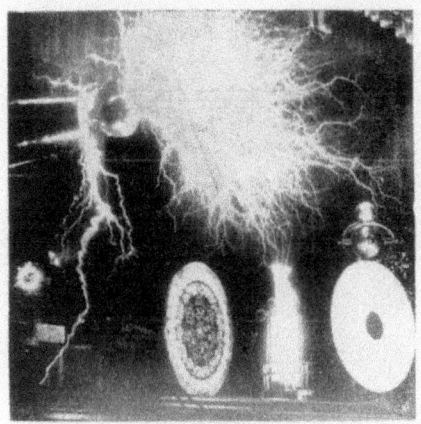

One of a dozen flyers that Ken Strickfaden distributed to bring attention to his lecture programs (courtesy of Ed Angell).

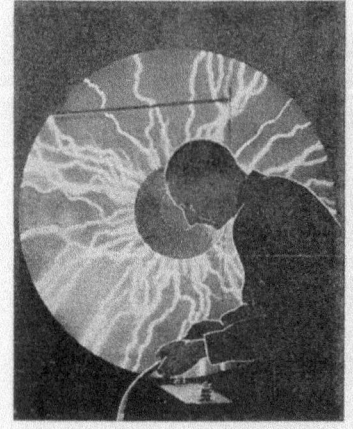
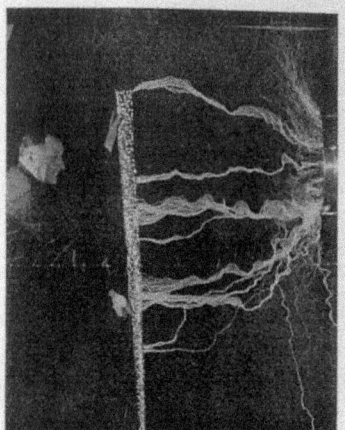
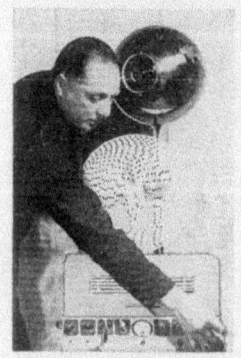

Another flyer used to publicize Strickfaden's lectures (courtesy of Ed Angell).

8 — On the Road Again — and Again

Science Presentations
by **KENNETH STRICKFADEN**
Music – Color – Electricity – Light – Sound

INSTRUCTIVE ENTERTAINMENT AS FEATURED AT FOUR EXPOSITIONS

MELODYNE — ULTRA-VIOLET FLUORESCENCE
GRAVITY NEUTRALIZER — STRATISMOBILE
ELECTRICAL LACE — LIGHTNING SCREEN
HARMONEYE — PYROGEYSER — ELECTROLIN
A MILLION VOLTS — MAGNA-STROBOSCOPE

SPECTACULAR PHENOMENA USED IN MOTION PICTURE PRODUCTIONS

July 19-20-21, Hollywood Woman's Club, Hollywood Boulevard, at La Brea.
Sunday, July 22, Temple of the Jewelled Cross, 118 North Larchmont Boulevard.

ADMISSION $1.00, Including Tax   DEMONSTRATIONS START AT 8 P.M.

An advertisement for a forthcoming Strickfaden lecture.

Girl Scouts, YMCA groups, veteran's hospitals, church-related organizations and other charitable institutions. The fees Ken received for other appearances depended upon the type and size of organization with which a contract had been signed. The number of requested performances per contract also played a role in determining fees. He once received the tidy sum of $1 for a demonstration at a recreational center. And Ken took in $3 for a program presented before a women's club. Strickfaden did not always record the fees gained for his services but once earned $1,287.25 for a short series of lectures. At times, he worked for a fixed fee plus a percentage of the gate. Under other agreements, the money pocketed depended on the gate receipts alone. Some lectures brought in $15, while others earned $75–80. His average intake per lecture fell somewhere in the $35–45 range. Earnings that exceeded personal expenses were forwarded home to Gladys. Ken's entrepreneurship spared him the necessity of standing in bread lines or visiting soup kitchens. Think of what Strickfaden's talents could demand today for a single appearance on the popular late-night television talk shows. In addition, Kenny would have fit in nicely on the children's science-oriented programs now so prevalent on the television networks.

The Strickfaden lectures were so well-received that he appeared before the same groups year after year. Ken's travels covered all of the contiguous 48 states, Hawaii and Canada. Some tours required several months before contractual agreements were fulfilled. The 1950 New York State journey, for example, during which Kenstric presented his amazing show at the school where I was teaching, began on September 22 and ended just prior to the Christmas holiday. His hectic schedule would at times require visits to as many as five schools in one day. And on some occasions, the schools were located in rural areas at distances of 25–50 miles apart. Although the majority of performances were presented before junior (middle) and senior high school students, Ken often received requests for appearances at colleges and universities. Lectures presented at the universities of Arizona, Kansas and Wisconsin were so enthusiastically received that he was immediately signed for a return engagement.

The following are but two examples of the hundreds of testimonials Ken received from schools and colleges:

> It is a pleasure to advise you that your assembly presentation yesterday of "Science on Parade," was received most enthusiastically by both teachers and students. I particularly want to commend you upon your ability to hold the interest of those thirteen hundred students for an hour and a quarter. Not the least feature in the success of your presentation is your own clever personality. In addition to the educational explanations and demonstrations which you gave, you are a real showman. The demonstrations themselves were fascinating in that they showed in a spectacular manner the fundamentals of some of the electrical phenomena and then followed with demonstrations of how these fundamentals were used in the modern wizardry of electrical science. Probably the demonstration of artificial lightning with its million and a half volts was the most interesting. I may say to you that our students feel that this was one of the finest assemblies we have ever had in this school [Principal L.J. Williams, Visalia High School, California].
>
> The apparatus designed and built by you was most efficient and the value of the exhibition to the students and to the general public was great. The reception you gave back stage was most instructive and interesting. Your method of presenting the facts was clear and concise, technicalities were omitted so that the layman could get a good idea of the subject. Your lecture is particularly valuable to students of electricity and physics and to the general public [E.P. Mathewson, Science Department, University of Arizona, Tucson].

Ken's Science on Parade presentation (later "The Kenstric Space Age Science Show") appeared time and again at motion picture studio events.

The Science on Parade show was later named the Kenstric Space Age Science Show.

Some of the studios where he presented demonstration lectures are Monogram (1), Columbia (2), MGM (3), Disney (4) and Warner Bros. (7) (the figures in parenthesis represent the number of contracts, not performances). He may have been called upon to give several performances per contract. Some of the studio engagements extended over a period of six to twelve months. Strickfaden did not record the income earned during the studio tours. Several special programs were presented before studio executives without receipt of payment. In those cases, the electrician may have benefited in other ways. The immediate question that comes to mind is whether Ken's studio appearances were ever recorded on motion picture film. Surely there must have been forward-thinking studio heads who seized upon the opportunity to make a permanent record of the events. Is there a motion picture film of Kenneth Strickfaden's lectures in the studio vaults just waiting to be discovered?

The possibility of the existence of a Strickfaden lecture on motion picture film came a step closer to reality with the appearance of two interesting television documentaries. Exciting clips of Kenny in action can be

An Elecstrick electric exhibition ready for display. Ken's lightning screen is the white-rimmed disc at the left.

seen in the A&E production *Mystery of Genius: Masters and Madmen* (1998) and the PBS documentary *Tesla — Master of Lightning* (2000). Although the scenes are very brief, they provide encouragement for further investigation.

Perhaps the largest number of people to witness a Strickfaden show at any one time occurred at expositions and fairs. In 1935, the electrician performed at the San Diego Exposition. A year later, he played an important historical role at the Los Angeles Electric Age Exposition. This event coincided with the inauguration of the transmission of electrical current from Boulder Dam. *The New York Times* for November 1, 1936 (RP4, p. 3), carried a photo of Strickfaden in the midst of long cascading electrical sparks. The caption, printed in bold letters, described the scene as "MAN-MADE LIGHTNING FROM BOULDER DAM." If for nothing else, Ken Strickfaden could make claim to being the first to energize a Tesla coil by the power of Boulder (Hoover) Dam. In 1939, Ken presented programs at the Los Angeles Home Show and the great San Francisco World's Fair. During the early 1940s, he performed at fairs and

8 — On the Road Again — and Again

Strickfaden shows were probably seen by the greatest number of people at expositions and fairs.

expositions in California and Canada. And in 1947, Strickfaden presented his science show at California's Centennial Exposition. Other equally important engagements include the Utah Centennial, California Pacific Exposition, Utah State Agricultural College, U.S. Department of the Interior, Los Angeles Veteran's Administration and the International Brotherhood of Electrical Workers. The following represent additional excerpts from testimonials found in Strickfaden's files:

> One of the most unusual and interesting assemblies of the year ... a great deal of scientific information in an amusing and rather spectacular way.
> Delighted in your spectacular electrical demonstration ... one of the highlights of our exposition.
> Frankly, we have never seen a more spectacular display ... audience expressed a wish for your return.
> Stimulating and instructive ... every university community should have an opportunity to witness your exhibition.

The Kenstric Science Show kept the gang awed and in stitches for an hour.

Ken's Canadian tour of the provinces in 1936 received favorable treatment from the press. One article included a photo of the electrician's "Gravity Neutralizer" which inspired an Ontario newspaper editor to forward a serious dissertation on a method of neutralizing gravitational forces. His theory was based upon the premise that the ether could be bent. Although no one has ever proven the existence of an ether, early scientists believed it to be a substance filling all space between the stars and planets. The editor theorized that employment of the "Flettner principle" would make it possible to easily move heavy objects.

College textbooks attribute to Anton Flettner an alternative method of moving vessels at sea by equipping ships with huge rotating columns in place of the traditional canvas sails. Scientists refer to the phenomenon of motion created by rotating bodies as the "Magnus effect." Although a ship equipped with Flettner's rotating columns successfully crossed the Atlantic in 1926, the system had its shortcomings and quickly succumbed to more efficient methods of propulsion. The correlation between Flettner's principle and the neutralization of gravitational forces is not clear. Perhaps the editor had in mind a scientific principle with which I am unfamiliar.

Kenstric, in his inimitable manner of veridicality, provided a clear and concise response to the editor's communication.

> Regarding the gravity neutralizer, the picture of which you saw in the *Toronto Star Weekly*, (I) will explain that this device is one of a number of spectacular electrical devices designed solely for the purpose of creating odd, fantastic effects for motion pictures.
>
> While this device is constructed on well known principles, and has been used in lectures to demonstrate electromagnetic repulsion, it has no other use nor does it promise to revolutionize any existing theories.

Perhaps the most memorable Strickfaden engagement took place at the Palace of Electricity during the California Pacific International Exposition of 1935–36. The Palace of Electricity program was jointly sponsored by the Bureau of Radio and Electrical Appliances, the San Diego Consolidated Gas and Electric Company, the Los Angeles Bureau of Light and Power and others. Among the exhibits were samples of marvels predicted for the future, while another area was set aside as a reminder of

8 — On the Road Again — and Again

the past. Of the latter, the inventions of Thomas Edison drew the greatest attention. But the magic of science was never more brilliantly displayed than the demonstration by which radio waves were used to produce popcorn. Another exhibit which amazed visitors was the transmission of music across a room in the form of a beam of light. But even these mesmerizing feats of science were to be eclipsed by a series of demonstrations given by a man named Strickfaden.

Initial attendance to the Palace of Electricity turned out to be far less than anticipated so the management decided to circulate a special flyer to promote the event. A photo of Ken Strickfaden and his equipment was included in the promotional. The following is a portion of the text:

> Most spectacular of all the features is the noncommercial "Electrical Wizardry Demonstrations" of Kenneth Strickfaden, creator of the electrical effects in more than a score of famous pictures such as *Frankenstein*,

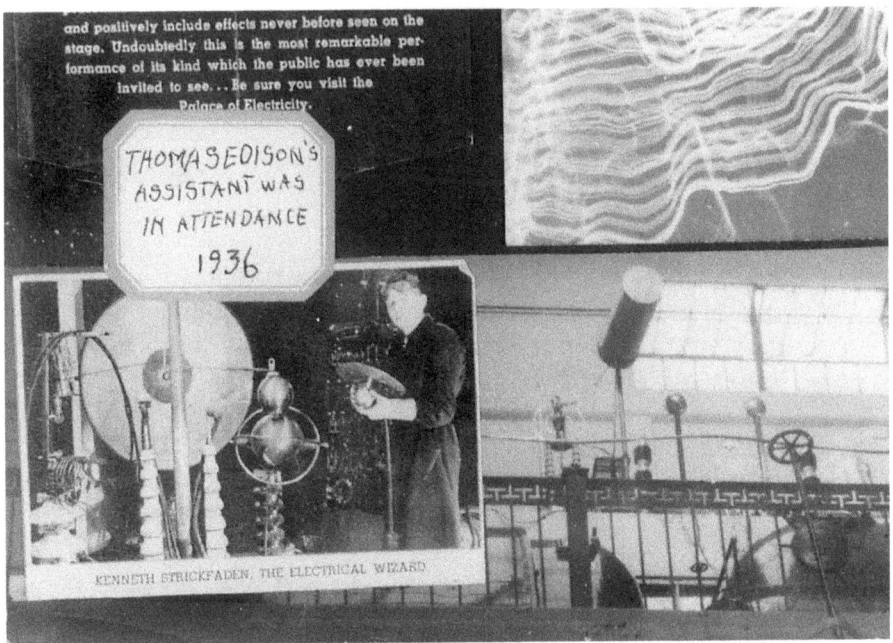

A photocopy of a section from Ken Strickfaden's scrapbook showing a portion of the circular advertising the Palace of Electricity presentation at the California Pacific International Exposition. Attendance increased by 88 percent and Ken found himself performing before standing-room-only crowds (courtesy of Ed Angell).

Flash Gordon, etc. These shows are presented four times daily as a courtesy to our visitors, and positively include effects never before seen on stage. Undoubtedly, this is the most remarkable performance of its kind which the public has ever been invited to see ... Be sure to visit the Palace of Electricity.

As the word of Strickfaden's show got around, the attendance to the Palace of Electricity increased by 88 percent! Ken found himself performing before standing-room-only crowds. At the exposition's closing, a survey of the total attendance revealed a record-setting 750,000 visitors.

Although Ken was reluctant to admit his positive influence upon young people, many who had witnessed his performances later gave credit to Mr. Electric as having been an important factor in their decision to obtain an education in science. Not a small number of the converts to science chose to follow a career in electrical engineering. One example is William H. Harrison, co-publisher of *Monsterscene* magazine. "Kenneth Strickfaden has long been a hero of mine. I'm sure that seeing his designs for the lab equipment used by a hundred mad scientists influenced me to pursue my own career in electrical engineering" (private communication to the author, 1/6/91). A teacher can receive no greater tribute than that as expressed by Mr. Harrison.

The proliferation of science centers, with their children's hands-on exhibits, is vindication of Kenneth Strickfaden's faith in science education. A most fitting tribute to this pioneer of science education would be to name a science center or electrical exhibit room in his honor.

Additional testimonials:

> I feel that your demonstrations were most worthwhile, and I can recommend you to any other school that is considering high-class programs which embody both educational and entertainment features [A.S. Bowhay, Principal, Santa Monica].
>
> Excellent from start to finish. I am sure this program was one of the best we have had this year [Jacob L. Neighbor, Principal, Hanford].
>
> We have heard only the finest comments concerning your demonstration and lecture. I believe that your program would be of interest to adult groups and to recreational center groups, and we shall be glad to recommend you accordingly. Mr. Clifton and I extend our belated thanks for your fine contributions to our Institute [C.C. Trillingham, Assistant Supt. of Schools, Los Angeles].

8 — On the Road Again — and Again

Upon completion of a lecture at a university, a group of engineering students raced backstage to meet the popular lecturer and to examine his unusual collection of apparatus. One of the students took a particular interest in a Tesla transformer. The following discussion ensued:

STUDENT: How long a spark will this instrument produce?
KENNY: Six feet.
STUDENT: If you build a larger one, will the spark be longer?
KENNY: Yes.
STUDENT: Why don't you build it"
KENNY: It wouldn't fit into my station wagon.

9

The Tesla Coil Connection

The time has come the unicorn said
To talk of many things,
Tesla coils and cyclosaurs
And a rotary gap that sings.
— The Ken Strickfaden Notebook

After Gutenberg's invention of the printing press, Nikola Tesla's discovery of the rotating magnetic field did more to advance civilization than any other scientific revelation. Its application to electrical generators and motors is what gives our homes heat and light. B.A. Behrend, a pioneering electrical engineer, provided an accurate summation of the importance of Tesla's discovery. "Were we to seize and eliminate from our industrial world the results of Tesla's work, the wheels of industry would cease to turn ... our towns would be dark, our mills would be dead and idle" (presentation of the Edison Medal to Tesla on May 18, 1917). Arthur Brisbane, dean of Hearst news editors, called Tesla "Our Foremost Electrician ... Greater Even Than Edison" (*The World,* New York, July 22, 1894, p. 17). Strickfaden considered Tesla "one of our greatest geniuses" (*Los Angeles Herald Examiner,* July 12, 1981, p. A-3).

Of Tesla's more than 100 patents, the instrument known as a Tesla coil is the only invention bearing his name. The Tesla coil is similar to an electrical transformer in that it converts electrical currents to either a higher or lower value depending upon the particular use to which it is being applied. But a Tesla coil differs considerably from the commonly known transformer in that it can also alter the frequency of the alternating

9— The Tesla Coil Connection

current being fed to it. For example, Tesla's apparatus can take the 120 volt, 60 Hertz (Hz) alternating current available in our homes and raise the voltage to hundreds of thousands while at the same time increase the 60 Hz frequency to millions of alternations per second. The frequencies at which Tesla coils function are called radio frequencies (RF). A Tesla (oscillation) transformer is a vital part of all high-power broadcasting stations. Guglielmo Marconi, often proclaimed as the inventor of wireless telegraphy, did not have much success in establishing long distance communications until incorporating a Tesla transformer in his transmitting and receiving circuits. It should be noted that in 1942, the U.S. Supreme Court judged Marconi's all important tuned four-circuit patent invalid due to prior disclosure by Nikola Tesla, Sir Oliver Lodge and John S. Stone. Stone acknowledged Tesla's prior work and declared the inventor "so far ahead of his time that the best of us mistook him for a dreamer" ("Fames of Nikola Tesla," *Liberty*, Oakland, San Francisco, July 11, 1917).

Nikola Tesla (1856–1943), inventor of the electrical system currently in use throughout the world, was once hailed as "Our Foremost Electrician ... Greater Even Than Edison." Although he held more than 100 patents, the Tesla coil is the only invention bearing his name (*Century Magazine*, February 1894).

Tesla originally devoted his high frequency experiments to the development of a superior system of illumination. It has taken the lighting industry more than 100 years to recognize the advantages of a high frequency illuminant. Several manufacturing firms have shown an interest in the production and marketing of an efficient bulb that functions on the same principle pioneered by Tesla.

Those fascinating lightning lamps advertised as "plasma globes" were invented by Tesla. The electrical wizard often astonished friends when holding an unconnected glass sphere in which fiery tongues of lightning would appear when a circuit elsewhere in the laboratory was energized. Edourd Remenyi, the great Hungarian violinist, was among the celebrities privileged to witness such a demonstration. The following is quoted from a letter the famous musician sent to Czech composer Antonín Dvořák:

> If you want to be blown up — down — to be pulverized, to be electrified, to be flabbergasted, to be electrically astonished, all you have to do is to come, and your family, to 35 South Fifth Avenue next Wednesday at half-past three P.M., and you will see things of which even you scarcely dreamt. [*Remenyi, Musician & Man*, by Kelley & Upton, A.C. McClurg & Co., 1906, p. 208]

While undertaking a search for a novel light bulb, Tesla discovered the tuned, inductively coupled, four-circuit arrangement that was to form the foundation for radio communications. Another Tesla discovery relates to the peculiar ability of radio frequency currents to produce flameless heat. Tesla lectured before medical institutions, suggesting that high frequency currents might have beneficial uses in the practice of medicine. His proposal spurred medical practitioners to investigate high frequency phenomena. Their experimental work resulted in a new field of therapeutics known as diathermy. The heat-producing capability of high frequency currents is also put to good use in the field of special welding and annealing. A modified Tesla coil can be found in the high voltage driving circuit of your television set. There are numerous examples where the Tesla coil has been used to advantage.

Although the Tesla coil was invented more than 100 years ago, it continues to be a servant of industry wherever high voltage

An illustration from a 1938 patent issued to Henry L. Transtrom for improvements in demonstrating high voltage effects. Transtrom was accidentally killed during a public demonstration of this feat.

9 — The Tesla Coil Connection

radio frequency currents are required. In addition to its technical properties, the Tesla coil is relatively simple and inexpensive to construct. Junior high school students in my classes were able to fabricate moderate-sized units capable of producing lightning-like discharges up to two feet in length. Electrical sparks of those dimensions represent potentials greater than 250,000 volts. Fortunately, radio frequency currents of those magnitudes are not as dangerous as an equivalent voltage of low frequency electricity. At high frequencies, low charge densities do not seem to produce nerve action (pain) or register the type of shock one experiences with low frequency house currents. This pheomenon is often referred to as the "skin effect." It becomes a different matter at high charge densities. Tesla safely demonstrated the skin effect principle by passing hundreds of thousands of volts of high frequency currents over his entire body.

The explanations in the previous paragraph should make it clear how the Tesla coil metamorphosed into a popular tool for stage charlatans and carnival hucksters. During the early part of the twentieth century, there existed a plethora of traveling shows featuring "human insulators" who claimed an invulnerability to the dangers of high voltage electricity. Some of the pseudonyms which performers applied to the trade are "Dr. Resisto," "The Human Battery," "The Electric Wizard"

Dick Aurandt, an electrical engineer and special effects technician, is connected to a 250,000 volt Tesla coil. This feat is not without pain or danger (courtesy of Dick Aurandt).

and "The Great Volta." It was also not uncommon to find a "Madam Electra," "Electric Lady" or an "Electrice" among the traveling exhibits.

When considering the Tesla coil's impressive characteristics, it should be no mystery as to why the motion picture studios were quick to recognize its potential as a special effects property. One of the first, if not *the* first film to feature a Tesla coil was the serial *The Romance of Elaine* (1915). Other silent cliffhangers in which Tesla's invention played a role were *The Black Box* (1915), *Wolves of Kultur* (1918), *The Great Radium Mystery* (1919), *Hidden Dangers* (1920) and *The Power God* (1926). Two silent feature films known to have utilized a Tesla coil were *Blow Your Own Horn* (1923) and *Metropolis* (1926). *The Romance of Elaine* was one of a trio of "Elaine" chapterplays featuring the popular Pearl White. The gentleman who came to the rescue in *Blow Your Own Horn* was a former shoe salesman named Warner Baxter. Of the above-mentioned titles, only *Wolves of Kultur*, *Metropolis* and *The Power God* appear to have survived and are available on home video. It is reasonable to assume that Ken Strickfaden enjoyed many, if not all, of the films discussed here. They

During the early part of the twentieth century, there existed a plethora of traveling shows featuring performers claiming an invulnerability to high voltage electricity. In many cases, the performance included an electric chair connected to a Tesla coil (courtesy of Mel Allen).

may have even played an influential role in the choice of career he was to follow.

The Tesla coil served as one of Strickfaden's favorite "mad scientist" props—an electrical instrument upon which he bestowed the title "mother-in-law eliminator." Ken had constructed his first model in 1914. As previously mentioned, a photo of an early Strickfaden-constructed Tesla coil appeared in *Electrical Experimenter* in November 1919. By 1931, the year in which Universal released *Frankenstein*, Ken had completed a variety of designs. Although his cone-shaped Tesla project appeared in that production, one has to carry out a diligent search to find it. When viewing the film, direct your attention to the extreme left side of the screen as Henry Frankenstein elevates the Monster (Boris Karloff) toward the laboratory's skylight. Film buffs can get a much better view of that model in *The Mask of Fu Manchu* (1932). The instrument is utilized in two scenes as a means of confirming the purity of a golden sword.

The creation scene from *Frankenstein* (1931). Strickfaden's Tesla coil (left of center) appears only briefly in the picture. Direct your attention to the left of the screen as the Monster is being raised to the roof (courtesy of Jerry Ohlinger's Movie Material Store, Inc.).

Strickfaden's "Meg Senior" Tesla transformer was put to good use in *The Clutching Hand* (1936), a serial in which Dr. Gironda (Paul Frazier) activated the transformer in a bogus lead-to-gold scheme. Science fiction and horror film fans are given an opportunity to observe this same apparatus in *Son of Frankenstein* (1939). Wolf von Frankenstein (Basil Rathbone) applied artificial lightning in an attempt to revive the comatose Monster (Boris Karloff). Benson (Edgar Norton), Frankenstein's loyal assistant, demonstrates a slight apprehensive response as the lightning-like sparks wriggle nearby. Apparently the scene was filmed in real time. In another laboratory experiment, several of the long writhing discharges appear to be seven or eight feet in length. Sparks of those dimensions equal a potential of approximately three-quarters of a million volts. This scene does not appear in either the VHS or DVD reissues now available to the public.

Other films in which Ken's Tesla coils are utilized include *Chandu the Magician* (1932), *The Lost City* (1935) and a multitude of Frankenstein copycat productions. Many supplemental mad scientist electrical

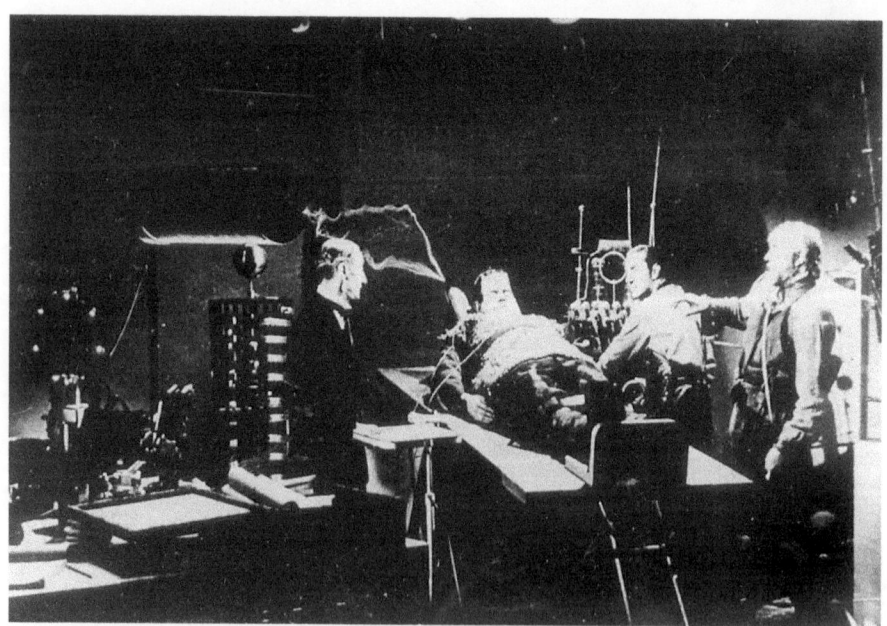

Benson the butler (Edgar Norton) and Ygor (Bela Lugosi) look on as Wolf von Frankenstein (Basil Rathbone) adjusts the laboratory apparatus in *Son of Frankenstein* (1939).

machines which Kenstric devised are rotating spark wheels, traveling (ascending) arc apparatus (often referred to as a "Jacob's Ladder"), weird pulsating bulbs (look for a neat one in *Son of Frankenstein* and similar films), fire rings and lightning screens. In addition to inventing spark-spitting machines, Ken constructed static props which do nothing but assist in creating a mood to fit a particular scene (simulated coils of wire, fake insulators, pseudo control panels, switches and other representations).

In 1937, an official at the Griffith Observatory in Los Angeles called upon Strickfaden for technical advice in the installation of a very large Tesla coil. Since then, this impressive instrument has been viewed by thousands of visitors to the popular museum. The lightning pyrotechnics and related thunderous buzz of the discharges have inspired many youths to follow a career in the field of electrical engineering. One of those lads was William C. Wysock.

> It was the Griffith Park coil, that I first saw as a young boy, that introduced me to Tesla. I never forgot the images that were etched in my mind.... Several years later, as a young teenager, my mother took me back to the Observatory so that I could once again see that beautiful coil. Those were wonderful memories, and it was that coil that got me started in building Tesla coils.

Wysock, an electrical engineer, has constructed numerous Tesla coils, one of them an exact replica of the Griffith Observatory transformer. The Griffith replica model has been placed on public display at Fry's Electronic Store in Fremont, California.

The Griffith Observatory Tesla coil is actually one of two identical units. They were constructed in the 1920s by Earle L. Ovington. Ovington used the coils to produce spectacular high voltage displays at the electrical shows held in New York City's Madison Square Garden. Ovington was acquainted with Nikola Tesla on a personal basis and the famous inventor often attended the Madison Garden electrical exhibits. Ovington had been an associate of Dr. Frederick Finch Strong of Tufts University. The two men were ardent admirers of Tesla and had collaborated on the construction of high frequency equipment for medical applications. Dr. Strong later became the owner of the Ovington transformers and eventually donated them to the Griffith Observatory. Space limitations at the institution allowed for only one of the units to be placed on display.

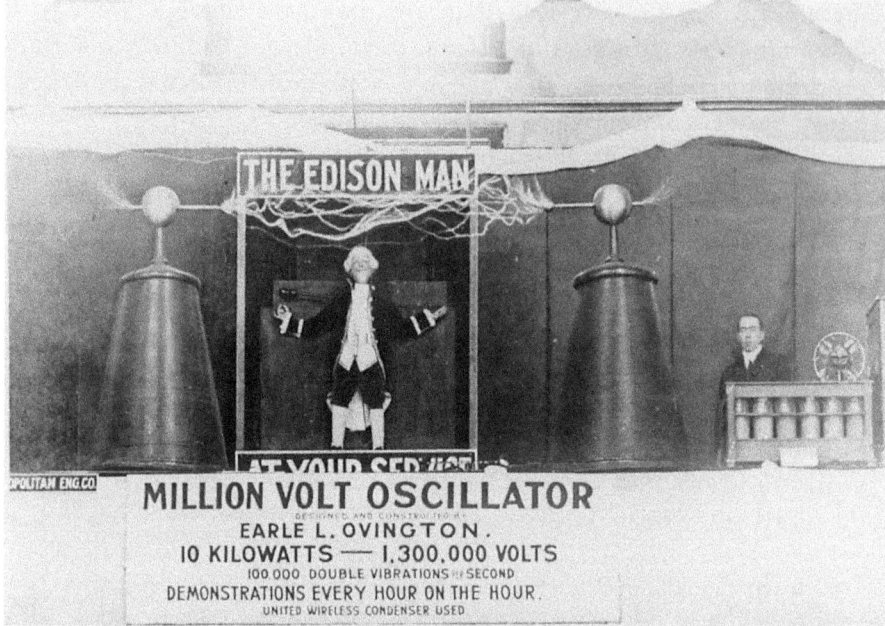

Twin Tesla coils, designed and constructed by Earle L. Ovington, were often displayed at the Madison Square Garden, New York City, electrical shows. The coils were later acquired by Dr. Frederick Finch Strong, who donated them to the Griffith Observatory. Because of limited space, only one unit was put on display (courtesy of Dr. E.C. Krupp, director, Griffith Observatory).

In 1985, there occurred a deterioration in the performance of the Griffith Tesla transformer. When Strickfaden's circle of wizards learned of the situation, technicians Richard Aurandt, John Foster, Edward Angell, Victor Hymowitz and other volunteers offered assistance in restoring the apparatus to its original efficiency of operation. The group's eagerness to help was inspired by the fond memories of their own childhood visits to the museum. This assemblage of dedicated engineers not only worked several days free of charge but also contributed valuable replacement parts from their own collections.

During the writing of this book, the Griffith Observatory Museum complex has been undergoing a major renovation. Included in the rebuilding process is an updating of the Tesla coil display. The spirits of Earle L. Ovington, Frederick F. Strong and Kenneth J. Strickfaden may be present during the rebuilding campaign. Visitors to the new museum who are familiar with the Tesla coil's history and have a basic understanding of the laws of physics by which it functions might be capable of visualizing three wispy figures merrily weaving around the Tesla coil as sparks pass through them and on into the air. All others will only see sparks.

> Ode to the Tesla Coil
> Here's to the fragrance of ozone
> combined with the smell of an
> overheated transformer.
> — Edward Aronson

10

"I Could Have Retired a Millionaire..."

Voltricks and Amperatus
— The Ken Strickfaden Notebook

    On November 8, 1932, the nation elected Franklin Delano Roosevelt president of the United States. His campaign promise had been a "new deal for the American people." Upon taking office, the fledgling coalition immediately established a number of programs under the National Recovery Administration (NRA). One of the many Roosevelt-sponsored programs which proved highly effective in reducing unemployment was the Federal Emergency Relief Act. This enactment established the Works Progress Administration (WPA). Citizens employed under the WPA provided labor for building schools, playgrounds, parks, water and sewer lines, levees, dams and so on. Between 1933 and 1940, the WPA put $20,000,000,000 worth of wages into previously empty pockets. Another New Deal program was the Civilian Conservation Corps (CCC). The CCC presented a semi-military atmosphere, but in place of guns the participants were armed with saws, hammers, shovels and other construction equipment. The CCC project served the nation's environmental needs such as the recovery of soil, water, plants and forests. This program removed a quarter-million unemployed from the streets and gave them work at $30 a month. Other actions taken under Roosevelt's leadership provided assistance to agriculture, banking, electric power, railroads and home-owner loans. "Happy days" were not yet "here again" but the pessimism brought on by the Great Depression was being diluted by an air of optimism. Incidentally, publications such as sheet music, magazines, etc., carrying the NRA symbol have become highly desired by collectors of Depression Era ephemera. The NRA logo can also be seen in motion picture films of that period.

One of the last films of the 1930s for which Ken Strickfaden supplied services was *The Ice Follies of 1939*. By 1940, the winds of war that had been eroding the European landscape were rapidly approaching America's shores. This bleak reality was offset by the good news of a sharp decline in the dependency upon bread lines and soup kitchens for feeding the nation's unemployed. The Great Depression was a matter of history by the time the United States entered the world conflict in December 1941.

In 1940, Kenny presented his Elecstrick lecture program on both coasts. Daughter Carolyn accompanied him to several shows including performances at the International Exposition held in Toronto, Canada. Ken worked on several films that year *Dr. Cyclops*, *Sky Bandits*, a pair of serials and Disney's *Fantasia*. Strickfaden's influence is also apparent in *The Devil Bat* (1940), *Man Made Monster* (1941), *The Ghost of Frankenstein* (1942), *The Man with Two Lives* (1942) and *The Strange Case of Doctor Rx* (1942). In addition to lectures and film activities, Ken assisted in technical work being done at KPAS radio. Film work for 1943 included high voltage effects for *Frankenstein Meets the Wolf Man* and the serial *Batman*. He also created impressive lightning bolts for the ritual scene in *Sherlock Holmes Faces Death*.

Between film commitments, Strickfaden continued to pound the lecture circuit. World War II was in full swing and many of the notebook entries characterized as "shows" involved gratis services to U.S. armed forces. Most of the performances given on behalf of the military were presented under the auspices of the United Service Organization (USO). Several appearances before military personnel took place at the Hollywood USO. The war had created an emotional patriotism not seen in this country since World War I. Everyone was doing their part to support the war effort. In addition to entertaining the men and women in uniform, Ken served as an instructor of industrial skills (electric and acetylene welding), training civilians for work in defense plants. The war had drained the pool of available skilled labor so courses were made available to help fill the void. Many of the newsreels showing men and women

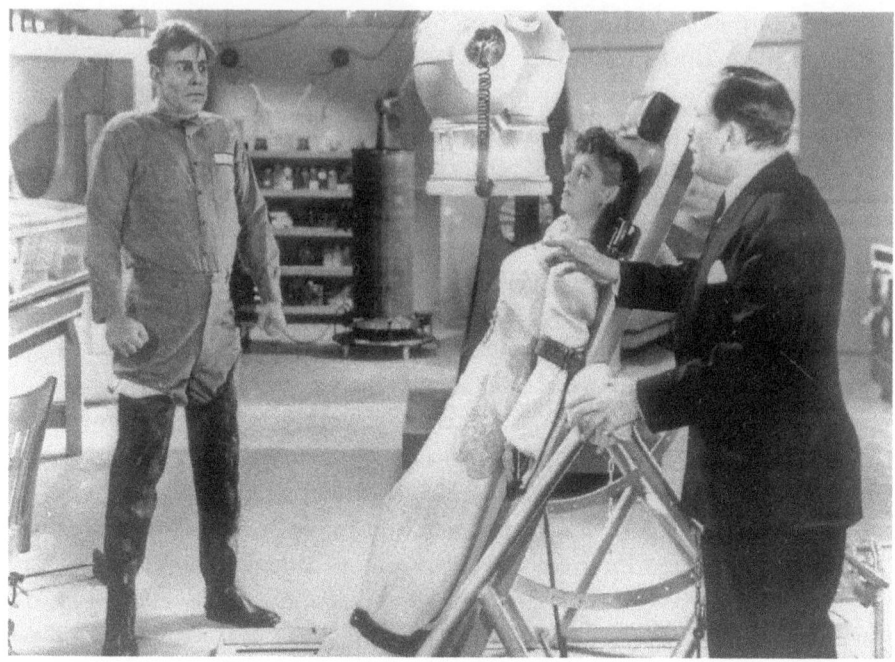

Man Made Monster (1941) featured numerous high voltage props. A large Tesla coil can be seen in the background. In this scene, Lon Chaney, Jr., confronts Anne Nagel and Lionel Atwill (courtesy of The Museum of Modern Art/Film Stills Archive).

welders in defense work may have been taken of workers who received their training under Strickfaden's watchful eye.

The highlight of Ken's film work for 1944 was *House of Frankenstein*. That year was not without its down side. Kenny's father, Francis (Frank) J. Strickfaden, passed away following a long illness. He spent his declining years under the care of the Strickfadens at their Santa Monica residence.

In 1945, the special electrical effects technician applied his expertise to Universal's *House of Dracula,* PRC's *Devil Bat's Daughter* and the Republic serial *Manhunt of Mystery Island.* The latter production featured several marvelous pseudoscientific props, not the least being a nuclear-powered transmitter designed to send energy to any location on Earth. This amazing invention was also capable of blasting a hole through the toughest natural or man-made material. Even more interesting was the Transformation Chair, a contraption which enabled the evil Mephisto

(Roy Barcroft) to alter his image. The Transformation Chair included ascending electrical discharges and an impressive slow-turning spark wheel.

Strickfaden's high voltage apparatus is nicely displayed in the Charlie Chan film *The Scarlet Clue* (1945). Mantan Moreland, providing his usual frightened valet role, accidentally switches on the equipment. Impressive bolts of man-made lightning can be seen flying about the room. Although an imposing rangefinder device is among the various lab apparatus, it plays no part in the action.

Mr. Elecstrick ushered in the 1950s with lecture tours at the University of Minnesota (1950) and Wisconsin (1951) as well as a return engagement at the University of Kansas (1952).

Ken and Gladys Strickfaden at their 26th Street home in Santa Monica (ca. mid–1940s) after the recent passing of his father. This is the house Ken designed, and paid for by the earnings from *Frankenstein*.

His schedule for 1950 also involved a contract for providing technical services to Nassour Studios. During that year, Ken re-signed with the School Assembly Association. Part of 1951 was given to fulfilling a contract with NBC. In 1952, the wizard presented a second series of lectures at the University of Wisconsin. Another tour, beginning in September of that year and lasting until May 1953, was devoted to science demonstrations at schools in the southeast.

The apex of Strickfaden's film work in 1953 was the box office success *The War of the Worlds*. Kenstric was up to his ears in activity in 1954. He signed a new contract with NBC, took part in experimental operations at the MGM sound shop, provided technical services to television station KTTV, prepared special electrical effects for the Hollywood Museum and continued to appear at fairs and shows.

It was a hot and humid morning in 1960 when Ken awoke to the realization that his body clock had slowed down. An arthritic condition brought on by years of hauling heavy equipment had taken its toll. He concluded that the time had come to rein in his highly demanding work schedule. Ken notified the IBEW of his intention to retire. Strickfaden had fulfilled 34 years of union service. His retirement, however, did not bring an end to his career.

A few years prior to Strickfaden's retirement, a representative for the Disney Corporation appeared at Ken's shop. The studio was looking for a method of synchronizing a soundtrack with the mouth, head and limb movements of a Donald Duck robot. Ken relished the challenge and resolved the problem with a clever electro-mechanical circuit that satisfied Disney's expectations. Ken claimed this to be the first application of "audio animatronics." There is no record of financial compensation for rendering this highly specialized labor and commercially valuable invention. Speaking in his customary humorous manner, the electrician declared, "I could have retired a millionaire had Disney paid for the service."

Although Ken publicly described the incident as an insignificant experience, he privately resented Disney's failure to demonstrate its appreciation in monetary form. One must wonder how Strickfaden would have reacted had he lived long enough to see female vocalist Peggy Lee win a legal challenge against the Disney Corporation over an analogous nonpayment indiscretion. Ms. Lee was awarded $2,000,000!

11

The Last Frankenstein Picture Show

Revamp old films, refilm old vamps.
— The Kenneth Strickfaden Notebook

Historians often apply the term "age of innocence" when analyzing past eras. If ever there was such a period coinciding with my growing up years, World War II brought it to an end. One of the improvements to come out of the post–World War II era was a revival of interest in science education. This is something for which Kenneth Strickfaden tirelessly dedicated his life.

Science education, however, was the last subject on my mind when graduating from Ithaca College in New York. It was my intention to establish a reputation as a great football coach — one which would stand alongside such gridiron immortals as Knute Rockne, Alonzo Stagg, Pop Warner, Bob Zuppke and others of their stature. After several failed attempts to obtain a teaching position, I came to the conclusion that all available coaching posts had been filled. But on the very first day of the fall school year, there arrived good news regarding a yet unfilled coaching position. Much to my mortification, the appointment required that I double-up and teach the junior high (middle) school science program. If confessions are in order, this might be a good place to begin. I was not one of those brainy high school students dedicated to burning the "midnight oil" preparing for tests or meeting homework deadlines. On the contrary, my attention was focused on girls and athletics. Any success that may have occurred in science classes was probably due to my instructor (who happened to be the athletic director). I suspect that he had a soft spot in his heart for student athletes. As to my struggle with Latin, geometry and other difficult subjects ... those are stories that best not be told. Here I was several years out of high school and working as a bona fide athletic coach and also the school's science teacher. As the radio personality Chester Riley would say, "What a revoltin' development *this* is!" The situation called for burning some of that leftover midnight oil.

Even though the predicament was rough and chaotic, I somehow managed to stay one step ahead of my students. Thanks to the research facilities at local libraries, that lead was stretched to several steps. Still, my heart wasn't fully dedicated to the task. I merely considered the science job as a way of getting a foot in the door. Consequently, both my students and I became clock-watchers waiting for the class bell to set us free. Such was the situation until a man by the name of Kenneth Strickfaden came to town. His science lecture program proved an inspiration to my students — and to *me*. "Hey," I reflected, "this science stuff is not only interesting but also fun and exciting!" In retrospect, I can say the experience was instrumental in launching my 28 year career as a science teacher. And thanks to Mr. Electric, the experience spawned the seed which some 50 years later germinated into this book.

What assignments Kenny Strickfaden accepted after 1960 depended upon the status of his health. During the years 1961–63, he did some television work and gave several lectures. One of his television contracts involved providing special electrical effects for a Steve Allen parody on the Frankenstein theme. In the autumn of 1962, Ken received correspondence from Richard Hall, administrator of the Committees for the Hollywood Museum Association, informing the electrician of his appointment as chairman of the Electrical Effects Subcommittee. The Hollywood Museum was founded as an education-oriented entertainment facility incorporating the arts of motion picture, television, radio and recording. The following is taken from Mr. Hall's communication:

> I am pleased to inform you that your appointment as Chairman of the Electrical Effects Subcommittee of the Los Angeles County Hollywood Museum has been confirmed by the Board of Directors. We feel honored to have you associated with us and we are sure you will enjoy your experience in helping to move this great project toward completion.

11— The Last Frankenstein Picture Show

On March 28, 1963, the various committees met on Paramount's Sunset Studios TV-2 stage. A portion of the agenda focused upon proposals for new exhibits. One motion receiving unanimous approval called for the replication of Frankenstein's laboratory. Other considerations which received popular support included a King Kong exhibit and demonstrations of electrical effects by Kenneth Strickfaden.

Ken served as a consultant to a Los Angeles engineering firm from May 1963 to February 1964. Part of 1964 was given to lectures in Arizona, an area he affectionately characterized as "Indian Country." Allan H. Trimpi was one of the many who attended the Arizona lectures. He later forwarded a letter (undated) commenting on Ken's performance:

> When I first personally saw your devices on display in Arizona several years ago, they were inspiring. I was frankly put in awe by the demonstration and the physical knowledge of electrical flow and its kinetic behavior. I searched library books and college physics texts to discover the practical knowledge, and only discovered that you have more knowledge of the subject in your fingertips than a shelf full of books on electrical behavior.

During the year that followed, Mr. Electric contributed to several episodes of *Lost in Space*, the Irwin Allen television production featuring Guy Williams and June Lockhart. In 1966, Ken returned to Las Vegas to provide technical services to KHJ television as well as some special effects for an ice follies show. He also provided electrical pyrotechnics for *The Munsters* and a parody called "Shrimperstein." During the years 1966–69, Ken picked up extra change working commercials for such high-profile companies as DuPont, Personna, General Foods and Union Carbide. Another film to his credit is *The Illustrated Man* (1969) starring Rod Steiger.

Sam Sherman, who produced and co-wrote the screenplay for *Dracula vs. Frankenstein* (1971), was determined to include the original lab equipment from Universal's 1931 epic. His visit to Strickfaden's shop was not without an unexpected surprise. Ken presented his distinguished visitor a frightening moment when he closed a switch on one of the high voltage devices. Sherman was in the unenviable position of standing on a grounded metal plate which became the target for cascading electrical fireworks. The startled producer made a hasty retreat as the sparks striking the plate began dancing close to his feet.

The equipment used in *Dracula vs. Frankenstein* was rented so Ken did not work on the set. When the film's technician experienced difficulty in getting the equipment to function, a request was made to film the high voltage apparatus at Ken's lab. The scenes shot at the Strickfaden shop would later be cut into the lab scenes used in the film. Ken had declined, fearing that the producer would, as Universal had done, continue to use the clips as stock footage in subsequent productions without proper compensation. Only when a contract was signed prohibiting further use of the clips without appropriate payment did Ken agree.

Sam Sherman may have been influential in getting the International Brotherhood of Electrical Workers to feature an article on Kenneth Strickfaden in the organization's *IBEW Journal*. Sherman was so impressed by the activities going on in Ken's lab that he conveyed a description to a relative connected to the union. The May 1972 issue displayed a two-page article on Ken titled "The Electrical Wizard of the Motion Pictures."

Young Frankenstein (1974) was the last major Frankenstein picture show for Kenneth Strickfaden. Although the set utilized many of the mad scientist accoutrements that appeared in Universal's 1931 epic, the two sets were not identical (courtesy of The Museum of Modern Art/Film Stills Archive).

11— The Last Frankenstein Picture Show

Upon learning of his brother Frank's tragic suicide, Ken took a brief hiatus from his work routine to attend Frank's funeral and to spend time with family. His notes mention work on a televised version of *Li'l Abner* (ABC 4/26/71). During the years 1971 through 1973, the wizard fulfilled commitments for providing special effects in commercials on behalf of Magnavox and the FBI and also a battery commercial. Motion picture work for this period included an industrial film titled *The Capable Computer* and the science fiction production *The Clones* (1973). Strickfaden next supplied services for the *Horror Hall of Fame* telecast (ABC 2/20/74) with Vincent Price. Scribblings among his copious notes feature references to "Strange New World," "Burbank Studios" and a parody titled "Frankenstruck."

The most noteworthy '70s film in which Strickfaden played an important role is Mel Brooks' *Young Frankenstein* (1974). The script called

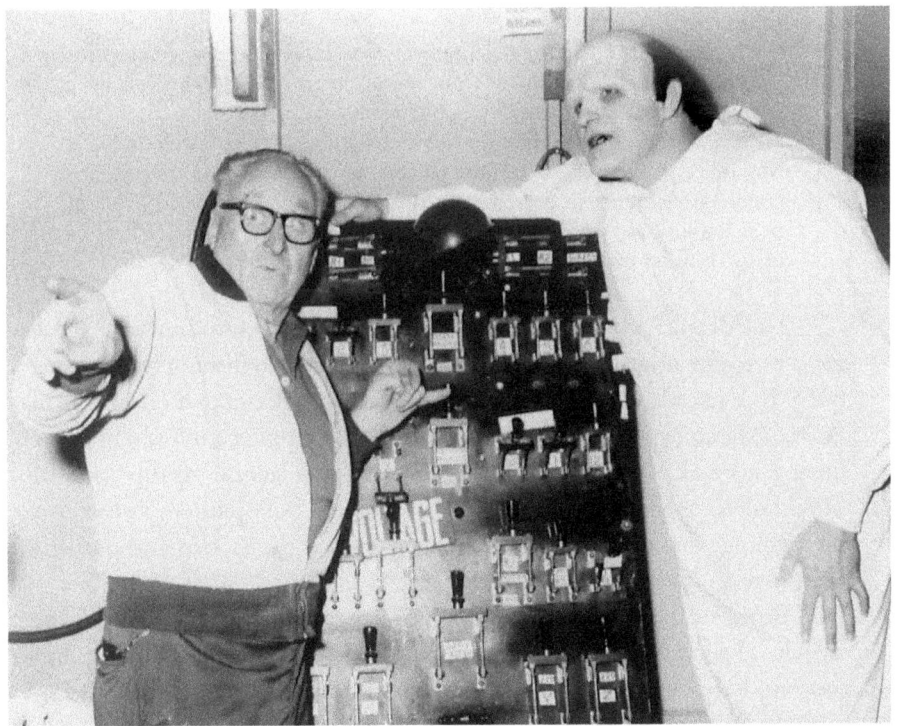

Ken Strickfaden appears to be explaining the control circuits to Monster Peter Boyle on the set of *Young Frankenstein* (1974).

for a re-creation of the trend-setting special electrical effects that Ken provided for Universal's 1931 epic. Although the mad scientist laboratory for *Young Frankenstein* featured some of the same Strickfaden-constructed accoutrements seen in the earlier four-star production, the two sets were not identical. Still, the conglomeration of Strickfaden's paraphernalia proved impressive. One who expressed an appreciation for Strickfaden's work was Gerald Hirschfeld, the Director of Photography. Hirschfeld's "The Story Behind the Filming of *Young Frankenstein*" appeared in the July 1974 issue of *American Cinematographer*. The following is an excerpt from Hirschfeld's article:

> The electrical wizardry really impressed me. Upon researching the picture it was learned that some of the original *Frankenstein* electrical laboratory equipment was still stored in the garage of the man who designed it for the film made in 1931. This man, Mr. Strickfaden, was on hand during all the laboratory filming to add his touch to the already fantastic array of bubbling vats and retorts and plastic tubes pumping blood solutions.
>
> He also built new electrical devices especially for *Young Frankenstein*. The laboratory was ablaze at times with "Jacob's Ladders"; these are spark-gaps that climb two V-shaped electrodes until the spark finally escapes at the top in a six-inch span of lightning. The "Melodic Melinda," a humorously named gadget, created arcs that jumped from contact-to-contact in prescribed rhythm, from waltz time to jive tempos. Radial lightning devices shot their arcs in giant six-foot circles, creating thunderous crashes on the set.

Mel Brooks' type of humor is well-known and one can only speculate as to the hilarity that may have occurred while filming his satirical farce. Ken revealed one incident when speaking before a gathering of film fans. As the story goes, beautiful Teri Garr stood sipping a refreshing drink during a break in the filming process. She was leaning against one of Strickfaden's machines, the "Digital Disputer." Ken had employed this high voltage device in a number of early films as far back as and perhaps even before, Universal's *Frankenstein*.

Brooks caught Ken's attention and gave a visual signal to close the switch. The machine immediately responded and commenced buzzing and zapping lethal voltages just inches from Garr's silky blonde hair. Taken completely by surprise, the terrified actress gave out with a loud shriek. She and the container holding the liquid refreshment parted company as the startled woman leaped for safety. A witness to the scene estimated the distance covered by Garr's spontaneous retreat had equaled, if not surpassed, the then current Olympic long jump record. The tirade of expletives erupting from the enraged star were so embarrassing that Ken could not bring himself to repeat Garr's coarse language when describing the event. Kenny sheepishly reported, "What she said is unprintable." The crew working the set watched with amusement as Garr, normally the epitome of loveliness, continued to express her outrage. In the meanwhile, Strickfaden had approached the whirling spark-spitting machine and took the same position where Garr had been resting. To the amazement of all, Kenny received no electrical shock. Although the device looked (and was) dangerous, the wizard had incorporated safety in its design.

Young Frankenstein marked the last Frankenstein picture show in which the original 1931 laboratory machines appeared collectively. And it is a sad fact that the film was the last (major) Frankenstein picture show for Ken Strickfaden.

Although the film industry has thoroughly documented Mel Brooks' comedic side, it has given less attention to the man's compassionate nature. An example of the latter endowment was revealed in *Young Frankenstein* when Brooks honored Strickfaden with a screen credit. Ken's contributions to the film are acknowledged during the audio commentary of the home video version. Included in this segment are several stills of Ken on the *Young Frankenstein* set. Incidentally, the electrician can be briefly seen in a segment of the American Movie Classics' "Backstory" production on *Young Frankenstein*. And Ken's special electrical effects legacy is appropriately recalled in the Turner Classic Movies documentary *Universal Horrors*.

12

"We Had a Ball!"

An elecstravaganza
— The Ken Strickfaden Notebook

Health problems or no health problems, Ken's demanding work schedule suffered but a slight reduction in activity. The ambitious electrician appears to have been blessed with a bubbling effervescence over which he had no control. However, he was now at an age where assistance became necessary, especially in regards to the hauling of heavy equipment. Among the long-time friends and admirers who eagerly rendered muscle power were Dick Aurandt, Ed Angell, Jim Shaffer and John Foster, to name a few. Mr. Foster, a retiree of the Los Angeles school system, had been a close friend to Ken and often accompanied the electrician on lecture and film assignments. Foster's daughters JoAnne, Dee and Mary adored Ken and unanimously embraced him as their "Uncle Strick." Ken proudly accepted the honor. John and Lois Foster would later play a compassionate role in providing Strickfaden with the comfort of living quarters during the wizard's declining years.

In 1975, after supplying services for a Milton Bradley television commercial and to Roger Corman's New World Pictures, Ken headed to New Mexico to be on location for the British Lion film *The Man Who Fell to Earth* starring David Bowie. Upon fulfillment of this contract, Mr. Electric made personal appearances at two science fiction conventions. Forrest Ackerman, a long-time Strickfaden fan, was one of the participants. Ackerman is famously known as a film historian, author,

12 — "We Had a Ball!"

Ken Strickfaden's circle of wizards. Clockwise: John Foster (back to camera), Dick Aurandt, Ed Angell, Jim Shaffer. Ken is visible in the background keeping a paternal eye on the activity. The device in the foreground is the Tesla coil used to provide special electrical effects in *The Entity* (1983) (courtesy of Dick Aurandt).

publisher and collector of film memorabilia. Ken jokingly bestowed upon Ackerman the title of "Foris Ackerloff" (after the horror film star, Boris Karloff). Ackerman reciprocated with several tributes referring to Ken as the "Lord of Lightning," "Electrical Vampire" and "Wizard of Watts."

In 1975, Ken provided equipment and technical assistance to the rock group KISS. One of the electrical gadgets he constructed for the musical troupe was a Tesla coil capable of electrical discharges 12 feet in length. Manmade lightning of that magnitude is equal to 1,000,000-volts! A year later, Ken leased equipment to a studio for the production of *Demon Dracula*. No film of this title was found in the references examined. Be that as it may, Kenny gave it a thumbs-down critique ("flop"). He next signed a contract with NBC for technical services for its television series *The Monster Squad* (1976).

Other films of this period for which Ken can be credited are *The*

Manitou (1978), *Coma* (1978) and *Sgt. Pepper's Lonely Hearts Club Band* (1978). Television work for 1978 included *Wonder Woman* episodes.

On Easter Sunday, March 26, 1978, Ken Strickfaden's world fell apart. Gladys Ward Strickfaden, his wife, partner and lifelong companion, suffered a stroke and passed away. Her death left a deep hole in Ken's life. It was a loss from which he never recovered. The chasm grew both wider and deeper when Strick experienced a falling-out with his daughters.

Strickfaden returned to work later that year, taking part in the first of a number of Bob Hope telecasts. Hope was the host of three TV specials in 1978. Ken's notebook scribblings for that period make mention of Cole Porter, a composer famous for film, television and stage musicals. Porter passed away in 1964. Mr. Electric continued to receive requests for special electrical effects in television commercials and was also hired to provide technical skills for another "Franky" spoof.

In 1979, Kenstric rendered services for a half-hour series telecast based on the life of inventor Thomas Edison. Attempts to confirm the Edison series were without success. Ken worked a second Bob Hope telecast in that same year.

Strickfaden presented several science lectures in 1979, two of which were given free of charge. The first demonstration presented on behalf of charities

Ken and Gladys Strickfaden on the fiftieth anniversary of their marriage. On March 26, 1978, Gladys suffered a stroke and passed away. Her death left a deep hole in Ken's life. It was a loss from which he never fully recovered (courtesy of Marilyn S. Throssel).

was before a senior citizen's group. The second appearance occurred at a home for battered children. Logbook notations listing *Star Wars* (1977), *The Empire Strikes Back* (1980) and *Raiders of the Lost Ark* (1981) were punctuated with the term "recording sessions." Ken had been a special effects sound technician as early as 1927.

In 1981, Ken received correspondence from Rufus B. Seder forwarding a plan for making a motion picture based on Margaret Cheney's *Tesla Man Out of Time*.

> I was thrilled to get your call, and very happy that you are interested in the Tesla project.... Bill Benenson is eager to send you a copy of Margaret Cheney's new book.... As I told you, we've been working on this project for ten months, and Bill has optioned Cheney's book. As far as we know, we are way ahead of anyone else in planning to make a dramatic feature about Tesla. Whether I will direct it, or whether Bill will produce it, nobody can say. But I am convinced that, if this picture is made, there is no one more qualified than yourself to oversee the special effects.

Mr. Seder forwarded a synopsis of the screenplay. Later the April 30, 1982, issue of *Variety* carried a full-page announcement of the forthcoming film by Bill Benenson Productions (BBZ Films Ltd.). Apparently, the plans for *Fantastic Vision: The True Story of Nikola Tesla* did not proceed beyond this point.

In 1981, Mr. Elecstrick's equipment appeared in a minor "Franky" production titled *Frankenstein Island*. That the film turned out to be a bomb had nothing to do with the quality of the special electrical effects. Here, again, Ken's high voltage apparatus performed marvelously. One prop that to my knowledge had never before appeared in a Strickfaden film is his "Psycho Gyro." This device consists of a high-speed gyroscope mounted inside a World War II ammunition can. Once the gyro attains its maximum rotational speed, the can will balance itself on just about any object and oppose attempts by anyone to alter its position. Spectacular as this mechanical apparatus may be, one must wonder as to its purpose in a film such as *Frankenstein Island*. Perhaps the director was intrigued by the oscillating container and concluded it would enhance the film's entertainment value — a boost it badly needed.

Strickfaden was now 85 and feeling the effects of deteriorating health. Furthermore, Ken faced the depressing prospect of having to move into a home for retired motion picture personnel. Still more distressing was the unpredictable fate of his valuable collection of special electrical effects paraphernalia. It meant more to him than merely an assemblage of transformers, coils of wire, machines, bulbs and so on. Ken looked upon his creations as a father looks upon his children. The man found solace and comfort when in the company of his technical achievements. Those moments of camaraderie enabled him to resolve or mollify personal problems and disappointments. Such an occasion occurred when Ken learned of the passing of brother Charles. Kenstric now had to face the reality that he was the last of the Strickfaden boys.

Of the many Strickfaden photos with which I am familiar, a multiple-exposed print showing the elderly wizard surrounded by sparking high voltage devices best sums up the man and his work. Kenny's pensive facial expression gives indication that he is either reflecting upon

A multiple exposed print of Ken in a moment of camaraderie. He often found solace and comfort when in the company of his technical accoutrements. The pensive expression on his face gives indication that he may be reflecting on life's past events or expressing a farewell to his creations. All sparking devices appear to be responding in unison as though understanding the significance of the moment.

12 — "We Had a Ball!"

ELECTRICITY·LIGHT
COLOR·MUSIC·SOUND

ELEC$TRIC

IMAGINEERED
INTERPRETAINMENT

KENNETH J. STRICKFADEN
853 TWENTY-SIXTH STREET
SANTA MONICA, CALIFORNIA 90403
TELEPHONE (213) 828-4256

85 YEAR OLD INFIRMITIES MAKE IT ADVISABLE FOR ME TO FIND A SUITABLE HOME FOR MY LABORTORY· THE TERMS ARE SIMPLE· THE ACCEPTED RECIPIENT TAKES ALL AND MAKES A REASONABLE DONATION, TAX FREE, TO A WORTHY ORGANIZATION · AND ASSUMES ALL RIGHTS AS TO USE· SALE· RENTAL· EXHIBITING ·

LABIS
THINKERY: LIBRARY· ENGINEERING FILES· RECORDS· DRAWINGS ·
INVENTERY: SHOP· BENCHES· MACHINERY· TOOLS· CABINETS ·
MUSARIUM: MASTER CONTROL· PANEL DISPLAYS · APPARATUS

STOCK
ELECTRICAL· TRANSFORMERS· MOTORS · RELAYS · SWITCHES ·
PHOTOGRAPHIC· DARK ROOM· CAMERAS · LENSES· OPTICS· LIGHTS ·
MECHANICAL· GEARS· BEARINGS· BENDING BLOCKS· PARTS ·
MUSICAL· INSTRUMENTS· BELLS· CHIMES ·RESONATORS· TUBES · CHORALE CELESTE· MELODYNE· HARMONEYE· WHIRLBLITZER·

TOOLS — SUPPLIES
11X48 SOUTH BEND LATHE· QUICK CHANGE· AUTO CROSS FEED· CHUCKS· ARBORS ANGLE WORKING NOTCHING· BENDING·SHEAR· WELDING· SOLDERING· PUNCHES · DRILLS· TAPS· VICES· STEEL BENCH 3X3X8 · 2 STEEL BENCHES 24X30X96· WITH 36 DR· DELTA SAWS· JOINER· BLADES· BUFFER· SANDER· GRINDER· 40 CABINETS· 5 BINS· 5 TABLES· 5 RACKS· 100 TRAYS· 50 BOXES· 48 TRAYS MAC. SCREWS· 20 TRAYS WOOD SCREWS· 20 TR. CAPS· 20 TR. RESISTORS · 20 TR. BRADS· NAILS· PINS· WASHERS· NUTS· BOLTS· FASTENERS· PARTS · COPPER· BRASS· ALUMINUM· IRON· COILS· STRIP· WIRE· SHEETS· SHAPES·

ON DISPLAY · **SPECIAL EFFECTS** · OPERATING
PROPS· SPECAACULAR CREATIONS· MAD LAB· USED IN MORE THAN 50 MOVIE AND TV THRILLERS· 2000 STAGE SHOWS· EXPOS· FAIRS

GOODIES
TESLA MEGAVOLT RESONATORS· TRAVELING ARCS· SCI-FI HI-FI· GRAVITY NEUTRALIZER· EDISON MEDICINE· DR·FRANKENSTEIN'S LAB · VULCANARIUM· RESONARIUM· NEBULARIUM · PANDERMONIUM· BLATS · SPACE BEACON · FIRELOSCOPE· TRANQUILIZER· ARTICULATED DISRUPTOR MORTALS PERMITTED TO PEEK BY APPOINTMENT ONLY ·

Ken Strickfaden

Kenny's "garage sale." He offered the entire contents of his lab, movie props, machine shop, etc., to anyone making a reasonable tax-free contribution to a worthy charity.

life's past events or expressing a last goodbye to his creations. All sparking devices appear to be responding in unison as though understanding the significance of the moment.

The charitable gentleman donated his Santa Monica home to the Methodist Church (in memory of Gladys) with the stipulation that the proceeds resulting from its sale be allocated to the welfare of deserving children. Strickfaden set aside two trust funds: one for Col. Farley's Boys Ranch Home in Texas, the other for the American Red Cross. He presented a gift of large movie panels to a Santa Monica cultural institution. Another set was put up for auction over KCET on behalf of charities. Strickfaden's entire Frankenstein laboratory was put up for sale. There are two versions of the story of the conditions by which the equipment would be disposed. In one, Ken is said to have stipulated the buyer provide a "reasonable" donation to a worthy charity. The second declaration, announced over national radio networks, stated the 1931 Frankenstein laboratory could be purchased for $1,000,000. A museum demonstrated an interest in the collection but a disagreement in regard to the terms negated the transaction.

As Ken prepared for the move into the Motion Picture and Television

---

THE ACADEMY OF MOTION PICTURE ARTS AND SCIENCES
AND
ACADEMY FOUNDATION
PRESENT

THE MAGIC MACHINES OF KEN STRICKFADEN

Monday, November 9, 1981 at 8:00 pm
In the Academy's
SAMUEL GOLDWYN THEATER
8949 Wilshire Boulevard
Beverly Hills, CA

Public ($3.00)   Academy Members (No Charge)

Above: An enlarged copy of the ticket sold for admission to Strick's Academy show (courtesy of William C. Wysock). *Opposite:* On November 9, 1981, the Academy of Motion Picture Arts & Sciences paid tribute to "The Magic Machines of Ken Strickfaden."

ACADEMY FOUNDATION

THE MAGIC MACHINES OF KEN STRICKFADEN
November 9, 1981
Guest Speaker: Vic Cox

FRANKENSTEIN   (Universal, 1931)

BRIDE OF FRANKENSTEIN   (Universal, 1935)

JUST IMAGINE   (Fox, 1930)

BUCK ROGERS   (Universal, 1936)

INVISIBLE RAY   (Universal, 1936)

MASK OF FU MANCHU   (MGM, 1932) 2 excerpts

YOUNG FRANKENSTEIN   (20th Century-Fox, 1975)

Discussion with Mr. Strickfaden and Mr. Cox

(Film prints courtesy of Universal, MGM, 20th Century-Fox, Films Inc., Em Gee Film Library)

   Ken Strickfaden was born in Anaconda, Montana in 1896. His career in the film industry began in 1921 in the Metropolitan Studios electric shop, where he was employed as a "chambermaid," fixing arc lights, cables, lamps and other appliances. He didn't stay long. In 1926, however, he returned to a similar job at Lasky Studios where he was allowed to experiment with sound effects as well as maintain electrical equipment.
   His imagination and curiosity led him to create apparatus at home for his own knowledge, since no demand existed for them then at the studios. Several years later, however, when sound movies and a public appetite for mystery thrillers came into their own, filmmakers wanted technological gimmicks in their plots and Strickfaden suddenly had a market for his self-acquired skills. He points to the sound effect of an electric chair in operation - produced off camera by sending high frequency current through a piece of wood - as his first film achievement with electrical legerdemain. One of the first films to show any of his devices was the 1929 Return of Sherlock Holmes.
   Eventually, as "Strick" says, "word got out that a wizard" was available to handle these special electrical assignments. Besides appearing in the original 1931 version of Frankenstein, Strick's machines have been in nearly all the sequels, spinoffs and spoofs to the classic gothic tale, including 1975's Young Frankenstein, for which he received a rare screen credit.
   In the mid-30's he left regular studio employment to become a fulltime free-lance electrical effects expert, eventually renting his skills and machines to virtually every major studio of the time. He also designed a traveling science show around his equipment and, billing himself as "Kenstric," he toured the country with it.
   Over the years Strickfaden has continued to experiment and develop new ideas in his Santa Monica workshop. He is, in his own words, "currently in quest of a 32 foot spark that will play music."

Fund Retirement Home, John Foster interceded and offered him living space at his Inglewood laboratory. Foster was a skilled electrician and mechanic who collected all sorts of precision scientific instruments. He specialized in microscopes, high-speed photography and electrical gadgets, and was a master builder of Tesla coils. The Foster laboratory was the kind of environment into which Ken Strickfaden could easily "melt." In addition, the man would then be located where John and Lois Foster could keep a vigilant eye upon his welfare.

On June 6, 1981, Strickfaden received the shocking news of the death of daughter Carolyn. She had been a victim of an automobile accident while on a trip through the Northwest. Carolyn had lived a troubled existence and Ken carried the burden of a father's guilt-ridden conscience in taking much of the blame for her turmoil. The grieving parent declared Carolyn's room "off limits." Although the door to her room remained

Ken addressing the spectators at the Academy show. Many of the adults in attendance had first seen a Strickfaden lecture during their high school years. Some even brought their chidren and grandchildren. Even at 85, Ken was able to demonstrate that the skills and wit of his heyday remained intact (courtesy of the Academy Foundation).

open, no one was allowed to enter Carolyn's space. Her death, however, was instrumental in bringing about a more harmonious relationship with daughter Marilyn.

Because of the tragic events that had come to pass, Kenny's view of the sky above was now obstructed by dark ominous clouds. But every dark cloud is said to have a silver lining. Strickfaden's cloud of despair turned inside out on November 9, 1981, when the Academy of Motion Picture Arts and Sciences paid tribute to "The Magic Machines of Ken Strickfaden." The grand event was held at the Academy's Samuel Goldwyn Theater on Wilshire Boulevard in Beverly Hills. The audience awarded Ken an enthusiastic welcome when the arthritic octogenarian hobbled onto the stage. Even at 85, Ken was

Ken and Dick Aurandt discussing the technical parameters of the "Digital Disputer." Aurandt first saw a Strickfaden lecture during his high school years. The experience inspired the lad to follow a career in electrical engineering (courtesy of the Academy Foundation).

able to demonstrate that the skills and wit of his heyday had not diminished. Many of the adults in attendance had first seen a Strickfaden lecture during their high school years. Some even brought their children (and grandchildren). A number of celebrities representing the entertainment industry were there to pay tribute to a friend and colleague.

Throughout the years, Ken had developed a special rapport with those he entertained. It was his custom to invite the audience to participate in, or comment upon, the many demonstrations. In his appearance at the school where I had been employed, one of the more popular students volunteered to take part in a demonstration. As Kenstric was about to complete the act, he brought forth a small musical instrument known as a kazoo. When the electrician blew into it, the notes of "shave-and-a-haircut, bay rum" were clearly heard. Just as Ken was about to play the last phrase, he touched the lad on the rear side with a rod carrying a harmless electrical charge. The boy jumped forward and gave out a shriek in synchronization with the final note of the tune. The student audience roared with laughter and the boy's popularity among his fellow students soared to new heights.

Audience comments were often a repetition of remarks Ken had heard over the years. "How is it possible to light an unconnected bulb?" asked one youngster. Strickfaden carried a mental file of replies. One favorite response was "Ahrr, it's magic." Another question repeatedly put before the wizard referred to the secret of surviving high voltage electrical shocks. "I eat rosenblitzen" was an explanation that never failed to bring a giggling response. Mr. Elecstrick often rendered a unique definition of electricity. "Electricity is life," he would say; "I'm just a big spark with hair."

Strickfaden and lifelong friend John Foster, who manipulated the controls at the Academy show (courtesy of the Academy Foundation).

When the demonstrations had concluded, the Academy presented clips from the motion pictures *Just Imagine* (1930), *Frankenstein* (1931), *The Mask of Fu Manchu* (1932), *The Invisible Ray* (1936), *Buck Rogers* (1939) and *Dr. Cyclops* (1940). A rousing cheer erupted from

"Meg Senior" Tesla coil is demonstrated by Strickfaden while other props await their turn. He described his equipment in empirical terms, declaring, "Everything you see here is made of junk." The fact that the Academy hailed the converted discards as "Magic Machines" is a tribute to Kenny Strickfaden's innovative and imaginative talents (courtesy of the Academy Foundation).

the audience when the scene from *The Mask of Fu Manchu* showed Ken doubling for Boris Karloff.

It should be made clear that Ken's equipment consisted of a patchwork of parts obtained from salvage yards, junk shops, old radio transmitters, antiquated medical machines, automobile graveyards, industrial surplus outlets or anywhere else a seemingly "worthless" property could be found and put to use. For example, one of the props appearing in *Son of Frankenstein* (1939) was from the cowling of a crashed airplane. Kenny provided an empirical description of his equipment when declaring, "Everything you see here is made of junk." The fact that the Academy hailed the converted discards as "Magic Machines" is a tribute to Kenny Strickfaden's innovative and imaginative talents.

It was with dismay that I learned of the Academy's failure to make a visual (film or video) record of the program. Surely this once-in-a-lifetime event deserved to be preserved for the benefit of current and future generations. To the Academy's credit, however, an audio tape of the program is available for the public's review at the organization's library.

Among Kenstric's records are notes made on the night of the Academy show. He listed the titles of the movies displayed, gave recognition to Program Coordinator Douglas W. Edwards, and acknowledged the assistance of friends. Underneath the heading "Demonstrations by Ken and his pals" are the names of John Foster, Vic Cox (emcee), Dick Aurandt, Jim Shaffer, Slim deCoursey and Ed and Janice Angell. At the top of the page is the declaration "WE HAD A BALL!"

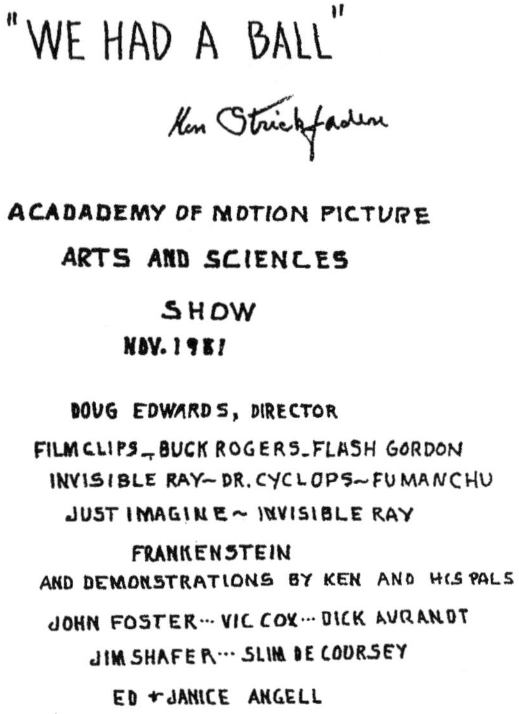

"WE HAD A BALL"

Ken Strickfaden

ACADADEMY OF MOTION PICTURE
ARTS AND SCIENCES
SHOW
NOV. 1981

DOUG EDWARDS, DIRECTOR
FILM CLIPS — BUCK ROGERS — FLASH GORDON
INVISIBLE RAY — DR. CYCLOPS — FU MANCHU
JUST IMAGINE — INVISIBLE RAY
FRANKENSTEIN
AND DEMONSTRATIONS BY KEN AND HIS PALS
JOHN FOSTER ··· VIC COX ··· DICK AURANDT
JIM SHAFER ··· SLIM DE COURSEY
ED + JANICE ANGELL

A page from Ken's Academy show notebook. He was always the first to give, and the last to take, credit. The misspelling of Academy is strictly Strickfaden humor.

13

No Ordinary Man!

> *Walk with equals or walk alone.*
> — The Ken Strickfaden Notebook

Although the term "genius" is generally assigned to the brilliant benefactors of mankind, it is at times bestowed upon unscrupulous characters such as clever embezzlers, crafty bank robbers, murderers and so on. Adolf Hitler, for example, was considered by many to have been a genius even though he had been directly and indirectly responsible for the deaths of 50,000,000 people. Inventor Thomas Edison defined genius in a phrase that is both narrow and simplistic: "Genius is one percent inspiration and 99 percent perspiration." The dictionary provides several qualifications for possible admission to this exclusive club: "A person considered having a strong influence; the personification of quality; a great natural ability (for a particular activity); great mental capacity and inventive ability; great original ability in some art, science, or music; or a person with a high degree of intelligence quotient." Several, if not all of the above proficiencies render an accurate description of the man about whom this book is written.

In the A&E television documentary *It's Alive! The True Story of Frankenstein* (1994), narrator Eli Wallach presents an appreciation for Strickfaden's talents:

> If ever there was a lost genius, then perhaps it was Kenneth Strickfaden. In Strickfaden's fertile brain was born the look and design of Frankenstein's laboratory. He began working as an electrician in a small independent

studio. But his real talent lay in designing weird electrical devices—bizarre machines that groaned and buzzed—that transformed invisible electricity into crackling kinetic sculpture.... It was so distinctive and so effective that Universal trotted out the same machinery time after time. It looked good in the movies and audiences seemed to love the electrical pyrotechnics. Strickfaden made a modest living renting the machines in this and other movies. His crackling gear made its final appearance in 1974 in *Young Frankenstein*.

Mel Brooks was fascinated by Strickfaden's work and made a personal visit to the electrician's shop when preparing the parody *Young Frankenstein*. He gives an account of the event in the above-mentioned A&E documentary.

> Every silly machine that goes bo-oop, bo-oop, bo-oop, bo-oop; zjide, zjidide, zjidide—and uh, there was one great one that did the lightning, the little lightning on his neck ... actually lightning bolts ... that went to his neck, all created by this—this Kenneth Strickfaden—a genius.
> Strickfaden was the original creator of the hardware for the first, I guess, three Frankenstein movies—and, he put these gadgets together and they were sensational, you know, especially in black- and-white with little zig-zags, radio waves and stuff. And we found him in a garage. No, we found his stuff in a garage. He was living above the garage in Santa Monica, and it was all there, intact. We dusted it, we plugged it in, it all worked. And everything you see in *Young Frankenstein*, every silly machine that goes bo-oop, bo-oop, bo-oop, bo-oop, bo-oop; zjide, zjidide, zjidide—all by this—this Kenneth Strickfaden—a genius.

Several references credit Strickfaden as having been an electrical engineer. Although he was highly knowledgeable in the electrical sciences, Ken's formal education ended with graduation from high school. From then on, Strickfaden attended the "school of hard knocks" all the while continuously honing those skills for which he later became so well-known. Had Ken continued his formal education beyond high school, he may have become a top-ranking physicist, electrical engineer, college professor, etc. But science's loss was our gain when Mr. Electric found a niche in the movie industry.

The fact that Kenstric lacked an advanced formal education did not discourage pedigreed electricians and scientists from visiting the 26th Street laboratory. One of the distinguished guests to appear there was Thorn Mayes, a General Electric research engineer. In a 1968 communication to Leland Anderson, also an electrical engineer who admired Ken's work, Mayes provides a brief comment on the experience.

> Last week, I was in Los Angeles and spent a most profitable morning with Ken. I wish I didn't live so far away as we have a lot in common and I learn a lot.

Politicians, studio employees, amateur electricians and a few claiming royal lineage were among the personalities who beat a path to Kenny's lab. Some of the Hollywood and entertainment-related individuals whose names appear in Ken's notes are Ken Bailey (Warner Bros. supervisor), Eddie Shipstad (entertainment entrepreneur), Sol Lesser (motion picture pioneer, producer and Hollywood Museum official), Forrest J Ackerman (Mr. Sci-Fi), Mel Brooks (producer, director, writer, actor), Andrew Stone (producer, director), Roger Corman (producer, director), Sam Sherman (producer, screenwriter, etc.), Al Adamson (director), and others,

Thorn Mayes (left), a General Electric research engineer, made several visits to Strickfaden's lab. He once wrote, "I was in Los Angeles and spent a most profitable morning with Ken. I wish I didn't live so far away as we have a lot in common and I learn a lot."

including a few leading Hollywood stars. Another visitor was Howard Gregory, an author of several successful books. Mr. Gregory spent part of a day with Ken after which he penned a note of appreciation (4/7/80).

> Thank you for your kind hospitality showing me your historic photos and your laboratory. I enjoyed your collection very much, especially when you threw those switches and the electrical display began crackling and climbing up those instruments. I was waiting for Karloff to come stalking into the room.

And then there is the man who approached Ken on behalf of Gypsy Rose Lee. Although Ms. Lee had appeared in such productions as *You Can't Have Everything* (1937), *Ali Baba Goes to Town* (1938), *My Lucky Star* (1939), *Belle of the Yukon* (1944) and other films, she was best known world wide as a racy burlesque queen. The conversation between Ken and Ms. Lee's manager was one of the electrician's favorite stories, and a tale which never failed to bring a twinkle to his eyes.

> While working at one of the major studios, I was approached by a gentleman who purported to be the personal manager of the famous entertainer Gypsy Rose Lee. After some pleasantries were exchanged, he carefully explained that Ms. Lee had seen a spectacular effect at an early vaudeville show and she wished to include it in her own live stage act which was currently showing.
> Her manager went on to explain that the effect was a performer standing on some weird electrical device and had large sparks coming off his fingertips. Now Ms. Lee's variation on this effect was to replace her tasseled pasties with shiny metal cones and have the sparks issue forth on command.
> With some reserve, I had to carefully explain to the manager that this effect was done with a Tesla coil and had some limitations in its use. I had to explain that the performer had to keep the sparks coming from a position well above his head and that I felt that the chosen portion of Ms. Lee's anatomy didn't lend itself well to that requirement. I also stated that this effect is not without some pain and that Ms. Lee's well developed chest was probably too sensitive to be practical. The gentleman left somewhat disappointed and I never heard from him again.

Of the many personalities who passed the entrance to Kenny's *sanctum sanctorum,* those receiving the warmest welcome were the junior scientists who had become mesmerized by his mad-scientist creations. Every once in a while, a youth carrying an electrical gadget would trot in looking to Ken for assistance. Gene Arntzen was one of those lads.

13 — No Ordinary Man!

I first met Kenneth Strickfaden in 1949 when attending the John Dewey High School in Long Beach. He had come to the school to put on one of his electrical shows. Mr. Strickfaden invited me to his home in Santa Monica to see his electrical equipment and help me with a Tesla coil. I was fascinated by all of the electrical props he made for serials and movies.

My last meeting with Ken was about 1959 when I had a job as a repair man for the Moviola Company. I went to the Warner Brothers Studios electric shop to see Ken and learned he was having lunch on Stage 16. It turned out to be the highest stage on the lot. Originally a normal stage, it had been raised for Busby Berkeley for his special camera shots.

The crew pointed to a ladder and told me Ken was on a catwalk at the very top of the stage. It was the tallest ladder I had ever been on in my life. Reaching the catwalk, and with the aid of a hand rail, I nervously made my way to a sleeping Ken. He had no fear of heights.

When I was visiting him at his workshop, he greeted me with a "Hello, Professor," which I would acknowledge with a "Hello, Mr. Electric."

I remember one Saturday seeing him up a power pole replacing a line transformer fuse he had blown. The neighbors had no knowledge of what happened because Ken had completed the repair in less than five minutes. What a guy!

At times, the steady stream of visitors became so intrusive that Gladys Strickfaden was forced to step in and salvage what little family privacy remained. One must wonder how Ken safely accommodated the crowds when his high voltage machines unleashed their lightning-like electricity. The scene must have been awesome, if not frightening. Neighbors were not oblivious to the hum of activity taking place at 853 26th Street. When their lights dimmed a notch or two, they knew it was playtime at "Stricky's."

Marilyn Throssel, Ken's daughter, disclosed a charming tidbit which aptly described her father's character. "Ken," she remarked, "had an elfin or leprechaun element to his personality." That trait was evident in the language Strickfaden applied at work, home and to each of his special effects devices. Just about everything, including food, was given the Kenstric touch. Any meal which pleased his sense of taste received a "that's larrapin" shout of approval. (Translation: darn good!) Kenny's favorite foods were hamburgers and chocolate malts, and his favorite color was purple (as evident by the purple-tiled bathroom). And one of the fanciful words he would often weave into a sentence is "salubrious."

Hardly any of Ken's machines were identified in standard scientific terms. He would take a commonly recognized word or phrase and reconstruct it to fit the occasion. For example, the name of a famous musical instrument known as "The Mighty Wurlitzer" was transplanted to a Strickfaden creation as "The Mitey Whirl-Blitzer." Other Kenstric contraptions took on such identities as Gravity Neutralizer, Zero Integrator, Retro Precessor, Promethean Flamer, Pyrogeyser, Solar Coronascope, Cosmoscope, Space Beacon, Novis Transducer, Syndroscope, Involuter, Resonarium, Cosmichordian, Transploder, Multistributor, Fire Ring, Mini Meg, Inductorium, Scintillator, Alpha-Gamma Converter, Cosmic Ray Diffuser, Videotron, Fireloscope, Brainwasher and so on. Ken applied the term "Imagineering" to describe his show long before it became a Disney trademark. And "Edison medicine" served as a Strickfaden signature years ahead of a rock group's CD of the same title.

Hardly any of Ken's machines were identified in standard scientific terms. Here he is shown with the "Multistributor" spark wheel. It appeared in numerous science fiction and horror films.

One of Ken's lesser-known inventions is the "Obersetzer." This device appears to parallel a commercially available attachment which converts a standard piano into an electrically operated player piano. I was not able to determine whether Strickfaden's "Obersetzer" and the commercial model are one and the same. No patent was found in Ken's files so he may have sold the principle outright. On the other hand, the "Obersetzer" may have remained an idea that Ken never got around to commercializing. It does, however, demonstrate the degree of creativity in the man's thinking processes.

If the genial electrician wasn't inventing something new, he could usually be found redesigning something old. Such is the case in regards to igniting flash (magnesium) powder for simulating lightning flashes. In the early years of motion pictures, some clever technician came up with the idea of pumping flash powder through a tube and igniting the volatile substance as it exited into the air. Strickfaden advanced the effect by an order of magnitude when replacing the compressed air with compressed oxygen. Voila, what a difference! Ken named his invention the "Magnalux" (great light).

One of the several Strickfaden notebooks I was privileged to review consisted of numerous pages filled with names, phrases, definitions and other verbalisms. The term fortune teller, for example, turned into "future foreteller." And Wizard of Oz became "wizard of ahs." Another Kenstric entry listed a "do it yourself suicide kit" for anyone contemplating self-destruction. Ken's definition for the essence of magnetic presence is "concentrated magnetism in motion as anticipated by Faraday, sought after by Einstein in his unified field theory, and actually produced by Nikola Tesla." Additional samples of Kenstric's articulations appear below the title of several chapters in this book.

During the 1930s, Ken volunteered to teach a seventh grade Sunday school class at the Santa Monica Methodist Church. Ralph E. Hedges was one of the children attending those classes. His communication to the author provided a description of Kenny's "fire-and-brimstone" sermons. "One saying that he told us has stayed with me ever since. It is 'The road to hell is paved with good intentions!'" But Strickfaden's Sunday school activities were not limited to Biblical instruction. Mr. Hedges disclosed information regarding a student orchestra that Ken had formed.

> Stricky led the orchestra and played the violin. We would come early every Sunday and practice the songs we were going to sing that day, and then play them as accompaniment to the singing. I'm not sure how we sounded but no one seemed to object to our music.

The Methodist Church owned a cabin named "Oak Lodge." The building was utilized as a retreat for church-related activities. It was also made available to youth groups. There came a time when Oak Lodge was in need of renovation. The church had no funds for the repairs so Strickfaden volunteered to put on a benefit performance. Mr. Hedges attended the event.

> He had an ultraviolet light demonstration with a number of items that shone brightly under UV. He had drilled holes in a metal disc which he fastened to a small electric motor, and which played musical notes when a jet of air was blown through the rapidly rotating disc.
> The grand climax was what he called his "million-and-a-half-volt generator." He had built a Tesla coil which caused rather spectacular sparks to jump off it. He had several demonstrations involving various pieces of equipment. At the conclusion of his program, he stood on it and raised his arms above his head, had someone turn on the current, and the sparks then jumped into the air from his fingers. With the lights off, it was very impressive to say the least.
> He had a gift of gab and all during the performance he was talking and explaining what he was doing. I'm sure I saw the show more than once as I believe he gave it a number of times.

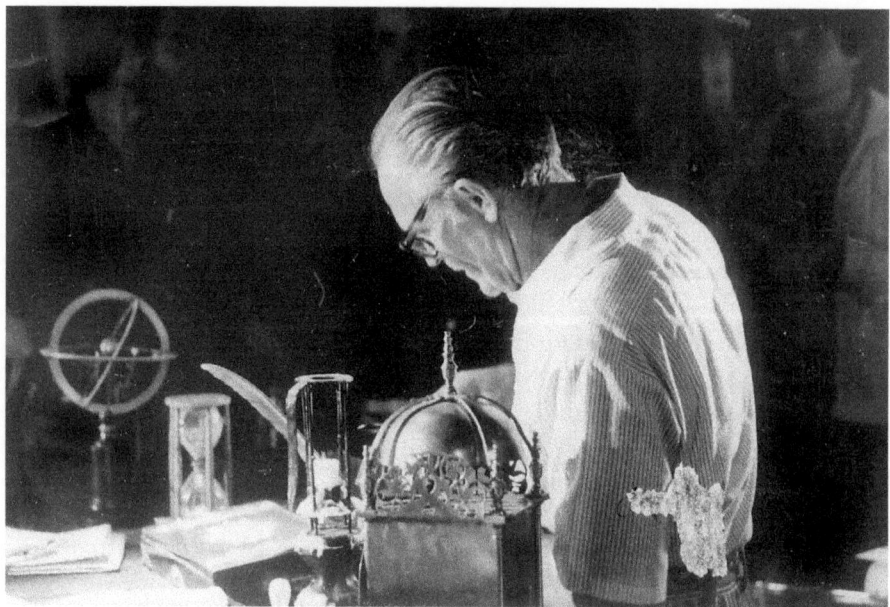

Steve Karkus, proprietor of Lightning Effects, Inc., has provided special effects for numerous films. Karkus held Kenny Strickfaden in high regard and considered him "a great special effects man, and a man of great character" (courtesy of Steve Karkus, Lightning Effects, Inc.).

13 — No Ordinary Man!

Steve Karkus with one of his many amazing special effects properties (courtesy of Steve Karkus, Lightning Effects, Inc.).

Steve Karkus, proprietor of Lightning Effects, Inc., has provided special effects for numerous films. In addition to his movie work, Steve has traveled worldwide giving demonstrations with equipment of his own design and construction. Like others in this field of entertainment, Steve held Strickfaden in high regard. "He was a great special effects man and a man of great character. I admired his sense of humor," stated Karkus. Mr. Karkus once visited Kenny's shop to discuss the various aspects involved in setting up a special effects program. The two men got along well and developed a friendly relationship. Karkus revealed the following experience during a brief visit to my home.

> I had worked on four Boris Karloff films during the late 1960s. By that time, Mr. Karloff's health had been in decline and it was necessary for him to use a wheelchair equipped with an oxygen tank. A nurse was available at all times.
> While making preparations for one of the scenes, I was having difficulty in getting a piece of apparatus to function to my satisfaction. Mr. Karloff was nearby and had taken notice of the frustration I was experiencing. His nurse came over and informed me that Boris wanted

to have a word. Upon approaching the veteran actor, I noticed a wry, humorous expression on his face. Karloff leaned a bit forward and whispered (in jest, of course), "Steve, don't you think we should call Kenny?"

Although Strickfaden appeared at times to be a plain and simple man, his total personality was an enigma. He rarely spoke of himself and was swift to direct the spotlight of praise upon others. When, for example, he was the recipient of acclaim for his unique contributions to the success of *Frankenstein* (1931), Ken's modest response was, "I built the machines but my friend Raymond Lindsay operated them. He should get the credit."

Kenny was a forgiving soul when it involved those taking advantage of his trust. That includes the colleague who borrowed a highly specialized and extremely valuable piece of equipment without any intention of providing for its return. And Strickfaden was never heard to say anything harsh about the young man who had been engaged to write his biography even though a request for return of the advanced collection of materials was denied. Additionally, Kenstric only spoke jokingly of having been ripped off by the Disney Corporation. It was of no surprise to Ken as he had witnessed a similar Disney trick involving animator Oskar Fischinger during the filming of *Fantasia* (1940).

In his declining years, Boris Karloff required a wheelchair equipped with an oxygen tank. A nurse was present at all times (courtesy of Steve Karkus, Lightning Effects, Inc.).

When one is given the privilege of examining the private diaries and correspondence of a person's estate, it is customary to apply some censorship and discretion prior to disclosing their contents to the public. In Strickfaden's case, no such restrictions were necessary. Kenny's *literae scriptae* contained no vulgarities, racial or ethnic slurs, mockery of religion, farmer's daughter jokes or any other ribald expressions one might expect to hear around "Tinseltown."

During Strickfaden's final years, he was continually plagued by a religious cult looking to enhance its agenda by the process of association. When he was aware of their presence, Ken would disappear into the workshop and lock the door. Another monkey on his back consisted of a group of "creeps" intent upon forcing the elderly electrician to sell them his collection of treasures. Kenny's constant refusals resulted in him becoming the target of verbal assaults.

Those who had the good fortune to be accepted into Strickfaden's inner circle were quick to develop a deep respect and intense fondness for the man. Kenny's wit, wisdom, benevolence and youthful radiance proved to be a winning combination of personality traits. Be that as it may, it would be unusual, if not impossible, for anyone to go through life without making enemies. It seems inevitable that Ken would have crossed paths with people whose personalities were as different as chalk from cheese. If such interactions resulted in antagonistic relationships, the number of hostile encounters permanently hardening Strickfaden's heart could probably be counted on the fingers of one hand; most likely the thumb of one hand.

Such laudatory remarks are not meant to convey an impression that Kenneth Strickfaden was a model of perfection. On the contrary, there were moments when Ken was far from being the consummate representation of humankind. His temper, while generally affable, could at times raise the temperature of water to its boiling point. On such an occasion, the man was not above taking a physical poke at the person stirring up his anger. And there were episodes when he would become consumed by his own little world to the point of endangering family unity. However that may be, it can be firmly stated that the few flaws in Kenny's temperament were dwarfed by the many positive traits of his overall disposition.

Strickfaden's daughter Marilyn disclosed some interesting reminiscences of her father.

> Dad had no journals that I know of, but made lots of sketches and schematics on his drafting board. He would then spend long hours in the shop converting the diagrams into a finished product. My father

would regularly make forays to aerospace or manufacturing companies where there were surplus items for sale. Some of what he located would not appear to be useful to a layman but he could visualize a use for his own special purposes.

Dad was always ready to visit with his cronies and interact with church youth groups and scouts. My father never smoked or drank alcoholic beverages so he didn't party. Partying to him meant having a hamburger sandwich and a chocolate malt.

My father always attended weekly Methodist Sunday school where he taught the sixth grade boys' class and participated in church services. He also presented electrical shows at no charge for local fund raisers.

I remember during the late 1930s and early 1940s when he would rent out a booth on weekends at Ocean Park Pier and also the Pike amusement zone at Long Beach, California. My mother would stand at the entrance and sell tickets to Dad's shows. Mom and Dad allowed me to examine the cash box so that I could remove the pennies for my collection. Such ventures were not big moneymakers because of the limited market and the problem of transporting heavy equipment.

A special feature of Dad's demonstrations was his unique sense of humor. Many attending his performances were schoolchildren and inserting a joke now and then helped to lengthen their span of attention.

At this point in the story, it should be apparent that Ken's true love was teaching the physical sciences. Strickfaden's effectiveness as an educator was greatly enhanced by his manner of showmanship. The man was a natural trouper who could easily have ended up at a carnival midway alongside jugglers and sideshow exhibitionists. Once again, the "Force" was with us when Hollywood prevailed over the circus and carnival industries.

It should also be evident that Mr. Elecstrick was not one to allow moss to grow underfoot. He seemed to have moved through life with "wings" set at full sail. How it was possible for Ken to simultaneously succeed at multiple pursuits and yet continue to meet personal obligations and relationships (family, friends, children, etc.) is nothing less than amazing.

And while on the subject of matters amazing: Whenever a question arose as to the status of an electrical circuit, Ken is known to have resolved the uncertainty by wiping two fingers across his tongue and then momentarily poking them into the outlet! Kenneth J. Strickfaden was no ordinary man!

14

Notes from Charles, the "Littler" One

Any author worth his or her weight in stationery knows that personal correspondence can provide vital information regarding a person's life. It was my intention to locate Ken Strickfaden's letters of correspondence to learn of his impressions of Hollywood, tales of motion picture experiences, life's desires, dreams and disappointments. Unfortunately, Ken did not carbon copy his letters. His files contained but a few incoming communications, some of which have been noted in this book.

Through the courtesy of Mrs. Marilyn S. Throssel, Ken Strickfaden's daughter, the author was privileged to receive photocopies of correspondence that Charles (Chas.) Strickfaden, the "littler" one, had written to Kenneth over a span of 24 years. The communications reveal the existence of a durable bond between brothers Charles and Ken. Even when Charles had reached adulthood and achieved a remarkable success as a professional musician, his lifelong willingness to give it up and become Ken's partner in a business of their own never diminished. Charles even dreamed of owning a cabin in the mountains where he and Ken could find respite from the drudgery of life's mundane routines. Charles idolized Ken and looked to him as his (secular) redeemer.

In all of the nearly 50 letters reviewed, the name of brother Frank Strickfaden appears on only two occasions. Frank, like his father before him, had left home at an early age. His absence during Charles' developing years precluded the possibility of a close relationship with his baby brother.

Charles' first letter to his 16-year-old brother Kenneth can be traced back to the summer of 1912. At the time, Charles was living with his mother in Portland, Oregon. Ken was living in Santa Monica with his father. Upon reviewing Charles' communications, it became apparent that here was a lad of 12 going on 17. It is possible that the separation and divorce of his parents were instrumental in nurturing a precocious maturity. Charles was very popular with his peers, especially the young ladies. That he rarely mixed with the womenfolk is not because of any dislike for female attention. It's just that he didn't want to be tagged a sissy by the neighborhood "toughs." In one of his early letters, 12-year-old Charles describes such an incident following a party given by one of his female admirers.

> After we had our eats, the girls wanted to go out and take a walk. Pretty soon, a bunch of tuffs came along. They had just got through tearing down the whole north Portland. Archie, the chief of the band, came up and grabbed Lucile. You know, of course, like the brave hero I am, I grabbed a hold of Archie and threw him over my head onto his back. Then the kids started to kick me. I let him up and he gave me a blow on the chin. All the while, Lucile was trying to bring me away. I then quick as a shot whirled my left hand and caught Archie on his chin. It knocked him down and blood began to stream from his cheek. His gang was so astonished that they walked away with him. Then Lucile wanted to hug and kiss me.

Charles developed into a strong, athletic boy who would later become a star playing high school football, basketball, baseball and track. He would also win honors in swimming, life saving and boxing. Charles enjoyed boating and learned to master the art of sailing. He was an avid outdoorsman who would rather than anything else be in the wilderness hunting grouse, tracking deer or trapping for fur. He became an excellent archer and once had taken a grouse while the bird was in flight. Although Charles loved guns, he quickly learned of their danger.

> By a foolish accident, my pal Harry got careless with an "unloaded" gun and shot me in the (blank). I had a heck of a time of it. It was a .38 caliber and it didn't go all the way thru. I could feel it almost coming out so I made him dig it out. He got a sharp knife and got it out making a cut in my rump about 3" × 9/32." I'm not dead yet but it is doubtful.

Not only did he learn that guns can be dangerous but Charles found that there are times when they can be mighty handy. Such was the case

14 — Notes from Charles, the "Littler" One

when he came upon several characters in the process of stealing his traps.

> I had a run-in with a nest of law breakers whom I caught stealing my traps. I backed up my argument by producing a .45 automatic which they didn't like. They haven't returned yet, but the traps have.

In addition to his fame as a high school athlete, Charles had established himself as a capable musician and was playing for two orchestras and one band. Teachers showered him with praise and predicted that he would someday make a good living as a professional musician.

> This summer I can make the coin playing. I've got the swellest saxophone. And the tone, why I can almost talk with it. The prettiest instrument you ever heard. At the senior dance recently, I had 'em all stepping. But instead of dancing, there was always a big crowd around where I played. Gosh, it's got a dandy tone and I can rattle off any old piece of music.

As Charles' reputation as a musician spread, he began to receive requests for services from band leaders working the nightclubs and dance halls.

> Tonight I begin to work at the Ocean Park dance hall playing the sax and clarinet. I work from 8–11 in the evening except Sundays and then a little longer. For a beginner, the manager said he would give me $75 then 85–90 and so on if I proved myself worth it. By the time school is out, I shall have made about $700.

The long hours devoted to non-school activities began to take a toll on both his health and school work. He failed to pass his senior math test and was required to take extra courses in order to graduate. Although he enjoyed making music, Charles expressed doubts as to making a living at it.

> I did not graduate because I need more mathematics so I can go to college. I figure that playing will never do me any harm. It is good side money and lots of fun and entertainment. But I don't believe I was made to sit on my tail and blow. It is too tiresome. Besides, it isn't a man's work.

Charles' failure to graduate from high school rattled Ken's customary happy-go-lucky temperament. He was concerned that Charles' musical activities were exposing him to the seedy side of life and warned of the detrimental effect it could have on his future. Ken urged his kid brother to avoid certain establishments known for their rowdy atmosphere. Charles gave assurances that there was nothing to worry about.

> Don't you ever think I'll go to the bad. The temptations are millions but never kid yourself cause I'm tough as ____ ____ and worth my weight in wildcats when I'm mad.
> I played at the Strand Cafe one night and said No after that. The smell of tobacco smoke and the sight of so many ignorant fools did not appeal to me.

In April 1919, Charles left Santa Monica and traveled to El Paso, Texas, to join an orchestra for a salary of $100 per week. He remained in Texas until August, stating, "I left El Paso — tired of my orchestra job. I quit and am on my way to college." He entered the College of Agriculture at the University of California with the intention of majoring in forestry. He participated in the school's musical and athletics programs. In addition to an already busy schedule, Charles founded a 50-piece jazz orchestra to help pay his college expenses. He also joined the glee club and was one of the few chosen for a tour of the Orient.

> Our glee club will make a concert tour of the Orient. There are 125 in the full glee club but only 20 will go on tour . . We will give concerts in Honolulu, Yokohama, Tokyo, Kobe, Nagasaki, Hong Kong, Manila, Shanghai, Fuchow, Peking, and Sing Tow. The ship's name is *Persia Maru*.

The Berkeley student left school during his sophomore year to accept a position with the Eddie Elkins musical ensemble. After two years with Elkins, he was hired to play for Max Fisher and his Ziegfeld Frolic Orchestra. Charles remained with Fisher for two years.

In 1924, Charles accepted a position with the famous Paul Whiteman Orchestra. He became a permanent fixture with the organization playing saxophone, clarinet, horn and oboe. During his stay with the Whiteman group, Charles studied oboe with Alfred Barthel of the Chicago Symphony Orchestra. After he gained a position with Whiteman, there occurred a downturn in the music business. Whiteman announced that he was forced to lay off ten members of the band. "He mentioned no names," Charles stated, "but upon inquiring, I found that

14 — Notes from Charles, the "Littler" One

A 1919 advertisement for a commercial establishment in El Paso, Texas. Members of the hotel's musical ensemble include Charles (Chas.) Strickfaden (shown playing the violin). Strickfaden played saxophone for the group. A handwritten note explains, "They got it kinda mixed" (courtesy of Marilyn S. Throssel).

I was elected to stay." Charles' importance to the band grew with each passing year.

> I have new duties now. I am now paymaster and jumbler of Paul Whiteman's finance. Each week, about $10,000.00 in cash is collected by me and passed out for the bills. I am in line to be promoted to first position in the sax section. We may go to Hollywood to make a movie.

The Whiteman ensemble was featured in several films, among them *King of Jazz* (1930), *Thanks a Million* (1935), *Atlantic City* (1944), *Lady, Let's Dance* (1944) and *Rhapsody in Blue* (1945). Whiteman also appeared in such films as *Strike Up the Band* (1940), *The Fabulous Dorseys* (1947), several minor musicals and Fox newsreel clips. Charles was seen with the orchestra in *King* and *Thanks*. Although he had left the orchestra in 1937, Charles was invited to participate in a reunion of former Whiteman band members for *Rhapsody*.

Even though Charles enjoyed the privilege of making out checks to such luminaries as Bing Crosby, the Jerome Kern estate, etc., he was much more than a "jumbler." Charles had caught the attention of the musical instrument industry. Companies such as Selmer, Buescher, Link, etc., were featuring Charles in their advertisements. His portrait appeared on musical instruction books and he was hired to write articles for *Metronome*, *Orchestra World* and other musical publications. The editors of *Metronome* nominated him as their candidate for the Musicians Hall of Fame. Sydney Berman, editor of *Orchestra World*, lauded Charles for his initial literary contributions.

> Thank you sincerely for an excellent column. I knew that we could expect as fine an article as you have sent in for the first in a series of "The Whiteman Bandwagon" and I am very glad to again thank you for joining our editorial staff [4/16/36].

Bandleader-crooner Rudy Vallee, worshiped by teenagers in the 1920s, included Charles Strickfaden's early 50-piece jazz orchestra among the "Ten Best Popular Orchestra (or Band) Leaders of All Time." Vallee went on to say, "These orchestras represent, in my opinion, the finest that were ever enjoyed on records, to dance to, or to just hear" (*The Book of Lists*).

Unknown to many who worked alongside Charles was his dissatisfaction with the frustrating demands of a musician's lifestyle. To Charles,

14 — Notes from Charles, the "Littler" One

the proverbial grass was always greener elsewhere. "I've been in the music business for 20 years. My earning capacity is excellent ... but no home or garden ... just living in hotels on the road."

> It was a haunting frustration to Strickfaden in the 1930s to be constantly reminded that people out there in the night were remaining in one place, sleeping in beds, staying close to home and fireside with wives and children, and never having to catch a train or leap from city to city and scramble after luggage. Strickfaden expressed this one night to Paul who replied, "Think Charlie; don't you suppose those farmers watch the trains go by and envy the travelers? It's just as frustrating to them to be stuck in one spot when everybody around is going someplace. Frustration, like money, has no home" [Delong, *Pops, Paul Whiteman, King of Jazz*, 1983, p. 190].

Little has been written about Charles after his 1937 departure from the Whiteman organization. Probably the best-kept secret of his musical career is his association with the classical music world. In the 1940s, he became a member of the Janssen Symphony of Los Angeles and often appeared as soloist. The Janssen Symphony was made up of the best musicians Hollywood had to offer.

> AN ALL AMERICAN program will be played by the Janssen Symphony when Werner Janssen conducts his all-American Orchestra in the third concert of the season at Wilshire-Ebell Theater Thursday evening, January 15.
> Janssen, a veteran of the last World War, served three years in the infantry. His orchestra of 45 members is composed of 39 men and 7 women — all Americans. Charles Strickfaden, English horn and oboe, is a captain in the American Flying Corps, and two other members of the orchestra are awaiting call.

The following excerpts (taken from newspaper columns) bring attention to Charles' solo performances with the symphony orchestra:

> In "The Swan of Tuonela" by Sibelius, Charles Strickfaden gave a splendid account of himself on the English horn.
> Sibelius' "The Swan of Tuonela" was hauntingly rendered, the lovely English horn solo exquisitely enunciated by Charles Strickfaden.
> Strickfaden's English horn quality also stood him up for an encore.
> "Quiet City," by Aaron Copland, for trumpet, English horn and strings, gave Charles Strickfaden opportunity which he bore with honors.

The other new work was Aaron Copland's "Quiet City" ... In this, the luminous beauty of Janssen's strings was perfectly matched by the suavity of Charles Strickfaden's performance with the reeds....

"Swan of Tuonela" was one of the outstanding features of the early part of the evening with an English horn solo by Charles Strickfaden played in magnificent style. With beautifully modulated phrasing and brilliant tone quality, the number brought repeated plaudits for the conductor and Strickfaden.

The program opened with Mendelssohn's Overture Ruy Blas, which was followed by Creston's Concerto for Saxophone and Orchestra with Charles Strickfaden as soloist. As music, the Concerto is inconsequential; as a show-piece filled with technical pyrotechnics, it is remarkable. Mr. Strickfaden disclosed amazing technical facility and tone quality of extraordinary beauty.

Werner Janssen, leader of the orchestra, was deeply moved by Charles' performance of the Creston and Sibelius compositions:

> I want to take this opportunity to congratulate you for the splendid job you did on Sunday night. There is no one living that could have done it as well as you and I am proud to have been the one to conduct your accompaniment ...
>
> As to "The Swan of Tuonela," I am happy to say that we are going to record this for a film short as well as for Victor and, of course, I planned this all with only you in mind ...
>
> Thanks for your wishes for our sixth season. They are greatly appreciated as you well know for wishes such as yours mean my life.

Charles' performances also caught the attention of such musical giants as Leopold Stokowski.

> When you played Debussy's "Rhapsody" at Camp Elliott, I asked the Los Angeles Philharmonic to engage you.... Sometime I would like to see you and talk over many things. If you have time, I wish you would spend an evening with me.

Charles recounted his experiences with Stokowski in an attempted autobiography.

> I was three times soloist for him. He made a new recording of *Fantasia* in which I participated. He recorded it with the Los Angeles Philharmonic but without the solo instrument. Then, in a large studio, I recorded the English horn solo part to the sound track.... Next day he called. "It was beautiful. I only wish Sibelius was there to hear it."

14 — Notes from Charles, the "Littler" One

Throughout his life, Charles carried an unwavering love and admiration for his older brother Kenneth. When the Strickfaden family's unity splintered, Charles and Frank moved away with their mother. Frank was embittered by the breakup and shortly after left to go out into the world on his own. When Charles was living with his mother, he missed his father and Ken. He later returned to live with Ken and his father but missed his mother. And when Ken flew the coop, his urge to be with his brother grew exponentially. "Well Kenneth," he wrote, "seeing that you won't come to me I guess I might as well have to come to you. But Kenneth, please come. I'm so lonesome for you." Those sentiments appear in Charles' letters from childhood and on into his adult years. The following are excerpts taken from notes Charles wrote to Ken. In the first quotation, Charles chastised his brother for the long interval between letters by fictionalizing the possible reason.

> The dirty villain crept up behind the man laboring over a work bench. In his hand he held a sledge hammer. Pausing for a moment in the shadow of a packing truck, he raised slowly and with a vicious blow smashed the skull of the unsuspecting laborer. Opening a door in the floor, he shoved the body in with a splash. It struck the sewer and that was the end of the career of K. Strickfaden.
>
> Just such schemes I've been hatching up in my mind that must have happened to you. Every time I come home from school, I expect a letter and don't get it. Tonight I was sure I wouldn't get one but you can see for yourself that you are not dead. For gosh sakes, don't keep us in suspense like that again. Write a letter and raise the devil about it, but write!
>
> It certainly does seem a long time that we have parted. I often remember how I used to come to your house way up there on the hill and such a good time I would have. I am very lonely now.
>
> I miss you like everything. There isn't a daw-goned fellow around here to do anything at any time or any place. I liked to ride around at night with you and not caring especially when we got in.
>
> I'll tell you absolutely frankly, I have ever since I was a little shaver kind of hitched all my future hopes on you. If ever a fellow missed a brother I sure have missed you. The things that I can always remember you by is the way you used to treat me. Just little incidents like riding me on your back made a deep impression.
>
> I don't hear much from you and if you knew how I missed you, you'd loosen up and exercise your arm. Your last letter for instance was exceedingly short. That is forgiven tho, because those few words meant a lot to me. "Chas. (you said), I want to see you make good and I know you will."

> I cannot eulogize enough the good and inspiring effect that your letters have upon me. Yours is a spirit which carries on while I seem to be clinging to a straw in a maelstrom of doubt.... Suffice to say that I am glad that I have a brother who offers solace in the form of enthusiasm, prospects for the future, and in presenting a view of an indomitable will to do and to succeed.

Several of Charles' letters contained reminiscences of Ken's high school days. His popularity with former teachers had not dulled even though several years had passed since graduation. The faculty often pestered Charles with questions as to his brother's whereabouts. Whenever time allowed, Ken would post a letter to his favorite high school instructors. His communications were so enthusiastically received that they would be read aloud to the students. "Mr. Stevens read your letter to the journalism class and showed them the pictures you sent," reported Charles. "It sure caused a bunch of fun." On several occasions, Ken's communiqués were printed in the school newspaper. Students would giggle whenever teachers recounted Ken's school pranks such as the time he frightened his female classmates by bringing a pet snake to the school dance.

Another interesting factor brought forth in Charles' letters is Ken's generosity. He was consistently sending money home to his father and Charles. Generally, his financial contributions to home varied between $40 and $500! Nan Strickfaden' s health had declined to the point where she had become dependent upon her family for financial assistance. Charles urged Ken to keep in touch with his mother and to provide for her living expenses rather than sending money home. When Charles was well-heeled, he would contribute to his mother's needs by sharing the wages earned from playing with musical groups.

Charles' pride in his brother grew by leaps and bounds when learning of Ken's success in the motion picture industry.

> Marion [Charles' first wife] and I saw a picture a short time ago called *Rainbow Trail* ... We were pretty sure that this must have been the one you worked on [letter dated February 2, 1932].
>
> We saw *Chandu* and I suspected that I had seen some of that apparatus before.... The confidence I have in your abilities is something to be considered seriously. I don't think that I could be surprised at the most astounding invention of genius coming from you [January 1933].
>
> We saw your [motion] picture and sure did get a big kick out of it. It has been running for several weeks on Broadway.... Your work alone is

the entire picture and the other fellows [in the band] who saw it say the same [March 22, 1935].

I dragged Marion over to the Great White Way to see the newsreel theatre. Some of the boys [in the orchestra] told me that famous brother of mine had some demonstrations on the screen. Your pictures were plastered out in front of the theater ... and name in lights on Broadway. I'm well proud of you [July 29, 1936].

Charles' letters make reference to a special saxophone stand that Ken had invented.

> This is a hurried note to explain that I have a party here whom I have interested in making and handling your baritone sax stand. I doubt whether or not there is a great demand but it is worth a try — and whatever profits are to be gained are entirely for you [April 1, 1932].
>
> The largest musical instrument manufacturers in the world are going to manufacture your stand this fall and put it on the market [1934].

Charles G. Strickfaden, a musician who developed techniques that extended the range of saxophone playing, who might have become the "Heifetz of the saxophone" had there been an equivalent selection of music available for his instrument, and who had achieved an unqualified success in his profession, neither acknowledged his accomplishments nor did he realize his lifelong dream of becoming a business partner with brother Kenneth.

> Tho I have made a success of music, I do not feel that I am a musician at heart.... What am I then and what do I want? Well, I am sort of a wanderer by instinct and in my blood flows a bit of the savage. Sprinkled with this there is a desire to write, to produce semi-art in photography and most of all to live a clean life in fresh air [January 19, 1935].

Charles Strickfaden enjoyed the remaining years of his life breathing the fresh air of Hawaii. He contracted leukemia during his late seventies and passed away at the age of 81 on September 11, 1981. The following is taken from his proposed autobiography and dated July 23, 1981.

> The battle is now nearly over ... and I already have one foot in the next [world]. My weight is 126 pounds. There is codeine for pain and blessed sleeping pills to take me under. I think I have slept for a solid week. Today, I forced myself to stay awake long enough to finish this, and to say — to my family, my friends, and to everyone I have known and loved — bless you forever.

15

"Re-Memories" (of early Santa Monica)

After a diligent search through Ken Strickfaden's papers, and making numerous inquiries, it appears that his letters of correspondence to brother Charles, and to anyone else for that matter, have suffered a fate not unlike Margaret Mitchell's South — gone with the wind. Shortly after Charles passed away, Ken set down on paper memories of his early days (ca. 1915) around Santa Monica. Ken's "Re-Memories" appear here courtesy of Ken's daughter, Marilyn S. Throssel.

Ken begins his look back in time with references to the lake and dam at Rustic Canyon which served as an early source of water for Santa Monica. Then there's the road to Sam Carson's cabin where brothers Ottie and Leo Carrillo (the actor) hosted some of the area's finest picnics. Carson was rather proud of being recognized as the "questionable son of Kit Carson." This same cabin became the property of Mary and Will Rogers (cowboy, comedian, actor) as a refuge from "friends" who had a habit of imposing upon their privacy. Rogers restored the building by incorporating a double (outside-inside) fireplace, hand-hewn ceiling beams, a corral with barns and a nearby berry garden. The property was later owned by Liz Persons, who added improvements for her string of race horses. The above described area is now part of a public park system.

Ken's remembrances include hikes to the canyon where one could drink clean fresh water from any stream, growths of tiger lilies eight feet in height, and ferns so tall that one could walk under them. Other sights

15 — "Re-Memories"

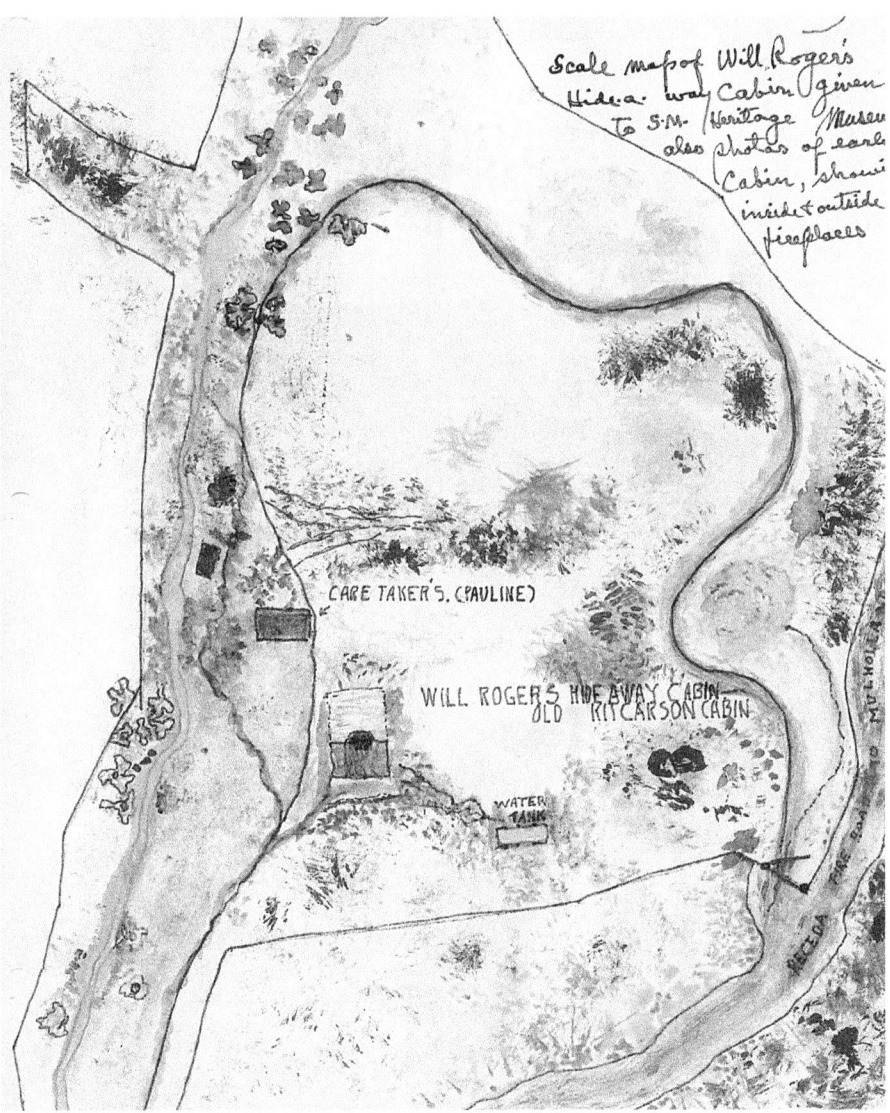

Map of an area near Santa Monica showing the location of Sam "Kit" Carson's cabin where actor Leo Carrillo staged large picnics and which was eventually owned by Mary and Will Rogers. Rogers was an actor and comedian whose crackerbarrel philosophy earned him international fame. The area is now part of a state park. From an original color sketch by Ken Strickfaden (ca. 1915).

recalled are flocks of frightened quail whirring away, bashful raccoons washing their "vitamins" at the shoreline, many deer that demonstrated little concern at his presence, and a profusion of silver-gray squirrels. That's where brother Charles harvested enough of the bushy-tailed critters to have a tailor convert them into two beautiful fur coats.

Strickfaden's notes provide a description of the automobile races along Wilshire Boulevard, San Vicente and Ocean Avenue where pioneer drivers such as Teddy Tetzlaff, Barney Oldfield, Gaston Chevrolet and Frank Wishart churned up clouds of dust. There is also the memory of the ill-fated auto mechanic who died in the lower branches of a tall eucalyptus tree after being hit by an out-of-control racer.

Reference is also made to "Bake" Loring's lunch room at the shore end of Santa Monica's Municipal Pier, where a hot dog could be had for five cents along with an equally inexpensive drink of soda pop. According to Ken, Loring's emporium of gustatory delights was established

"Bake" Loring's lunchroom at the shore end of Santa Monica's Municipal Pier. Photo (ca. 1920s) by Ken Strickfaden (courtesy of the Santa Monica Public Library Image Archives).

around 1900 and still going strong in 1915. Bake also owned a lunch room on the street behind the high school where an entire eight-inch pie cost but 15 cents. Any customer whose pocket could not yield the necessary funds was given the opportunity to buy half a pie for eight cents. Another small lunch room stood on Seventh Street where a 300-pound giant called "Tiny" served up hefty portions of chili beans for ten cents.

There was always a group of youngsters swimming around the Santa Monica Pier. But if the sewage treatment plant adjoining the pier was in operation they were forced to swim far into deeper waters. The boys would bring tire irons for harvesting barnacles from the piles under the wharf to be used as bait to attract bass, sea trout and other edible fish. Sometimes their catch was sold to unsuccessful fishermen on the top side of the wharf so that wives could retain faith in their providers.

There was a Japanese fishing village up the coast, rudely called "Skibbyville," where one could sneak around the hillside and get a distant view of the rough-and-tumble wrestling matches put on as cultural entertainment for the fishermen. The contestants were giants who put on what appeared to be a fierce battle. The affair ended in a fish-fry with all the trimmings.

Strickfaden recalled the delightful picnics at Beverly Glen where the horse-and-buggy teams starting at the old Christian Church would be driven up Nevada Avenue (Wilshire Boulevard). A quartet would sing every 15 minutes at the beautiful roadhouse and soda fountain near the bridge at Topanga Canyon. Deeply tanned swains of surf and sand would rendezvous at the 99 step stairway leading from Wilshire Boulevard road down the Palisade bluffs. The group consisted of Ken and Charles Strickfaden, Harry Hoag, "Wuzzy" Gunther, Irv Montgomery, Paul Walter, Earl "Screech Owl" and Ray Charles, Leo Reithmiller, Cliff Eshelman, "Curly" Baker, and Eddie Sands.

There were daring owl hunts over the Palisades where the bravest of the group would be tied to a thick hawser and lowered down to where six balls of fur nestled in their cliff abode. The birds, raised in a covered chicken pen, were fed ground squirrels harvested from the sparsely populated Gillette Regent Square development. The owls were tagged with such names as Cleo, Phoebe, Theo, Tom, Dick and Harry. They soon grew quite tame and were fond of sinking their talons into an extended forearm in anticipation of an evening meal.

Another group activity was the "wild safari" hikes to the town of

Filming on the beach north of Santa Monica Pier. Photograph (ca. 1920s) by Ken Strickfaden (courtesy of the Santa Monica Public Library Image Archives).

Saticoy to pick apricots. Participants were Lawrence Lazenby, Jack "Gunboat" and Bernard Evans, "Peach Basket" Les Storrs and a host of other stalwarts who were so fond of apricots that they were willing to endure hot weather, dusty orchards, various annoying insects and long hours just to enjoy good fellowship and meals of apricots prepared in every imaginable way.

In the vicinity of the present Sears store stood the Kalen Film Studios. Early westerns were made up the coast at Inceville. Other studios were Bison and Biograph.

There was a huge picture of Thomas Edison at the Venice Hall Ballroom where dancing contests were held. Many brawls occurred there following the football games between Santa Monica and Venice High Schools. Bathing beauty parades were staged on the beach near the Sebastian Cafe in Venice.

Ken recalled helping to fight the big fire on Venice Pier. He and friend Carl Spangenberger were credited with rescuing the pipe organ in the California Theater. The piers were crowded with numerous entertainment

A bathing beauty contest at the Sebastian Cafe in Venice. Photograph (ca. 1920s) by Kenneth Strickfaden (courtesy of the Santa Monica Public Library Image Archives).

establishments and concession stands. A sampling of the marts include Sharkie's Bowl, Noah's Ark, The Bamboo Slide, The Coal Mine, Paris After Midnight, Willard's Temple of Music, palmists by the score, The Shooting Gallery, The Diving Bell, Giant Dipper roller coaster, Pig Slide and Unger's Mystic Egyptian Temple where a blindfolded psychic sitting on an elevated throne would call out your name.

How interesting it would have been had Ken written a "Re-Memories" of the early days of Hollywood.

16

Saying Goodbye to Mr. Electric

*I place my soul within God's palm
Before I sleep as when I wake,
And though my body I forsake,
Rest in the Lord in fearless calm.*
— Hebrew prayer, "Eternal Lord"

By the time Kenny had reached his eighty-seventh year, he was no longer in control of his mad scientist and laboratory properties. The majority of his most important special effects gadgets came under the control of Ed Angell and John Foster, two of his closest associates. At the time, Angell was owner of the Hollywood Set Shop. One of the first films in which he utilized Strickfaden's apparatus was a cutesy short titled *Frankenweenie* (1984), a production which inaugurated the career of director Tim Burton (*Beetle Juice, Batman, Edward Scissorhands* and others). Some remaining properties were distributed locally in sales to amateur and professional technicians.

Mr. Electric's last year on this earth was anything but a happy experience. In addition to suffering the pain of deteriorating joints, he had to contend with the deleterious effects from hardening of the arteries. On his good days, Strickfaden was the same cheerful comedic character of earlier years. At other times, he would lose consciousness of reality and have difficulty recognizing even the closest of family and friends.

Ken celebrated the Thanksgiving and Christmas holiday seasons of 1983 with the John Fosters. Although this assemblage of friends provided a joyous atmosphere, those occasions effectively churned up tender

16 — Saying Goodbye to Mr. Electric

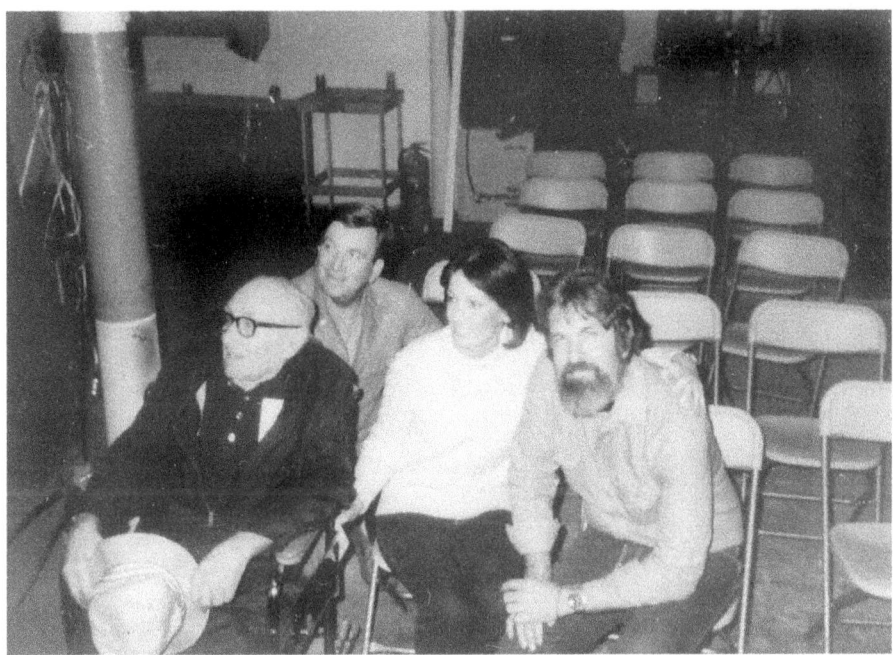

One of the last photos taken of Ken prior to his passing in February 1984. Janice and Ed Angell are seated. The man at the rear is unidentified (courtesy of Dick Aurandt).

memories of family gatherings with Gladys and the children. And always in the back of his mind were recollections of his childhood years with brothers Frank and Charles. Ken would become deeply depressed and fall into an uncontrolled weeping. He was well aware of the reality that time was running out.

When living at Foster's laboratory, Ken followed a routine. He would rise early in the morning, have his customary glass of milk or cereal (Strickfaden did not drink coffee) and head in the direction of the machine shop. There, Mr. Electric would sit before a large drafting table and design new and exciting special electrical effects gadgets. Ken Strickfaden did not live long enough to enjoy the Leap Year Day of February 29, 1984. The ailing octogenarian was rushed to Inglewood's Centinela Hospital where for several hours he desperately clung to life. According to the coroner's report, death resulted from "congestive heart failure, cerebral vascular accident, and renal failure."

On the very day, and close to the hour, of Strickfaden's expiration, the electrical system for the City of Los Angeles shut down. It matters not whether the technical breakdown resulted from human error or had been the act of a higher authority, no tribute, planned or unplanned, could have been more appropriate. But even in death, the man had taken steps to divert attention from himself. It was Ken's request that there be no funeral service. His body was buried at Santa Monica's Woodlawn Cemetery on March 5, 1984.

Kenstric's passing, however, did not diminish his role as an influential force in films. Strickfaden's mad scientist apparatus made Hollywood history when it appeared in Douglas Trumbull's revolutionary Showscan production *New Magic* (1984).

The news media ignored Ken's desire for anonymity. Burt A. Folkart, staff writer for *The Los Angeles Times*, composed a chronological summary of Strickfaden's professional achievements (3/3/84, p. 7). A review of Kenny's motion picture work was written by Forrest Ackerman for *Starlog* magazine (6/84, p. 66). Edward Angell, whose career in special

Together again. The Strickfaden gravesite is located in Woodlawn Cemetery on 14th Street at Pico Boulevard, Santa Monica. The gravestone is set in Section E, Lot 131, Block 17 (courtesy of Marilyn S. Throssel).

effects can be traced directly to Strickfaden's influence, wrote a tribute to his mentor for *TCBA News* (Vol. 3, #2, p. 2).

> It is with great sadness that we, the Tesla coil builders of the West Coast, report the passing of our long time friend and inspirational helpmate, Ken Strickfaden. For many of us, Ken started the spark that led to a long and rewarding romance with high voltage electrical devices.
> While most people thought of him as the creator of the Frankenstein laboratory equipment, his real purpose in life was that of a teacher of scientific principles. We all mourn his passing.

Of the many tributes published in media and trade journals, both prior to and after Strickfaden's passing, none summed up the man's contributions to science fiction and horror films so succinctly as did journalist Victor Cox:

> Without his electrical inventiveness, a host of mad scientists (and a few heroes) would never have happened... [*Los Angeles Times Calendar*, 11/18/81, pp. 1, 6, 25].

17

A Sampling of Mad Scientist Films

In writing this book, it was not my intention to provide an analytical review of the nearly 100 motion picture productions in which Kenneth Strickfaden had a hand. But it is my opinion that a publication such as this would be lacking if special attention was not directed to a sampling of films in which his equipment is prominently displayed. Excluded from this chapter, however, are the well-known Frankenstein series, *The Mask of Fu Manchu* and other motion pictures of their caliber so adequately described in numerous publications devoted to genre films.

The criteria by which the titles in this chapter were selected had nothing to do with their star rating, box office success, reputation of the cast, the director or quality of the script. The major emphasis in the selection process merely requires that a film provide an ample display of the art of Strickfaden's high voltage effects. Titles are listed chronologically by year.

More likely than not, the type of films in which Ken's machines play a pivotal role are those based on the mad scientist theme. Generally, the plots incorporate such conceptions as world domination, theft of a military weapon, personal wealth, brain switching and so on. And again more likely than not, the script will feature a death ray or robot weapon whose owner declares: "With this invention, I will rule the world."

Chandu the Magician (Fox, 1932), 74 min. Cast: Edmund Lowe, Bela Lugosi, Irene Ware, Henry B. Walthall, Herbert Mundin, June Vlasek, Virginia Hammond. Directors: Marcel Varnel, William C. Menzies.

Chandu (Lowe), a student of Eastern mysticism, has learned the secrets of invisibility and the power to control men's minds. His bag of tricks also enables him to walk over hot coals and through fire without injury.

Robert Regent (Walthall), Chandu's scientist–brother-in-law, has invented a death ray machine with the power to destroy cities halfway around the world. Roxor (Lugosi), an evil man bent upon gaining world domination, steals Regent's death ray but doesn't have the knowledge required to make it function. Roxor kidnaps Regent and his daughter to force the inventor to put the ray gun into operation. Chandu sets out to save the Regents. Regent succumbs to Roxor's threats and sets up the machine for operation. Unknown to Roxor, the scientist adjusts the machine so that it will self-destruct. Roxor, thinking that he now has the power to carry out his evil desires, points to the long-handled switch and declares: "At last, I am king of them all. That lever is my scepter. London, New York, Imperial Rome — I can blast them all into a heap of smoking ruins. Cities of the world shall perish. All that live shall know me as master, and tremble at my word." Roxor activates the switch and destroys himself, but not before Chandu and the Regents make their way to safety.

The film includes two scenes in which the viewer is

One of the many forms of traveling (ascending) arc devices Strickfaden used in films. A high voltage spark forms at the base of two diverging electrodes. Convection currents resulting from the arc force the spark to rise. The length of the spark increases until it reaches the upper end and extinguishes itself. The process is repeated as another spark forms at the bottom.

given an opportunity to examine Strickfaden's apparatus. Electrical equipment making up Regent's laboratory are a traveling (ascending) arc, "Cosmic Ray Diffuser," "Multistributor," spark wheel, double Tesla resonators and a complex nonfunctioning construction containing various electromechanical components. The latter concoction and the "Multistributor" were among the lab apparatus in *The Mask of Fu Manchu*.

The Vanishing Shadow (Universal, 1934), 12 Chapters. Cast: Onslow Stevens, Ada Ince, Walter Miller, James Durkin. Director: Louis Friedlander [Lew Landers].

Robots, invisibility, death rays and numerous scientific gadgets assist the scientific genius Stanley Stanfield (Stevens) and electrical wizard Prof. Carl Van Dorn (Durkin) in avenging the death of Stanfield's father by Wade Barnett (Miller) and preventing him from gaining control of Stanfield's shares of his late father's newspaper. Also assisting is Gloria Grant (Ince), a newspaper reporter and estranged daughter of Barnett. Grant has changed her name in protest of her father's questionable business activities as well as his past abusive treatment of her late mother.

One of the most effective instruments Stanfield employs to overcome Barnett's gang of thugs is a special belt named "The Vanishing Ray." It enables the wearer to become invisible. Only his shadow can be seen when in a state of invisibility. Other scientific inventions in Stanfield and Van Dorn's anticrime arsenal are a handgun death ray, electric ray torch, hand-held remote control (similar to today's television remote) and a remarkable radio-controlled robot. The serial is complete with car, airplane, and train collisions as well as other narrow escapes that add excitement to the plot. *The Vanishing Shadow* is a delightful serial to watch — which begs explanation as to why film writers have treated it so lightly.

In this serial, the first of Strickfaden's chapterplay films, can be seen a rotating spark gap, "Meg Senior" Tesla coil, traveling arc devices, "Cosmic Ray Diffuser," radio test gear and numerous static props that do nothing but provide an illusion that they are important to the plot. One strange device draws attention even though it is a non-functioning prop. It consists of two large bulbs with attached components. Strickfaden had a remarkable imagination for concocting (non-workable) apparatus made up of unrelated electrical components.

17 — A Sampling of Mad Scientist Films

Air Hawks (Columbia, 1935), 69 min. Cast: Ralph Bellamy, Tala Birell, Edward Van Sloan, Douglass Dumbrille, Robert Middleton, Victor Kilian, Wiley Post. Director: Albert Rogell.

Two airlines compete for a mail contract. Barry Eldon (Bellamy), owner of the independent ITL, is being pressured to sell his company to the larger Consolidated. Shortly into the film, we are shown a secret science laboratory where electrical experiments are being undertaken by an inventor named Schultz (Van Sloan). As generators hum, and spark wheels spit out electrical flames, Schultz directs a ray gun at a model bridge. The target is completely vaporized. He then focuses in on a model airplane. This, too, goes up in flames. The owners of Consolidated hire the demented scientist to shoot down Eldon's ITL planes. Schultz mounts the apparatus inside a large van which features a slide-away roof. He drives the mobile lab to an area located along the routes followed by ITL's airplanes. Eldon now faces a crisis as his planes begin to disappear. With a bit of sleuthing by Eldon, Renee Dupont (Birell) and a newspaper reporter nicknamed "Tiny" (Kilian), the trio are able to locate the position of the van and blow it to smithereens.

In addition to the fancy ray gun, other Strickfaden machines making up the mad scientist's lab are a traveling arc, double Tesla resonators, the "Cosmic Ray Diffuser" and an assortment of interesting electrical and radio gadgets.

Sky Bandits (Criterion Pictures, 1940), 52 min. Cast: James Newill, Dave O'Brien, Louise Stanley, Joseph Stefani, Dwight Frye. Director: Ralph Staub.

The Yukon Gold Mining Company has been shipping its gold by air freight but the planes never reach their destination. Sgt. Renfrew of the Royal Mounted Police (Newill) and his sidekick (O'Brien) have been assigned to solve the mystery. They believe the planes are being destroyed by a mysterious force.

Deep in the Canadian wilderness is a secret lab owned by a mentally unbalanced inventor named Speavy (Frye). A group of gold-hungry thieves take control of the lab and bring in a Prof. Lewis (Stefani) to oversee the experiments. The crooks have conned Lewis into thinking that targeting planes is part of a secret government national defense program.

The lab is equipped with numerous electrical gadgets and has a sliding roof panel which allows a ray gun to be aimed skyward. Renfrew and his fellow Mounties locate the lab and capture the criminals.

The Strickfaden props include a ray gun, spark wheel (also used in the 1932 film *Sherlock Holmes*), the ubiquitous "Cosmic Ray Diffuser," a large pulsing light bulb (standard Strickfaden stuff), radio sets and a large nonoperational inductor (coil) that previously appeared in such films as *Frankenstein* (1931), *Shadow of Chinatown* (1936), *The Fighting Devil Dogs* (1938) and other Kenstric films.

The Monster and the Ape (Columbia, 1945), 15 Chapters. Cast: Robert Lowery, George Macready, Ralph Morgan, Carole Mathews, Willie Best, Ray "Crash" Corrigan. Director: Howard Bretherton.

A remote controlled robot, high voltage electricity, secret passages, surreptitious television transmissions, an ape, a mad scientist and a lot of action keep viewers entertained through 15 chapters of *The Monster and the Ape*.

Prof. Arnold (Morgan) of the Bainbridge Research Foundation has invented a remote controlled robot called "Metalogen Man." The robot receives its energy from a rare metal known as metalogen. According to Arnold, the rock-like material provides power to the robot "on the theory of the interradiation principle." Arnold demonstrates his robot before a group of highly respected scientists. Among the distinguished guests is a demented professor of science named Ernst (Macready). He is jealous of Arnold's accomplishments and prepares a scheme to

The ubiquitous "Cosmic Ray Diffuser" appeared in numerous mad scientist films. It produces a visual (sparking) and audible (clanking) effect in a sequential rhythmic pattern.

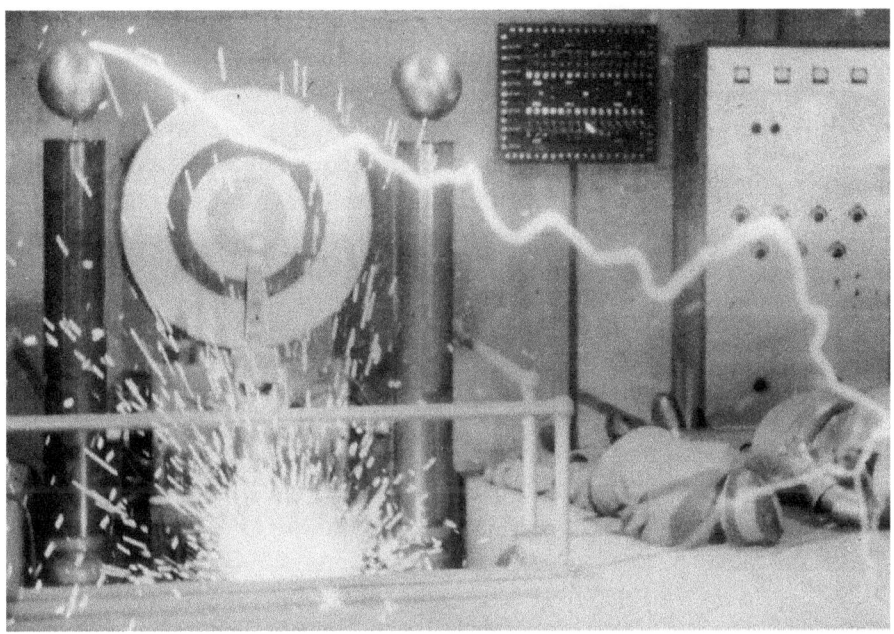

A scene from *The Monster and the Ape*'s Chapter Ten, "Forty Thousand Volts" (1945). Ken Morgan (Robert Lowery) lies unconscious as man-made lightning threatens electrocution. Thanks to movie trickery, Morgan survived the cascading bolts. The disc between the twin Tesla coils is Strickfaden's lightning screen.

obtain the metalogen and the robot. Ernst is assisted in his criminal acts by several characters of low morality and Thor, a semi-tamed ape (Corrigan). Upon gaining possession of the highly prized metalogen, Ernst boasts, "With this, and my knowledge of the metalogen man, I've practically got the world in the palm of my hands."

Ken Morgan (Lowery) and Babs Arnold (Mathews) support Prof. Arnold and provide the action and romantic interest in the film. Prof. Arnold's chauffeur, "Flash" (Best), contributes comedy.

Cheating is obvious in several chapter endings. One conspicuous discrepancy occurs at the close of Chapter Three. Morgan is rendered unconscious and falls onto a moving conveyer belt used for transporting materials into a furnace. He completely disappears into the flames. But in the recapitulation introducing Chapter Four, Morgan miraculously regains consciousness and rolls off of the belt long before reaching the fiery furnace.

The mad scientist's laboratory is fitted with an impressive array of electrical equipment (most are non-functioning props). A most interesting lab component is Strickfaden's lightning screen, a disc about three and a half feet in diameter. It can be seen creating very brief fingers of electrical sparks over the face of the disc. Although the electrical discharges last but a few thousandths of a second, each individual spark leaves a fingerprint of itself lasting several seconds. The effect is quite impressive when the screen is operated in darkness.

Master Minds (Monogram, 1949), 64 min. Cast: Leo Gorcey, Huntz Hall, Billy Benedict, Alan Napier, Glenn Strange. Director: Jean Yarbrough.

Confusion and mayhem occur when the Bowery Boys become involved with high voltage experiments being undertaken at an abandoned house. Sach (Hall) develops psychic powers after reading a book on the life of Nostradamus. A scientist (Napier) kidnaps Sach with the intention of carrying out brain-switching experiments with Atlas (Strange), a wild man captured in a South American jungle. The fun begins when the Bowery Boys discover the location of the lab and Whitey (Benedict) accidentally closes the main switch controlling the high voltage equipment.

Master Minds displays an amazing array of Strickfaden's equipment, and sparks are as plentiful as in any film of this type. Equipment making up the laboratory are a lightning screen, traveling arc devices, large (non-functioning) inductor, "Multistributor," a master switchboard, "Cosmic Ray Diffuser" and other electrical gadgets.

Long, impressive sparks jump between two ball electrodes during the brain transfer process. The heavy electrical discharges appear to be four to five feet in length and represent approximately 400,000 volts. But as Ken Strickfaden has been known to say, "Photography can stretch a spark of a few inches into laboratory length."

Jesse James Meets Frankenstein's Daughter (Circle Productions, 1966), 82 min. Cast: John Lupton, Cal Bolder, Narda Onyx, Steven Geray, Rayford Barnes, Jim Davis, Felipe Turich. Director: William Beaudine.

This mixture of the science fiction and western genres failed to produce a box office smash.

Maria (Onyx), a descendent of Baron Frankenstein, is engaged in experiments with the goal of bringing the dead back to life. Her experiments have failed due to the lack of a living brain with which to work. In ride Jesse James (Lupton) and sidekick Hank Tracy (Bolder). The two men get mixed up with a gang of stagecoach robbers and Tracy is wounded. He is taken to Maria's laboratory for medical treatment. Tracy is precisely the specimen needed for Maria's brain-switching experiments. The operation is successful and Tracy is converted into a zombie-like robot named Igor. Igor kills Maria and then turns against Jesse but is shot by James' girlfriend (Turich). The film ends as Jesse James and the local sheriff (Davis) ride off into the sunset.

The Strickfaden laboratory equipment used in this film is comprised of a diathermy machine, spark wheel, "Cosmic Ray Diffuser," blinking neon lights, double pole resonator, radio test equipment, small (non-functioning) inductor and a pair of neat sparking medical helmets worn by Tracy and Maria during the brain transfer process.

18

The Strickfaden Legacy

Although the technique of projecting images in motion is by itself a special illusion, the art of special effects by masking techniques, double exposure, slow motion, filming in reverse, etc., have been a part of filming since its inception. Kenneth Strickfaden's inventions and innovations in the field of special electrical effects added a dimension to filming techniques. As is the case for most artists, their legacy is usually limited to one or more images or work form. Ken's legacy is rather broad in that it consists of images, sounds and also the special equipment necessary for producing his art. Strickfaden's contributions merit recognition.

Even though he was satisfied that his images were permanently engraved in motion picture history, it was Ken's desire to have his tools continue to function in the industry long after his passing. To this end, he transferred what was called "The Strickfaden Collection" to friends John Foster and Ed Angell. Both men had extensive working connections in the motion picture business.

After Ken's complete retirement from motion picture activity, the equipment was put to use in a number of projects for both sound and visual effects. The film *Tron* (1982), which was considered groundbreaking for the time, used Ken's favorite variable traveling arc invention to generate sound for the battle scenes. In 1984, a Disney short titled *Frankenweenie* was the directorial debut for Tim Burton. Burton based the visuals for this production on his favorite laboratory scenes from *Frankenstein* (1931) and incorporated as much of the Strickfaden equipment as he could crowd into a very small set. In the case of Burton, it can be said that Ken posthumously played a small part as star maker. Other projects in which the Strickfaden legacy is evident are *Brainstorm* (1983), *The Adventures of Buckaroo Bonzai* (1984), *New Magic* (1984) *The Terminator* (1984), and *Powder* (1995).

With the passing of John Foster in 1993, and Ed Angell's retirement in 1994, it was time to locate a new home for Ken Strickfaden's equipment. A number of feelers were put out to film industry leaders who had some vested interest in securing the collection. One of the more important film companies to express an interest was Universal Studios. After a cursory examination by Universal, it appeared that preserving Ken Strickfaden's place in motion picture history was of lesser importance than the company's then-current involvements in the entertainment field.

When it came down to a last resort for finding a home for Ken's equipment, the Planet Hollywood organization was contacted. At the time, Arnold Schwarzenegger headed the restaurant chain and seemed a natural choice because Ken's equipment was used to generate sparks that appeared in his epic film *The Terminator*. Additionally, the Planet Hollywood chain was well-known for its displays of famous motion picture artifacts. Among its marvelous collection are such recognizable motion picture memorabilia as Judy Garland's blue and white gingham dress from *The Wizard of Oz*, Scarlett O'Hara's green gown from *Gone with the Wind*, the Butterfield stagecoach on which John Wayne rides in the classic film *Stagecoach*, Charlie Chaplin's jacket from *The Great Dictator* and Darth Vader's costume from *Star Wars*. But Ken Strickfaden's part in motion picture history was not included in Planet Hollywood's business plans.

Because the collection had been housed in Dallas, Texas, the next logical prospect was The Studios at Las Colinas. The Studios had been running a very successful tour for a number of years and it appeared to be a good location for a permanent home

On February 15, 2003, The Studios at Las Colinas made arrangements to sell its Strickfaden holdings through Odyssey Auctions in association with Julien Entertainment, Inc. But instead of offering the collection as a complete package, the Las Colinas group decided to dispose of Strickfaden's properties in individual lots. Held at the Sofitel Hotel in Los Angeles, the sale was advertised as the "Monster and Magic" auction because it also incorporated the collections of Blackstone the Magician and that of Forrest Ackermen. The following excerpts are taken from two separate announcements preceding the event:

From the collection of special effects genius Kenneth Strickfaden comes the original laboratory equipment used to bring Boris Karloff to life in *Frankenstein*. Other pieces of Strickfaden wizardry in this collection appeared in *Bride of Frankenstein*, *Son of Frankenstein*, *The Munsters*, the Universal Flash Gordon serials, *Dracula vs. Frankenstein*, and Mel Brooks' *Young Frankenstein*.

The sale features property from the fabled collection ... once owned by Kenneth Strickfaden — the Hollywood special effects genius. Strickfaden, who built props for *Flash Gordon* and *The Wizard of Oz*, created "Megavolt Senior." The device — " it produces 1 million volts of lightning-like bolts — was used in several Frankenstein movies and *The Terminator* starring Arnold Schwarzenegger. It could command $65,000 or more.

The variable traveling arc was one of Ken's favorite inventions. The rate at which the electrical discharge ascended could be varied. In *Tron* (1982), it was used for sound rather than visual effects. From an original color photograph (courtesy of Doug Norwine).

The properties put for sale were among Strickfaden's most important creations: Megavolt Senior, Megavolt Junior, lightning screen, Fireloscope, Nebularium, Digital Disputer, Involutarium, traveling (ascending) arc units and his unique and reliable switchboard, all used time and again in science fiction and horror genre films. Not listed among the sale items are Ken's invaluable Multistributor, the conical Tesla coil used in *Frankenstein* and *The Mask of Fu Manchu* and the ubiquitous Cosmic Ray Diffuser.

Not any of the properties were sold because tentative buyers found the minimum bidding prices too high. It is unfortunate that Hollywood had neither the desire nor the foresight to establish a permanent display of the original Frankenstein lab setting with which illustrated lectures describing the filming of the 1931 production would be available to the public. Fortunately, the story of the filming of *Frankenstein* is given extensive coverage on the film's DVD. Kenneth Strickfaden's legacy is noted, albeit briefly, in the disc's bonus elements.

> The use of his machinery in the *Frankenstein* series was most impressive and had a great deal to do with the lasting quality of the films. They were most convincing.— Ray Harryhausen*

*From a communication to the author on September 19, 2001.

19

A Final Word

Kenny was the most amazing man I've ever known.
— Gary Landis, film and TV technician

Considering the heights of perfection to which the special effects industry has ascended, there appears to be no superlative that adequately describes the current state of achievement. Perhaps "mind-boggling" would suffice as an empirical characterization of the situation. A list of films which best show what has been done with modern equipment and techniques might include the Star Trek and Star Wars series, *Jurassic Park* (1997), *Titanic* (1998) and other blockbuster productions. Technicians are now able to reproduce images of long-dead icons in new settings such as Fred Astaire dancing with a vacuum cleaner, Humphrey Bogart as a jewelry salesman and John Wayne selling beer. Equally startling are the scenes in *Forrest Gump* (1994) in which Tom Hanks visits with celebrities who have passed to the other side. The ability to electronically resurrect the dead makes Henry Frankenstein's experiments appear both amateurish and inhumane.

Except for special productions such as the Terminator series (in which Tesla coils are put to use), most of the high voltage special electrical effects are now created by a skilled computer engineer. Computer-generated electrical lightning is added to a film after the scene has been completed. This method of producing special electrical effects not only protects the participants from the threat of injury by electrocution but also allows control of the dimensions and direction of the electrical visu-

19 — A Final Word

Artwork (courtesy of Doug Norwine).

als. Unlike the excitement that permeated the set of *Frankenstein* (1931), people no longer come from miles around to watch when the big switch is pulled. Gone (in most cases) are the real live bolts of man-made lightning with their accompanying acrid scent of ozone gas, the odor of overheated transformers, as well as the white-hot carbon particles falling to the set below.

As sophisticated as today's state of the art may be, it too will be surpassed by tomorrow's technical advancements. With the revolutionary digital video technology now available, the day of the standard system of projecting pictures by film onto a screen appears to be nearing its end. One can only speculate as to what future advances in optics, electronics and metallurgy may bring to the entertainment processes.

Regardless of what marvels the future may provide, Ken Strickfaden's basic approach to the physical sciences will never lose its intrinsic entertainment value for pure imagination, innovation and sheer excitement. As long as video technology and late night black-and-white television programs are available, the special electrical effects created by Frankenstein's Electrician will for many years continue to win, entertain, and inspire new generations of fans.

Ode to Kenstric

Forever young,
And always sunny;
Remaining active,
And so funny;
I wish he had lived
to one hundred twenty.
— Harry Goldman

Appendices

Appendix A. Photographica

To say that Kenneth Strickfaden had been bitten by the photo bug would be an understatement. From the time he entered high school, Ken began pointing a camera at hundreds of subjects including amusement sites, battlefield scenes of World War I (few survive), family and friends, as well as his own laboratory apparatus and equipment. Ken used a variety of cameras, mostly the type designed to accept a negative of approximately 3 × 4 inches.

He reproduced the photos using a printer or enlarger of his own construction. Time has taken its toll in regard to the subjects Ken photographed. Most no longer exist. Fortunately, many of the negatives created during his lifetime remain intact. The following pages represent a small selection of the hundreds of photos taken by, and of, Kenneth Strickfaden.

The early days. Strickfaden assembling a mad scientist apparatus.

Strickfaden holding a "Melodyne" musical disc. The large lens at the right appeared in *Son of Frankenstein* (1939).

Strickfaden dodging lightning bolts spewing forth from the "Megavolt Senior" Tesla coil.

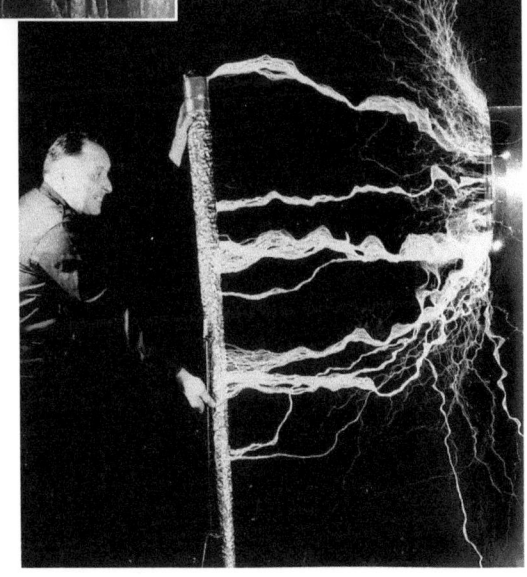

160   Appendix A

Above: Strickfaden creating a form of electrical art. He is the only technician known to perform this trick.

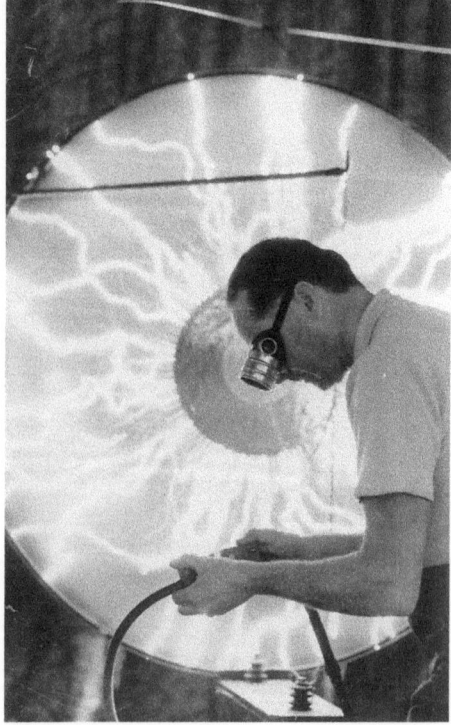

Left: The inventor is silhouetted by the high voltage discharges from his lightning screen apparatus.

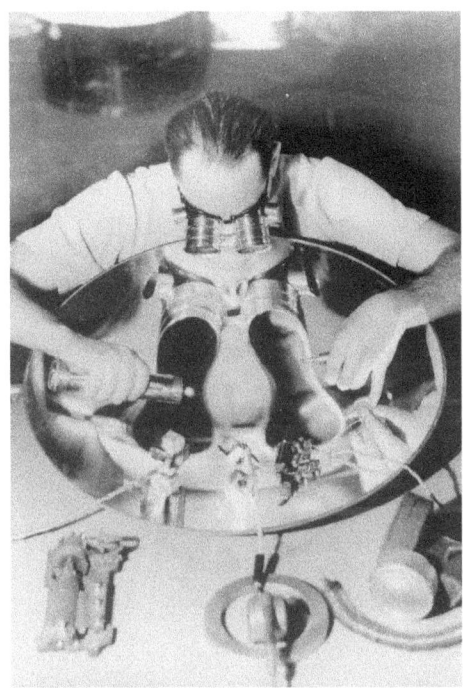

Left: Strickfaden creating distorted images with the "Nebularium" mirror device. This apparatus was used to project giant shadows in the Universal's *House of Dracula* (1945).

Below: Strickfaden standing fearlessly before a high voltage arc. His reliable switchboard can be seen in the foreground while the famous "Mcg Senior" Tesla coil appears in the background.

Strickfaden silhouetted by a shower of spidery sparks emanating from the pyrogeyser device.

Ken served as sound technician on many films. This photograph may have been taken on the set of *The Rainbow Trail* (1932) or *Mystery Ranch* (1932).

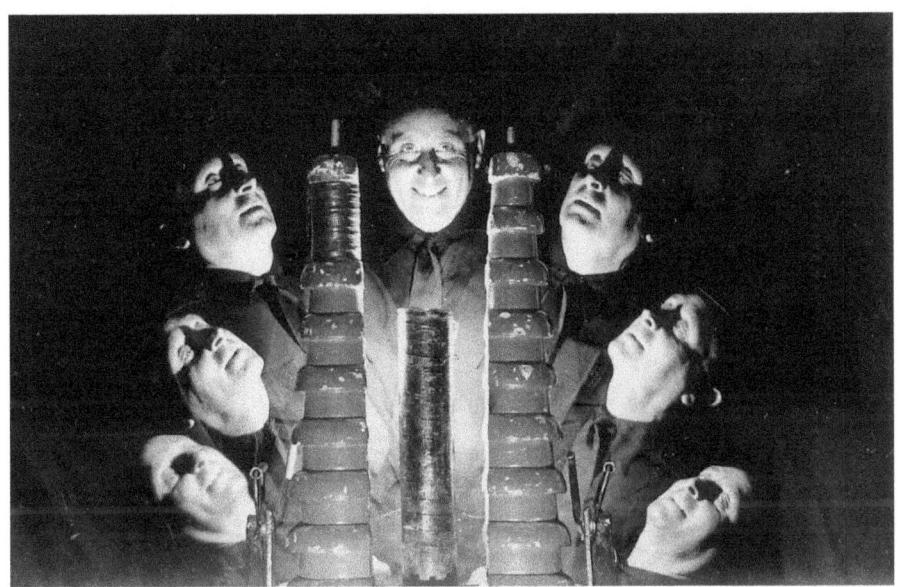

Above: Strickfaden in an example of his photographic multi-exposure talent. This photographic feat was accomplished long before the availability of computer trickery.

Right: Strickfaden's 15-year-old daughter Marilyn modeling a science fiction caricature. The nose cone once served as an ornament on the Strickfaden family Christmas tree.

Left: Paul Walter, one of Strickfaden's lifelong friends. Walter majored in theology and became an evangelist. He is shown holding a switch box that controlled Strickfaden's "Magnalux" invention. It was used in numerous films to simulate flashes of lightning.

Below: Car trouble on his way to Las Vegas to appear at one of the nightclubs.

The "Cosmic Ray Diffuser" appeared in *Frankenstein, Bride of Frankenstein, The Vanishing Shadow* and many other science fiction and horror productions. It produced a visual (sparking) and aural (clanking) effect in a rhythmic pattern.

Strickfaden's conical Tesla coil created life in *Frankenstein* (1931) and tested for gold in *The Mask of Fu Manchu* (1932). The individual lightning bolts appear as a single mass due to the effects of a time exposure.

Hark! A Martian cometh.

Carbon electric arc.

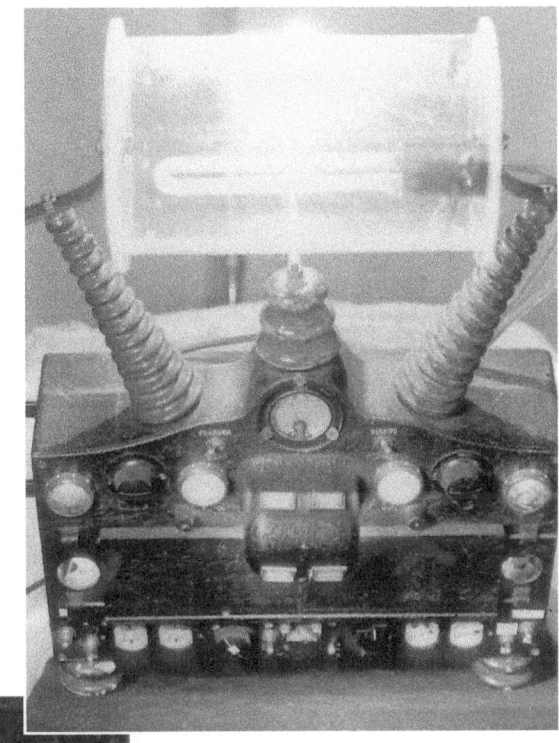

"The Fireloscope" can be seen in *Dracula vs. Frankenstein* (1971) and similar horror films.

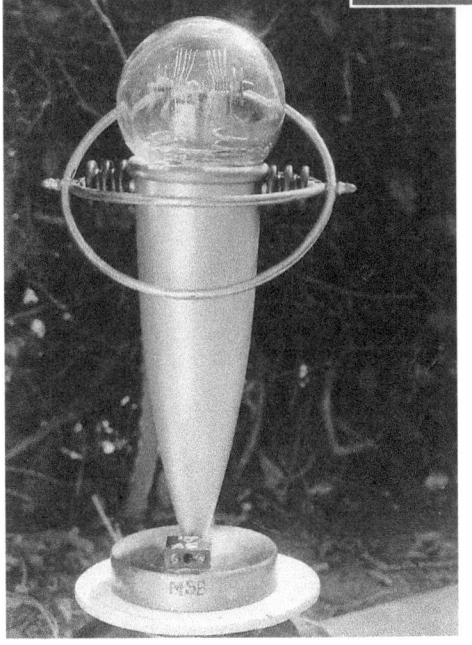

The "Space Beacon" can be seen in films ranging from *The Mask of Fu Manchu* (1932) to *Murder by Television* (1935) and beyond.

Appendix B. Technical Notes and Sketches

Kenneth Strickfaden was a doodler, scribbler and note taker. Although his notes were not written with publication in mind, this writer takes the position that they provide an insight into Strickfaden's character and scientific mind, and his approach to the career he loved. The following are but a sample of the numerous notes found in his files. Many of the original sketches were drawn with watercolors.

Technical Notes and Sketches

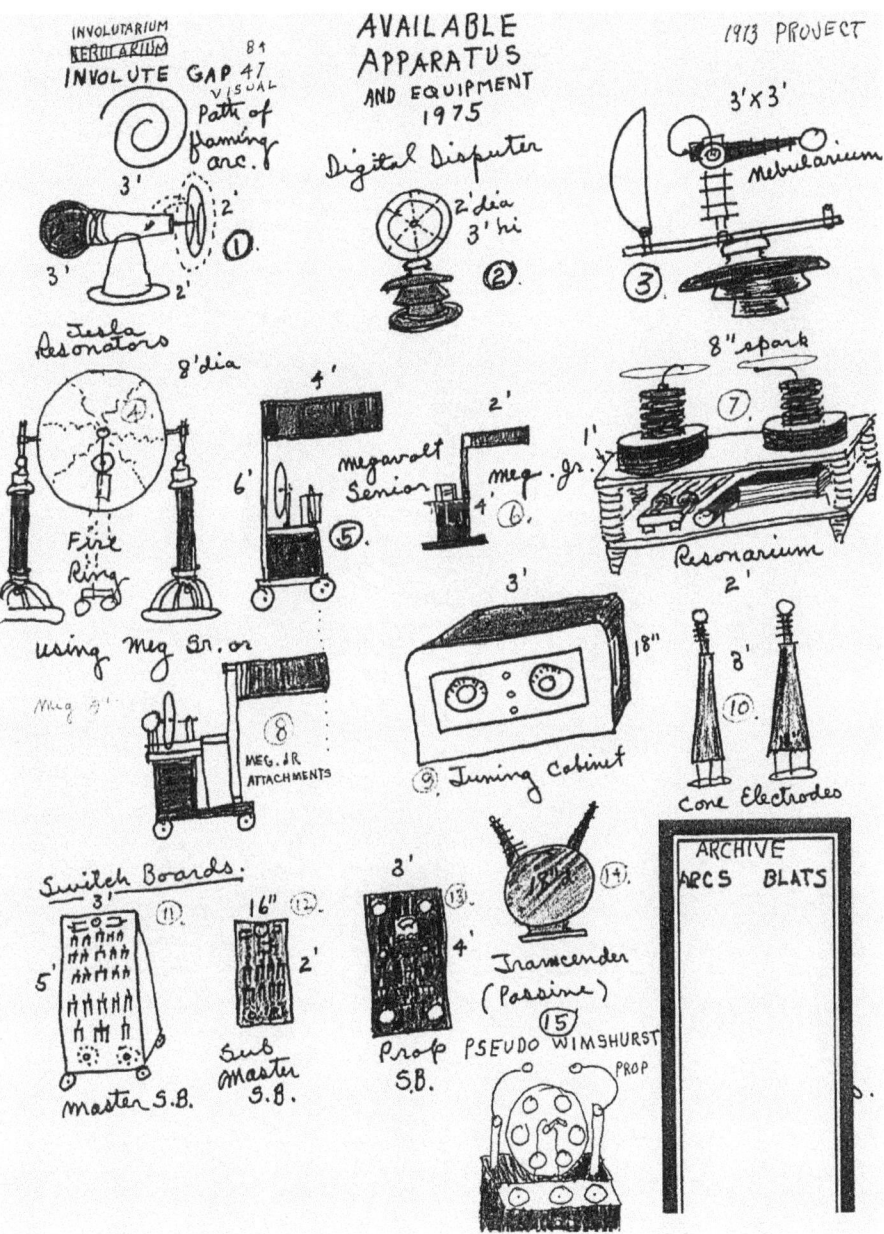

Appendix B

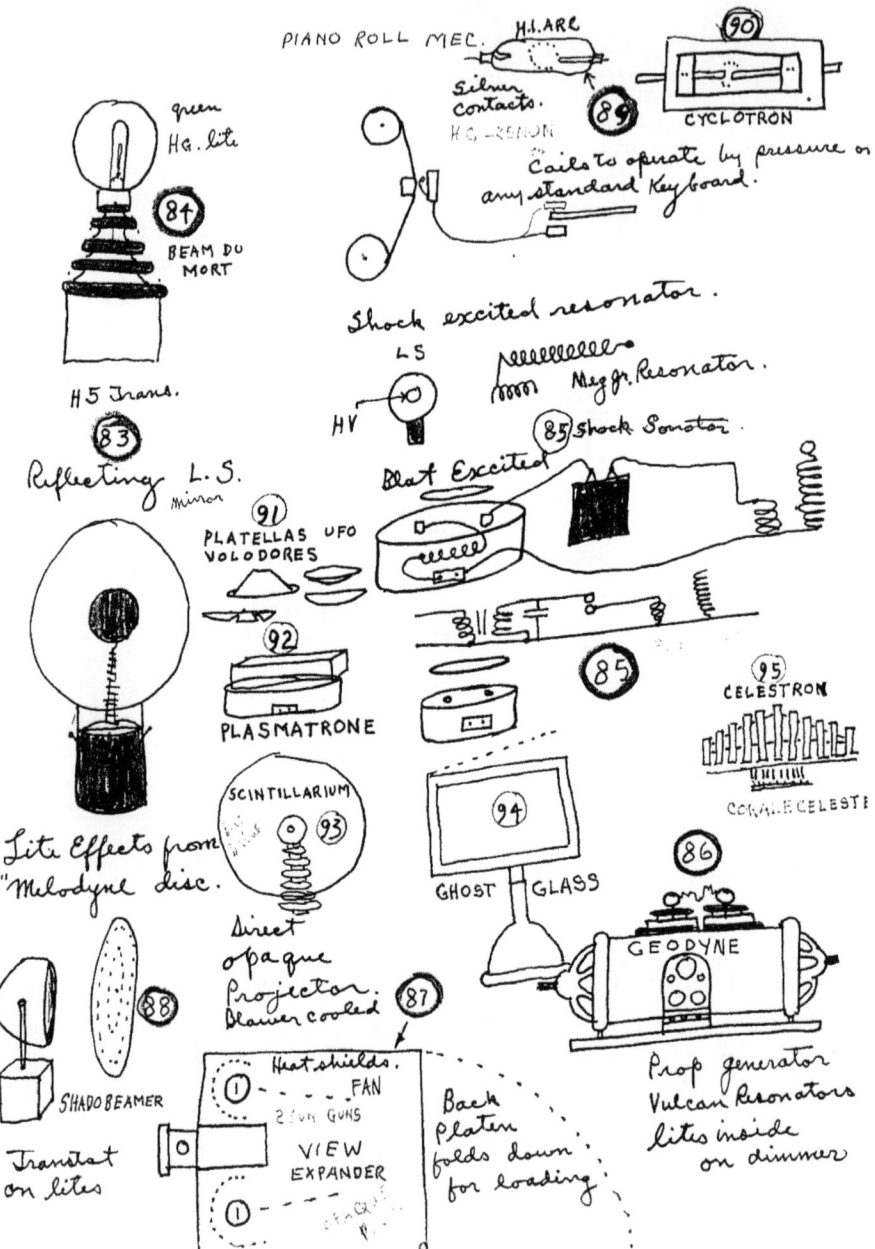

Technical Notes and Sketches

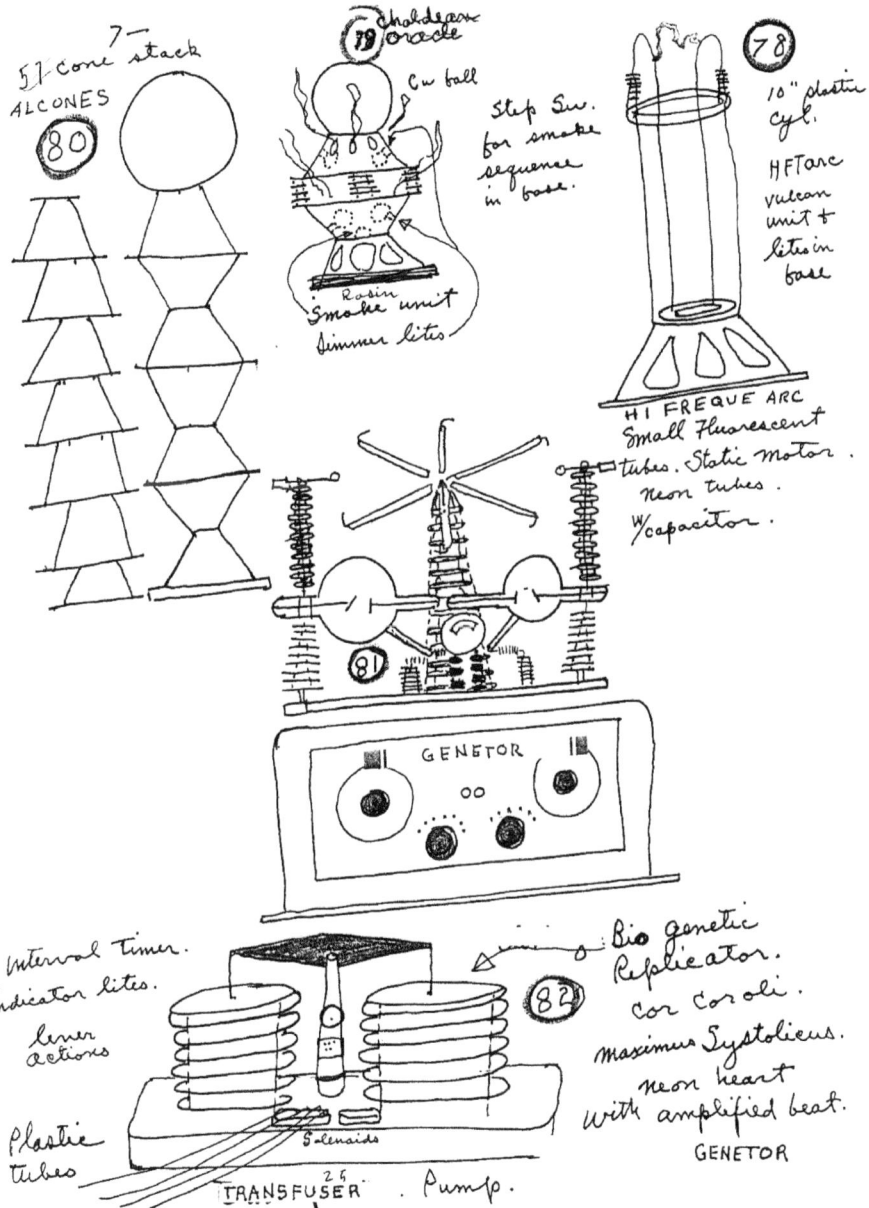

Appendix B

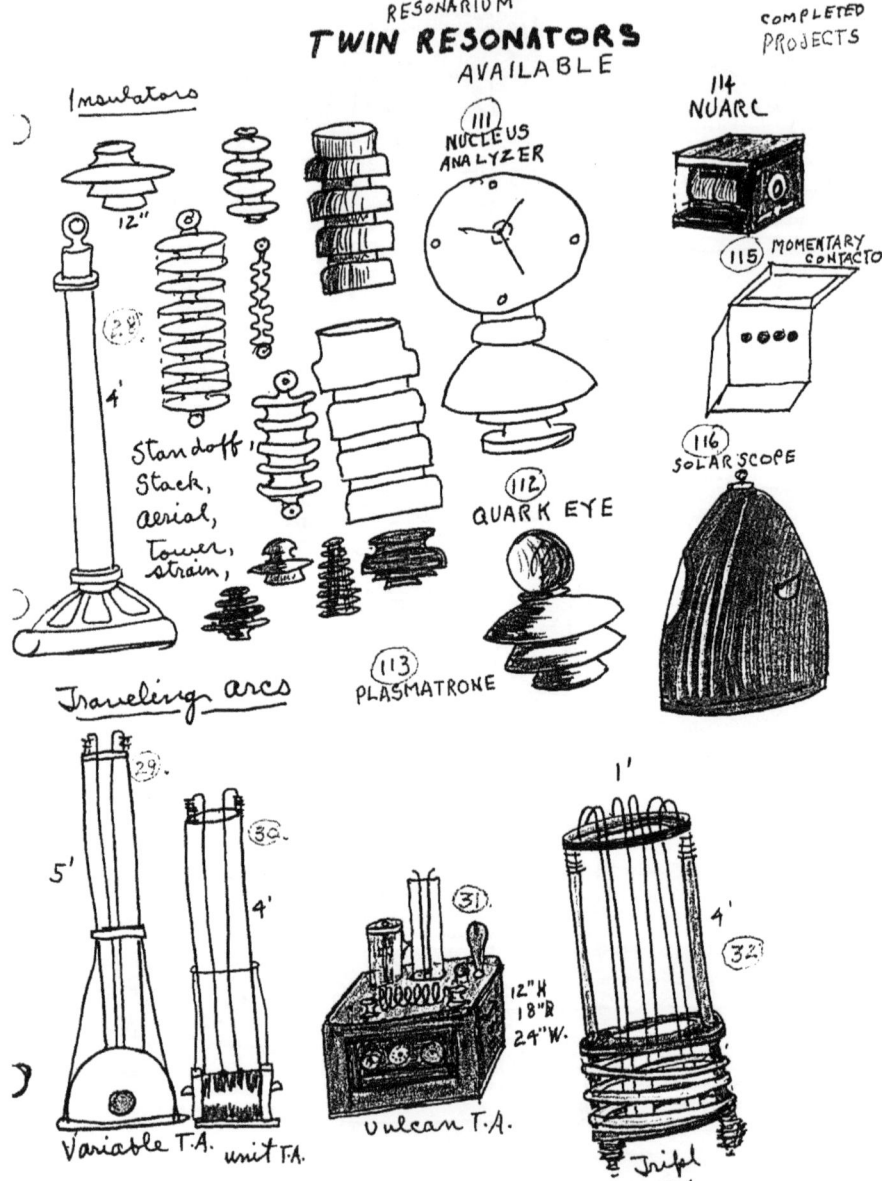

Technical Notes and Sketches

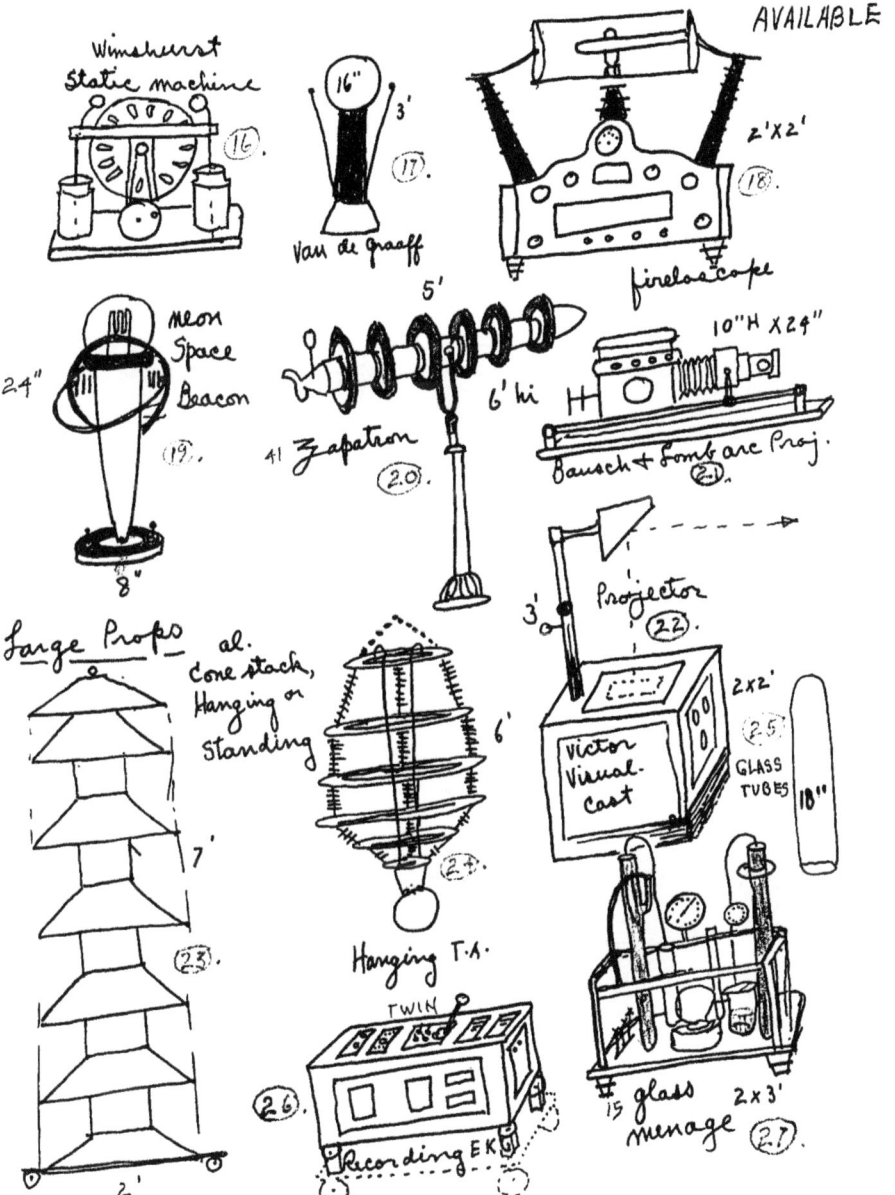

Appendix B

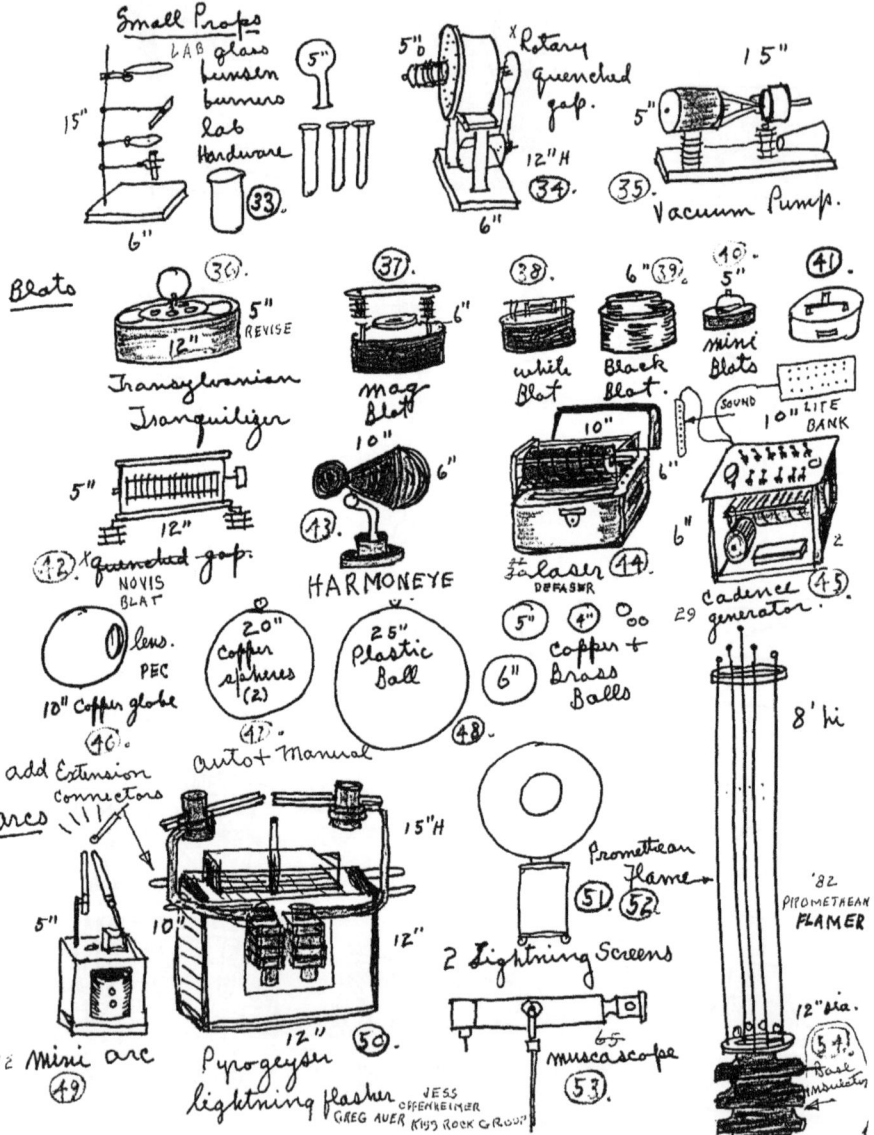

Technical Notes and Sketches 175

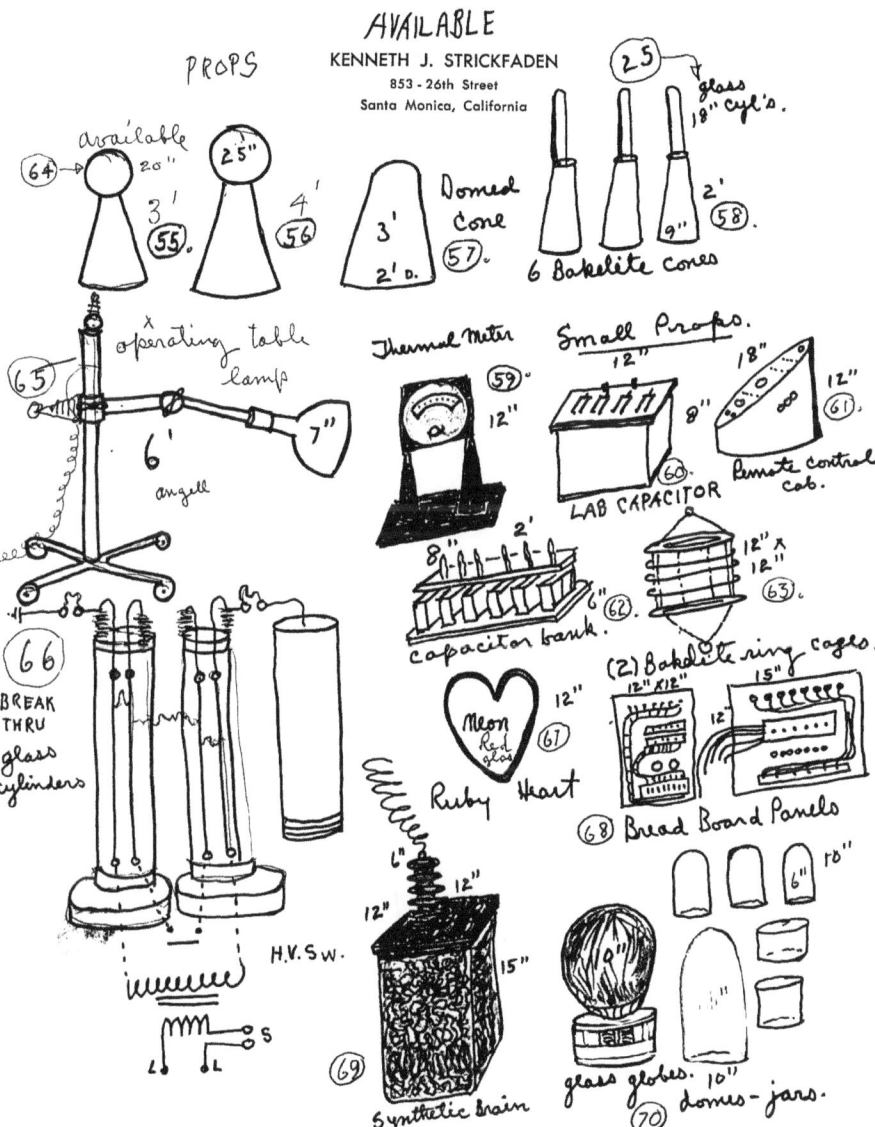

Appendix B

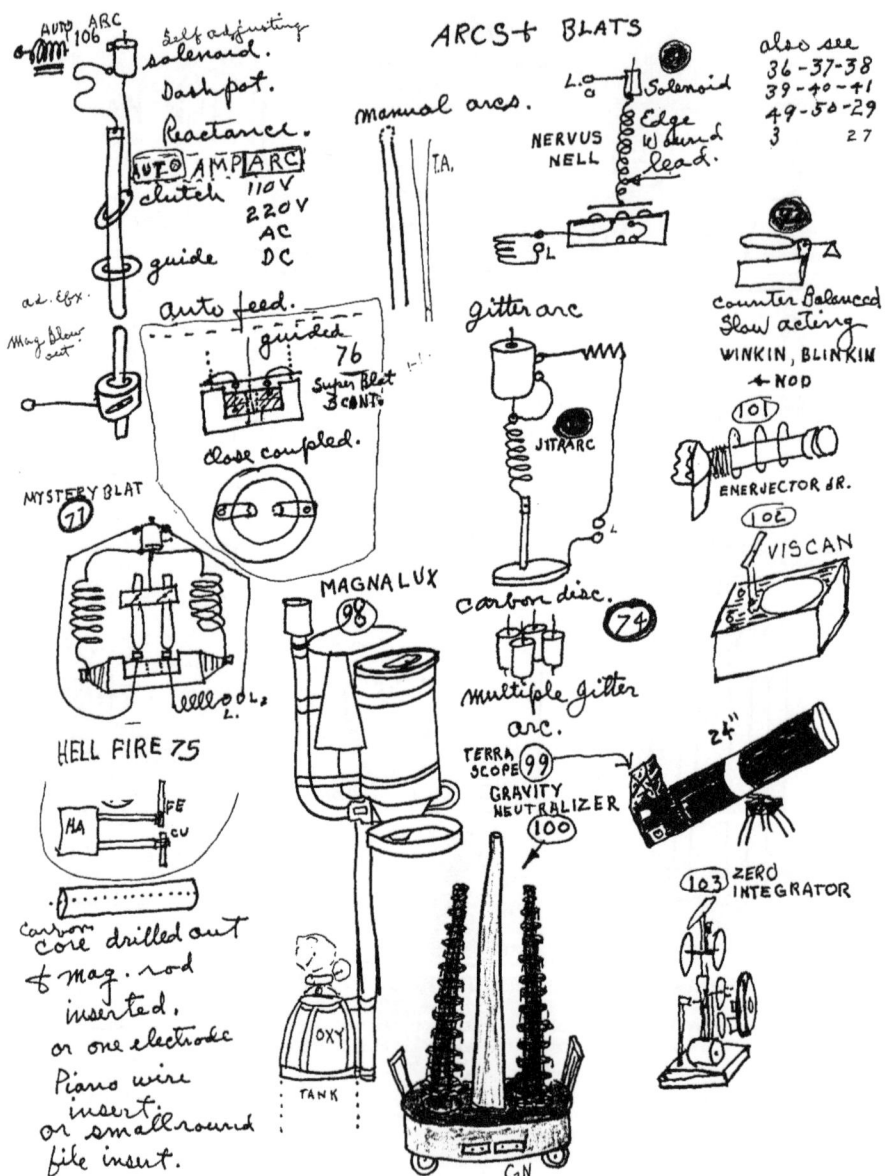

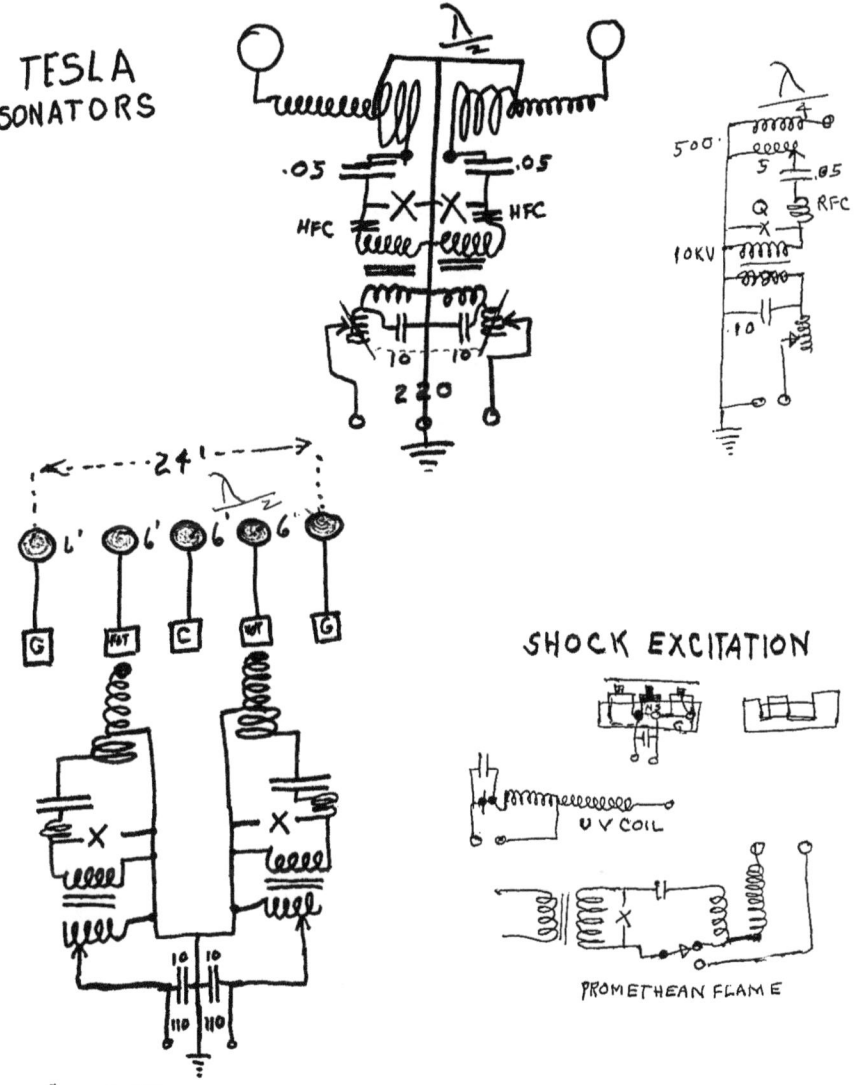

Appendix B

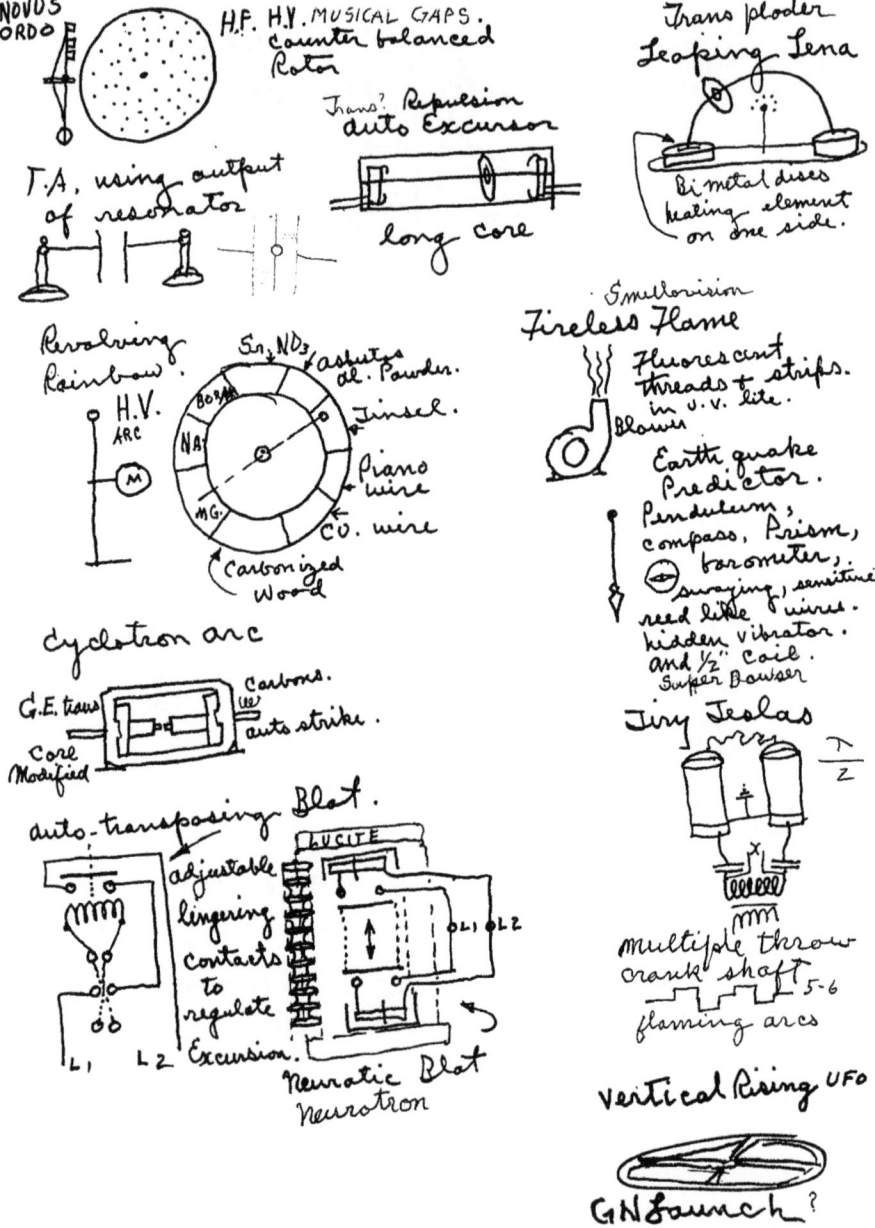

KENNETH J. STRICKFADEN
853 - 26th Street
Santa Monica, California

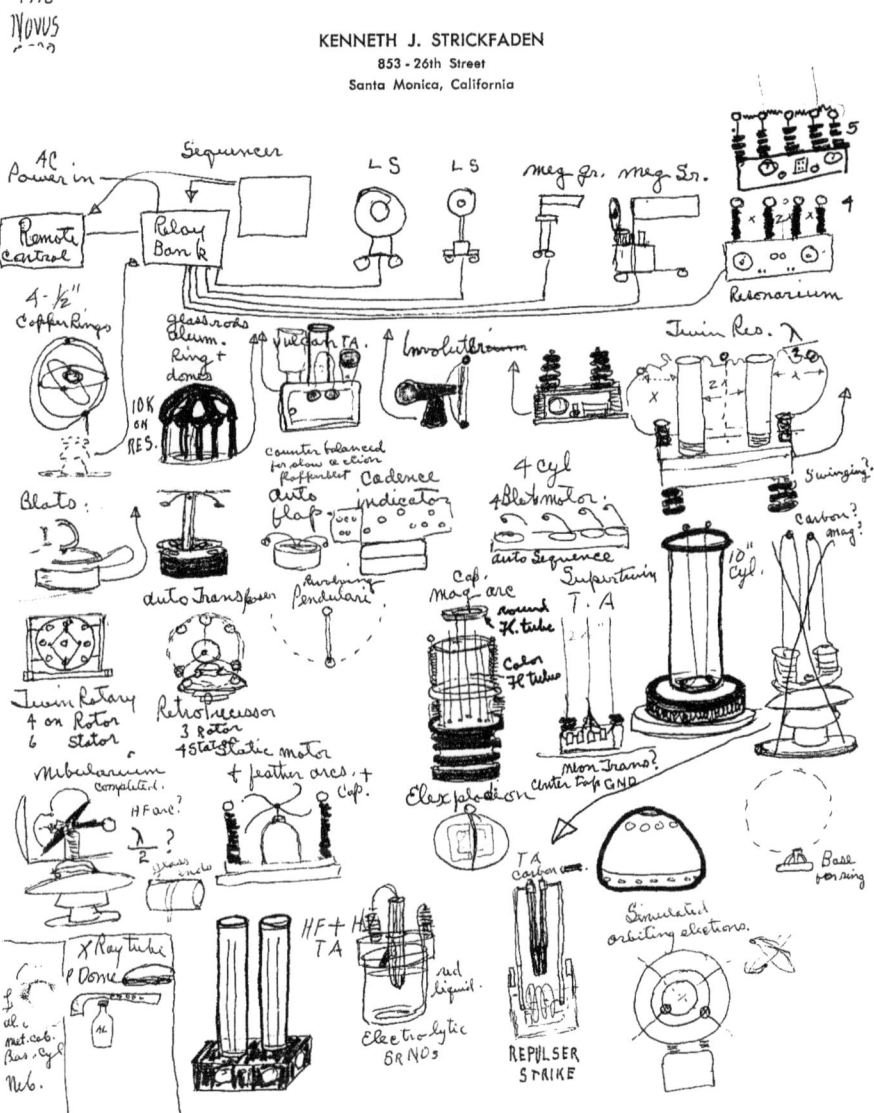

Appendix B

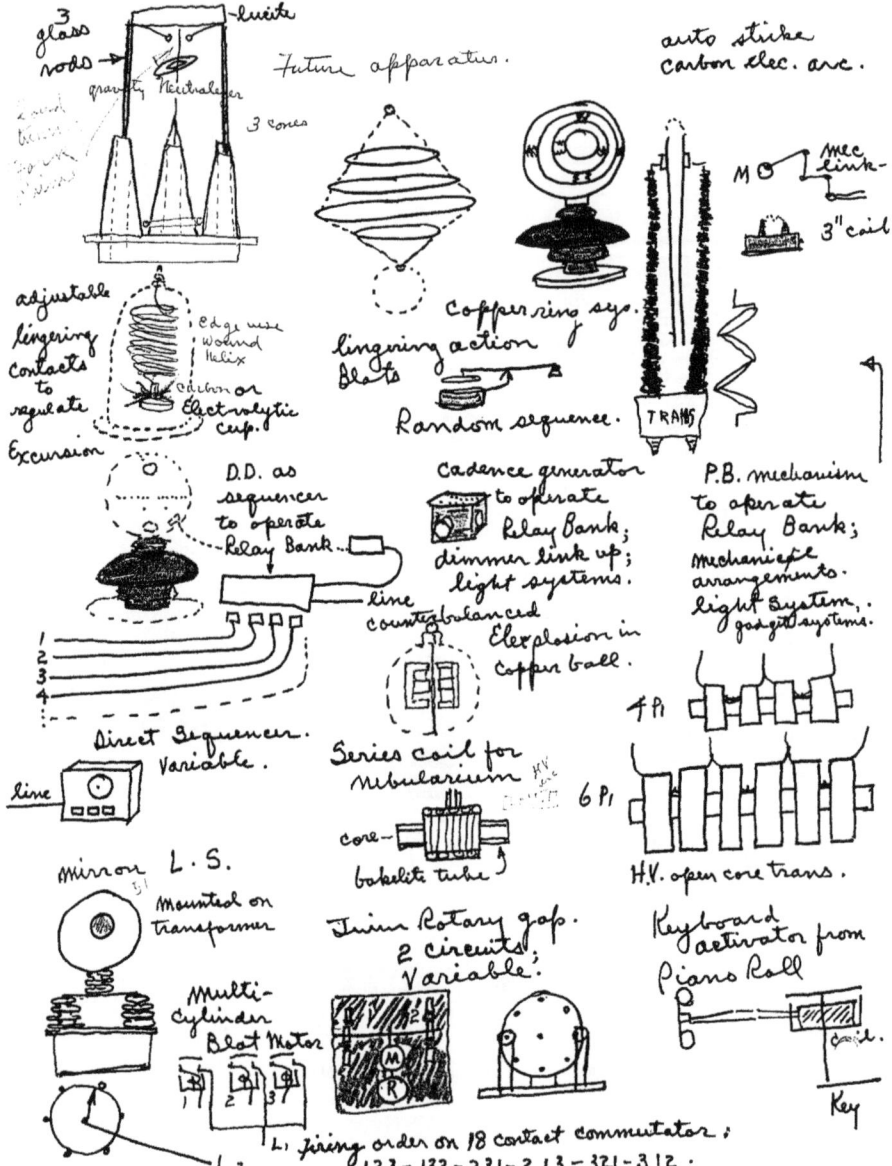

Technical Notes and Sketches

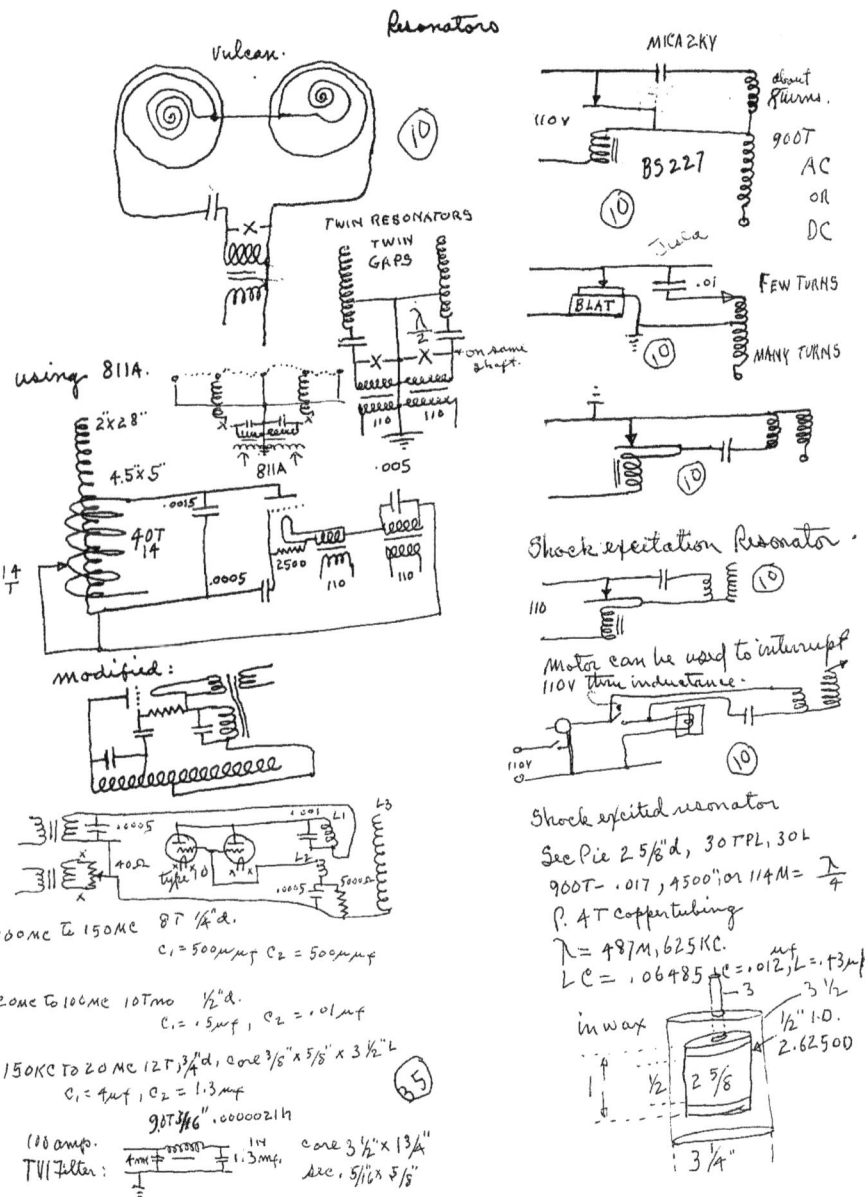

Appendix B

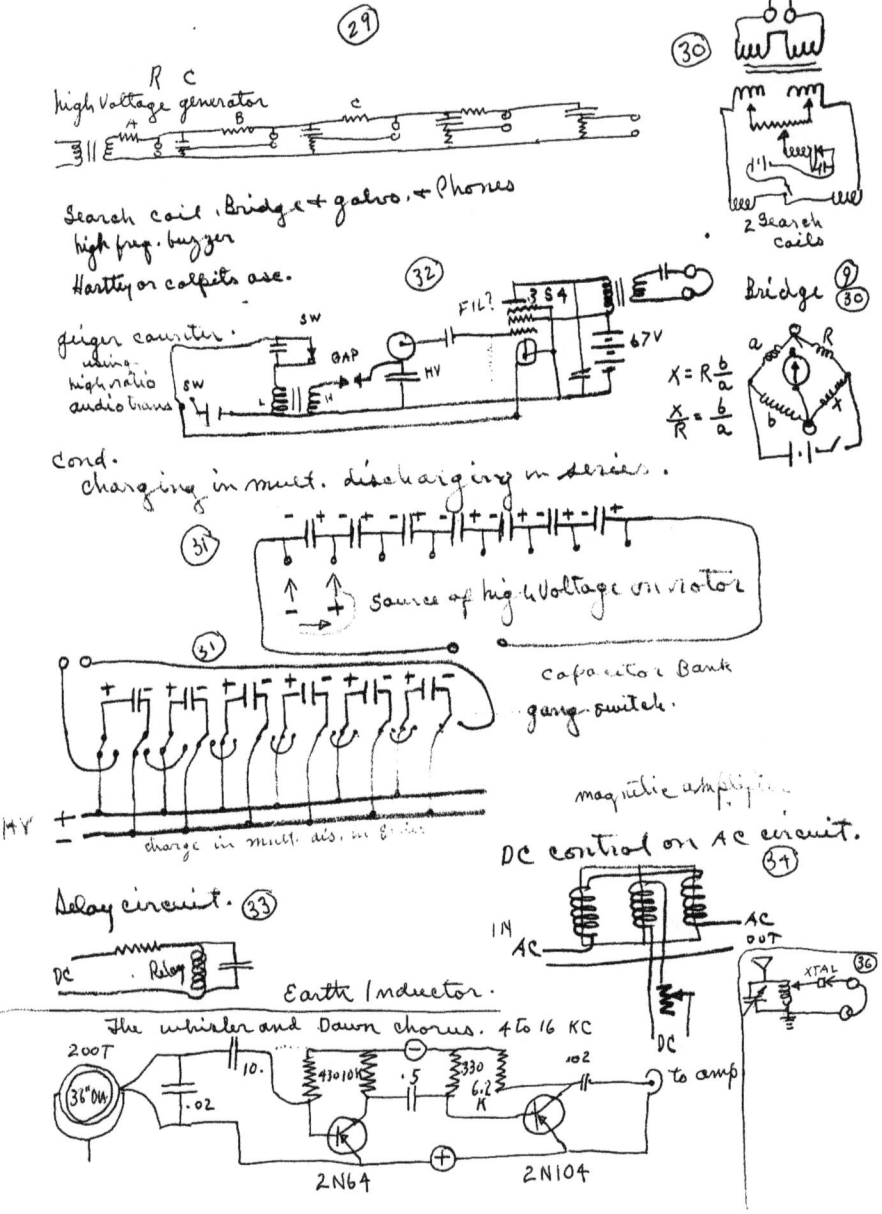

Technical Notes and Sketches

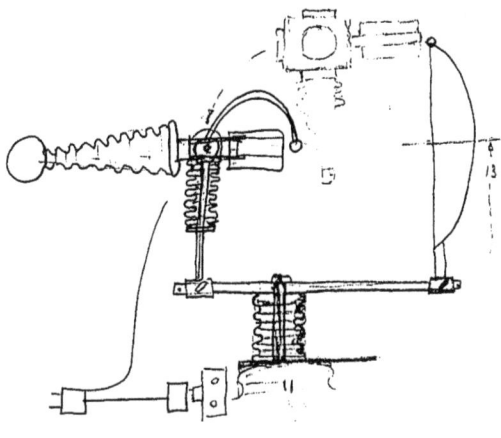

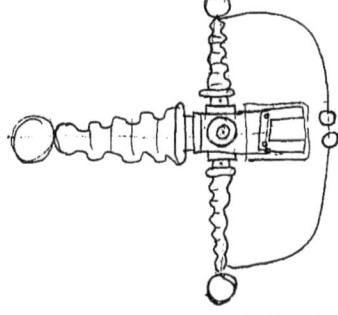

Above: Construction details for the "Nebularium." The device was used in *Frankenstein* (1931), *The Mask of Fu Manchu* (1932), *Bride of Frankenstein* (1935), *House of Dracula* (1945) and others. Strickfaden also named it a "Nucleus Analyzer."

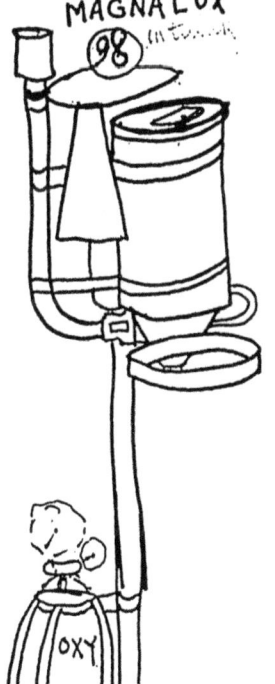

Left: Diagram for the "Magnalux" (great light) machine. It was used to simulate flashes of lightning.

Appendix C.
Miscellaneous Illustrations

A selection of sketches found on Ken's postcards, parcels and envelopes as well as some samples of official documents, correspondence and miscellaneous literature.

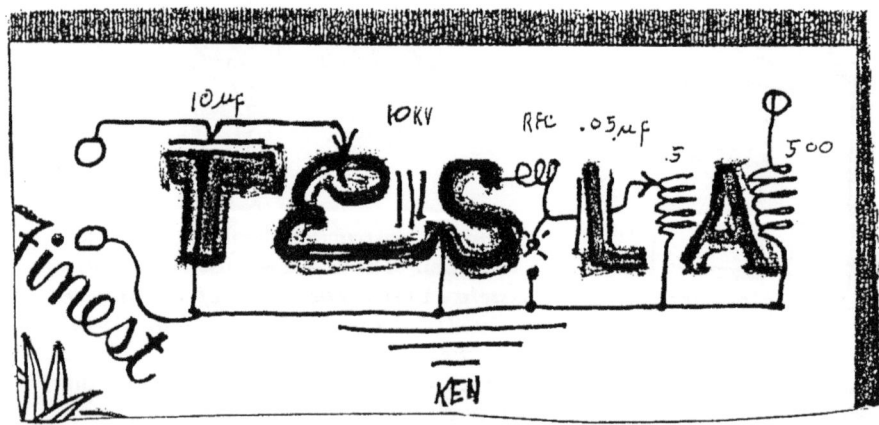

The top from a box which Ken Strickfaden had used to send the author technical data and materials. The letters in "Tesla" are connected by a diagram representing a Tesla coil circuit.

Miscellaneous Illustrations

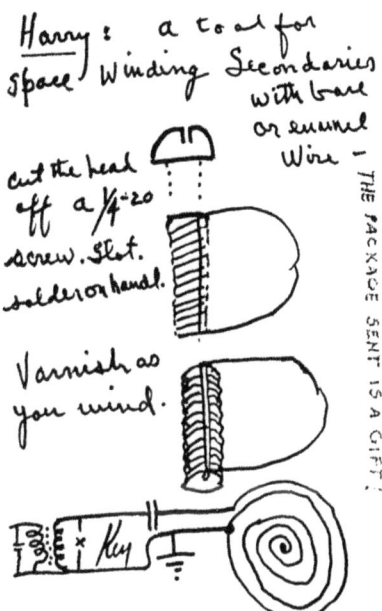

Left: A postcard message from Strickfaden following shipment of the package mentioned (see facing page). He provides instructions for space-winding turns of wire of a Tesla coil. The circuit at the bottom represents the connections for a Tesla coil.

Below: A sketch (original in color) in which Strickfaden caricatured friends attending his eighty-seventh birthday celebration. A bit of Strickfaden humor is revealed in the memo "Ken and Rolls were their [*sic*] to lend dignity [*sic*]." The author considered it an honor when Ken decorated the sketch with a TCBA decal.

Appendix C

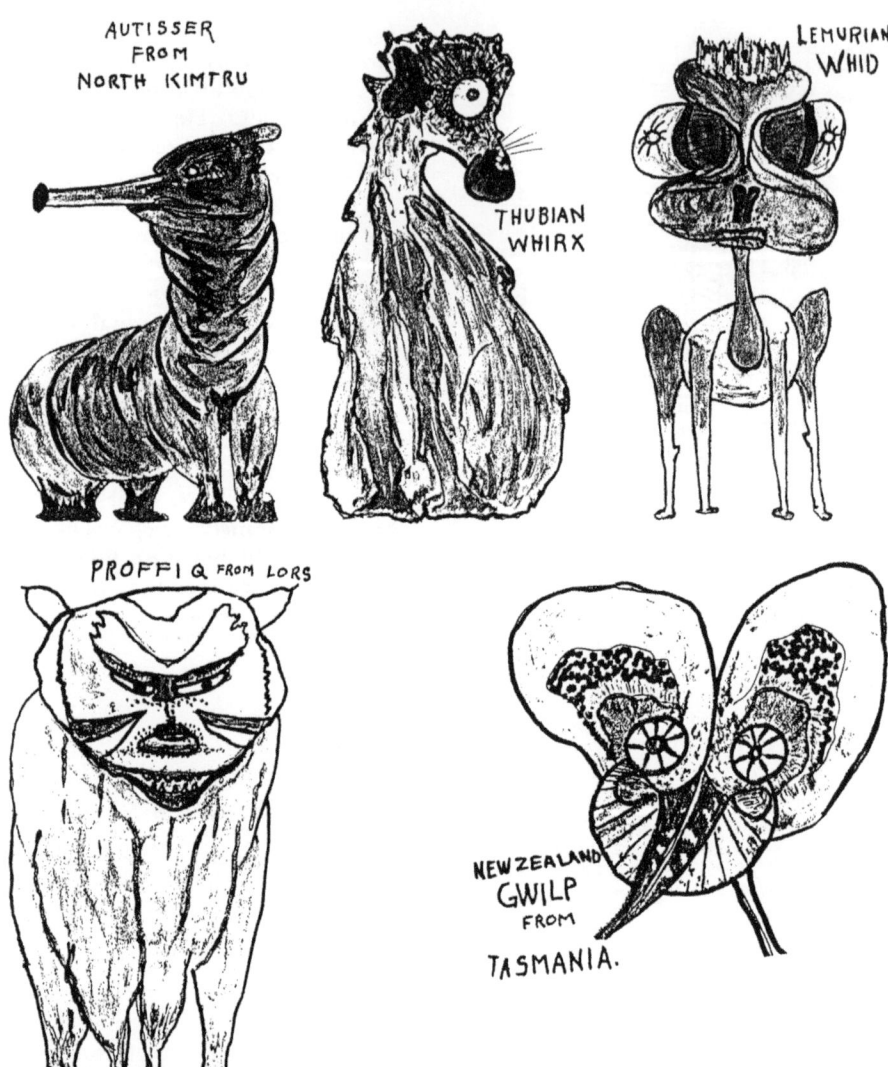

These are samples of the numerous watercolor sketches found in Strickfaden's notebooks. The conversion to black and white greatly reduces the striking effects of the artwork.

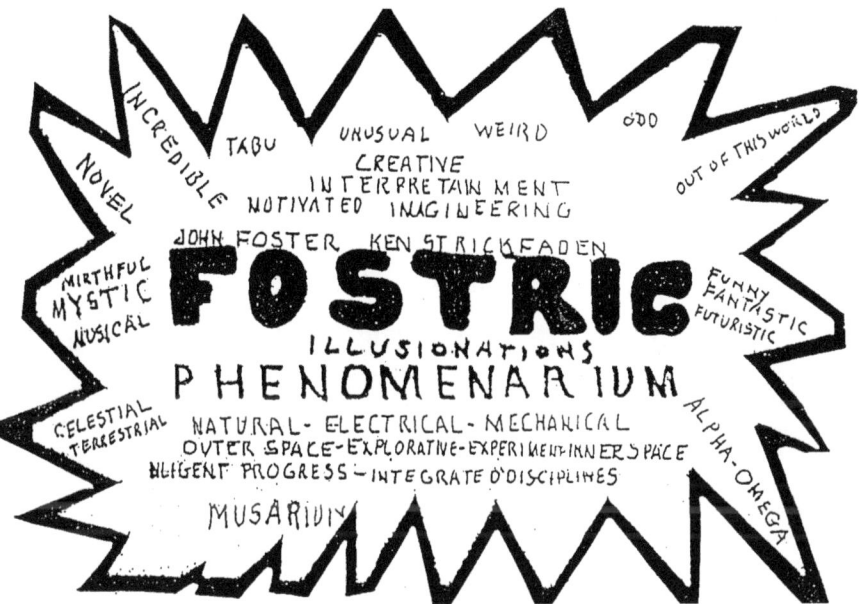

A humorous (black and orange) announcement declaring the partnership of John Foster and Kenneth Strickfaden. The two senior citizens enjoyed presenting science demonstration lectures to schoolchildren.

An identification card announcing Strickfaden's enlistment as a private in the 478th Pursuit Squadron, 3rd Army, December 9, 1923.

Appendix C

Santa Monica High School
Santa Monica, California.

his Diploma Certifies that

_____ Kenneth Strickfaden _____

has satisfactorily completed the four year's course of study prescribed by the Board of Education..

Given at Santa Monica, California, this ___twenty-ninth___ day of ___June___ in the year of our Lord one thousand nine hundred and sixteen

W. F. Barnum, PRINCIPAL

PRESIDENT BOARD OF EDUCATION

CITY SUPERINTENDENT

Kenneth Strickfaden's high school graduation diploma from Santa Monica High School, June 29, 1916.

CITY LICENSE 1930-1931
CITY OF SANTA MONICA   No. 2171
FROM JULY 1, 1930, TO JUNE 30, 1931

Electrick Laboratory .... having paid $6.00

10 per cent penalty for delinquency

into the City Treasury, is hereby granted license to transact the business of _Research Dev. Laboratory_ .... in the City of Santa Monica for the term above mentioned, in conformity with the provisions of Ordinance No. 451 (Commissioner's Series) and all Ordinances amendatory thereto.

Location _1348 15th St_

NOTE—Ten per cent penalty is added to all Licenses remaining unpaid after August 1st.

Commissioner of Finance ex-officio City Clerk.

(Place this in a Conspicuous Place)

A city permit to operate a commercial establishment. At the time, Strickfaden's home and shop were located at 15th Street. *Frankenstein* was more than a year away.

Miscellaneous Illustrations

During World War II, Ken contributed to the war effort by training civilians for work at shipyards, airplane factories and defense plants.

An IBEW certificate presented to Ken on his retirement from the union. For 34 years Strickfaden was a union member.

Appendix C

COLUMBIA PICTURES CORPORATION
OF CALIFORNIA, LTD.
1438 GOWER STREET
HOLLYWOOD, CALIFORNIA
HOLLYWOOD 3181

June 30, 1938.

Mr. Kenneth Strickfadden,
853 26th Street,
Santa Monica, California.

Dear Mr. Strickfadden:

The following is our agreement and understanding:

    1. You do hereby agree to furnish and supply all of the electrical equipment required by us for special effects in the laboratory sequences and in the sequences involving the process shots of the airplanes in connection with the production of our photoplay entitled "WINGS OF DOOM".

    2. You also agree to furnish and supply such equipment and apparatus as may be necessary or required by us for dressing the laboratory sets used in connection with said photoplay.

    3. All of the above equipment shall be transported and delivered to our studio in Hollywood, California, at your expense, and you agree to furnish such apparatus and equipment at such time or times as we may request.

    4. As rental for the equipment above mentioned, we agree to pay to you the sum of One Hundred and Thirty Dollars ($130.00), which sum shall entitle us to the use of all of said equipment during such time as we may require the same in connection with the production of said photoplay; provided, however, that in the event we shall require the use of the equipment, hereinabove in Paragraph 2 described, beyond the time that we require you to render your personal services, as hereinafter provided, we agree to pay, as rental for such equipment during the additional time, at the rate of Fifty Dollars ($50.00) per week, or pro-rata for any fraction of a week.

    5. You also agree to render and perform your services for us at the times and in the manner required by us in connection with the installation and operation of all of the equipment above mentioned. For such services we agree to pay to you the sum of Five Hundred and Twenty Dollars ($520.00), which you

agree to receive in full payment for such services; provided, however, that in the event we should require your services for more than six (6) days on the set, in connection with the photography of said photoplay, which days need not run consecutively, we agree to pay to you additional compensation at the rate of Eighty-Six Dollars and Sixty Cents ($86.60) per day, for each such additional day that you are required to render your services on the set in connection with the photography of said photoplay.

If the foregoing accords with your understanding, kindly acknowledge the same in the space provided therefor below.

                        Yours very truly,

                        COLUMBIA PICTURES CORPORATION
                        OF CALIFORNIA, LTD.

                        By_____
                                   Vice-President

AGREED TO AND ACCEPTED:

Kenneth Strickfaden
Kenneth Strickfadden

A contract between Columbia Pictures and Kenneth Strickfaden enlisting his services and equipment for the motion picture *Wings of Doom*. This may have been a working title as the references examined did not list this film. Notice misspelling of Strickfaden.

SPECIAL TECHNIQUE FOR THE
SUCCESSFUL TREATMENT OF
STREPTOCOCCUS INFECTIONS
"(STREP THROAT")
COMMON "COLDS"
INFLUENZA ("FLU")
SINUS INFECTIONS
ACNE; IMPETIGO
BRONCHITIS, ETC.

OFFICE TREATMENT ONLY
FOR APPOINTMENTS PHONE
HI 8041
PHONE BETWEEN 1 AND 3 P.M.
OR BETWEEN 6 AND 7 P.M.

FREDERICK FINCH STRONG, M. D.
6129 FOUNTAIN AVENUE
HOLLYWOOD, CALIF.

Nov 21;7/51

Dear Mr Strickfaden-

    I tried in vain to get you on the phone but no one answered. Hope you are still well and everything is going finely with you.

    I am now in my eightieth year and still taking patients. our rent has been raised and we will be compelled to move if we can find a cheaper place. I shall hate it as we have been here for thirteen years and it had grown to seem like home. My five meter ultra short wave(which I call my "VITAL N RMALIZER) Do you know anyone with High Blood-pressure.Thirty two years ago I was running a systolic of over Two hundred. The Met. Life Co rates High Blood pressure as PUBLIC ENEMY NO1 it kills 600,000 annually (more than Cancer and tuberculosis combined I am now running a norm l pressure of about 185 and am feeling very well dispite my age. Are you still doing ELECTRICKS? I have all my tesla apparatus and dont know what to do with it. Do you know anyone who would take it off my hands. We are sadly in need of money and I would sell all my H-F apparatus for fifty dollars. You have no doubt seen the million volt coil which I gave to the Planetarium. Can you not come up and look over my High-frequency "JUNK-PILE". Today Jose Iturbe came in and played for us. He is going to try to sell my piano forme He says % IS A VERY GOOD PIANO" I also want to sell my harp We shallbe very glad to see you again. If this reaches you please call me up

                your old High-frequency friend

                    Frederick F. Strong

A commuication from Dr. Frederick F. Strong requesting assistance from Ken Strickfaden in the sale of equipment. Strong donated the large Tesla coil that has been for many years on display at the Griffith Obseratory Museum.

Mr. Ken Strickfaden
853 - 26th Street
Santa Monica, CA

June 22, 1977

Dear Mr. Strickfaden:

I am Archivist in the History Division at the Los Angeles County Museum in Exposition Park. Included in our collections are many old historic photographs and negatives of Los Angeles and Southern California. Visiting us today is a teacher from Santa Monica, Barbara Williams, doing research on Amusement Parks and Merry-Go-Rounds with the Santa Monica Redevelopment Dept. They hope to restore the old Carousel on the pier there.

She has just told me your work in the motion picture industry, and in particular of your interesting photo collection. Because photographs make up such a large part of our collection (three-fourths of our visiting public researchers come in to see the photo collections), I know how really important such material is to the history of this area. The fact that you as the photographer know the background history of these photos makes them doubly important, as I am sure you realize.

I hope you have considered making plans and may actually have made arrangements to place your collection in a Southern California institution. Photographs are such an important part of our local history where the physical change has been so great in just the past fifty years. I hope you will be able to have your collection remain here in the Los Angeles area at an institution that would make the material available to the public researchers.

Sincerely yours,

John M. Cahoon
History Division
Archivist

Commercial Photographer

Giles W. Mead, *Director*
C. F. Gehring, *Assistant Director*
Leon G. Arnold, *Assistant Director*

NATURAL HISTORY MUSEUM LOS ANGELES COUNTY
Los Angeles County Museum of Natural History • 900 Exposition Boulevard • Los Angeles, California 90007 • Phone (213) 746-0410

A communication from the Los Angeles County Museum of Natural History concerning the eventual location of Ken Strickfaden's collection of historical photographs. It is unfortunate that Hollywood did not demonstrate a similar concern for the future of his Frankenstein laboratory properties.

Appendix C

8949 Wilshire Boulevard
Beverly Hills, California 90211
(213) 278-8990

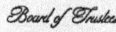

Board of Trustees

GENE ALLEN
EDWARD ASNER
LINWOOD G. DUNN
HAL ELIAS
ARTHUR HAMILTON
FAY KANIN
TOM MANKIEWICZ
MIKE MEDAVOY
MARVIN E. MIRISCH
WALTER MIRISCH
CHARLES M. POWELL
FRANK E. ROSENFELT
ROBERT E. WISE
RICHARD D. ZANUCK

Officers

MARVIN E. MIRISCH
President

FRANK E. ROSENFELT
Vice President

RICHARD D. ZANUCK
Vice President

FAY KANIN
Treasurer

HAL ELIAS
Secretary

JAMES M. ROBERTS
Executive Secretary

GYTE VAN ZYL
Legal Counsel

November 30, 1981

Mr. Ken Strickfaden
P.O. Box 1130
Inglewood, CA   90308

Dear Mr. Strickfaden:

I am writing to convey the Academy's appreciation for your help in making "The Magic Machines of Ken Strickfaden" the success that it was. I thought the entire evening went quite well, and the audience seemed to love it.

Enclosed you'll find some photographs I thought you might find interesting, and I hope you'll accept them as a token of our thanks. You'll also find a second group of photos that I would appreciate your giving to Mr. Foster along with our thanks.

Yours sincerely,

Douglas W. Edwards
Program Coordinator/Exhibits and Special Film Programs

DWE/rr
encl.

A letter to Ken from Program Coordinator Douglas Edwards following the Academy's tribute to "The Magic of Machines of Ken Strickfaden" (November 9, 1981).

March 4, 1995

Dear Mr. Goldman:

I have just read the article that you wrote in the Jan./Feb. 1995 issue of FILMFAX. It was given to me by Lois (Mrs. John) Foster.

Kenneth Strickfaden is my father. The article about him, and his electrical apparatus, is very complete and had several information bits that I have never known about before!

I am the last family member left, but I have 4 children and 4 grandchildren. I am going to see that each of them receive copies of your article, as it is very inclusive of the major parts of his life. Better than a story book, in fact.

Thank you for writing such a careful and complimentary description of the good, and interesting life that he led.

Sincerely,

Marilyn S. Throssel

Correspondence from Ken Strickfaden's daughter commenting upon the author's article "Mr. Electric," which appeared in issue #48 of *Filmfax*, January/February 1995.

The originals were in brilliant colors.

Appendix C

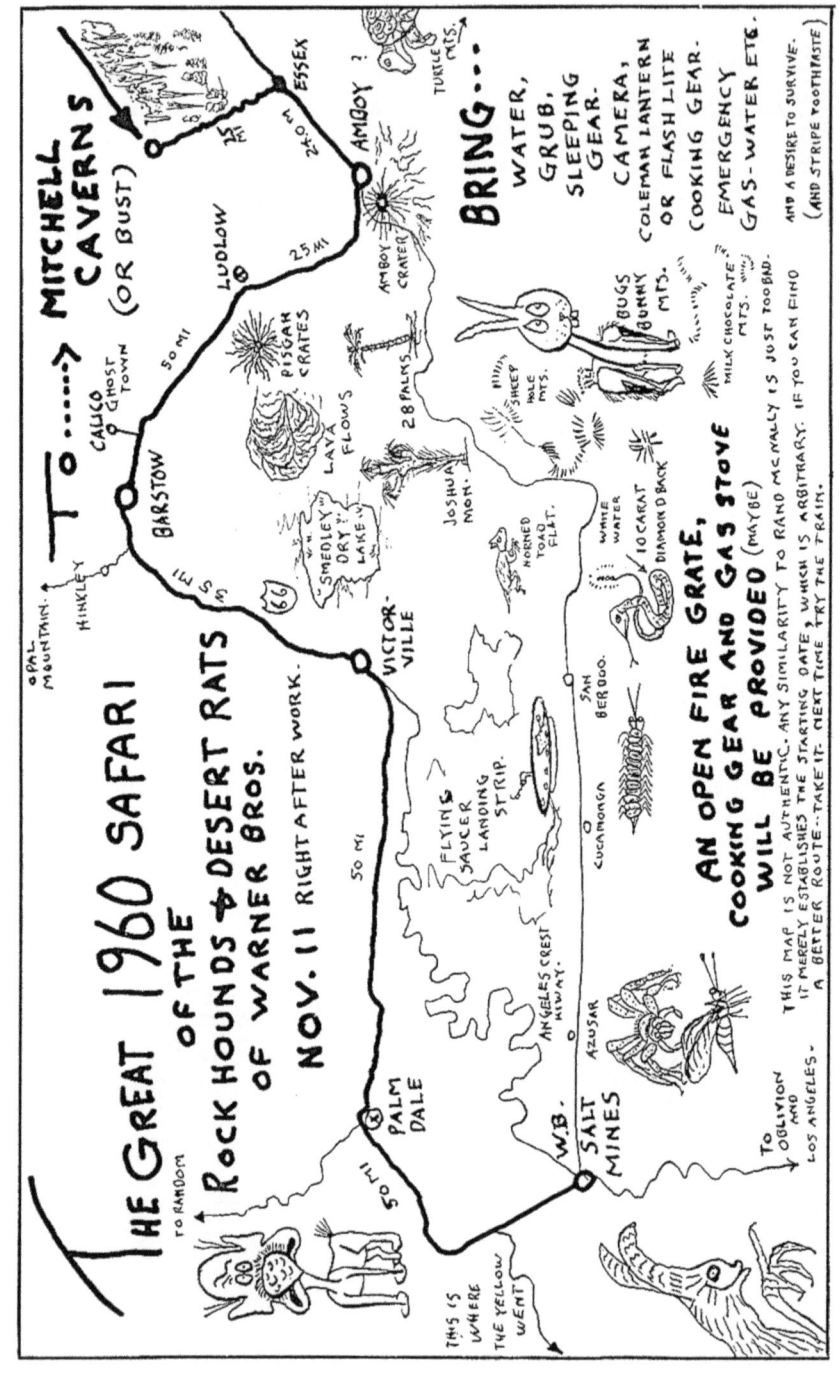

7001 FRANKLIN AVENUE · HOLLYWOOD, CALIFORNIA 90028
Telephone 1~~876~~~~xxxxx~~~~6~~~~xx~~1   851-3313

May 22, 1972

Kenneth J. Strickfaden
853 26th Street
Santa Monica, California

Dear Mr. Strickfaden:

Sorry to be so long in answering your letter offering us the monster goodies. I would be delighted to use some of the effects in The Castle, the reason I haven't called you before this is, I simply can't find the correct place to use them. We are involved in another project at the moment and as soon as it's finished I would like to give you a call and at your convenience, get together with you.

Again, thanks for your interest in The Magic Castle, and I will be calling you very shortly.

Best regards,

Milt Larsen

jc

Above: Correspondence from the Hollywood Magic Castle regarding the placing of Ken's apparatus on exhibit.

Opposite: Strickfaden's map providing instructions for finding the location of a weekend jamboree to be held by employees of Warner Bros. Kenny's humor is apparent in such remarks as "This is where the yellow went," "To oblivion and Los Angeles," "Flying saucer landing strip," "This map is not authentic. Any similarity to Rand McNally is just too bad... If you can find a better route, take it. Next time take the train."

Appendix C

LOWELL THOMAS, *President*   BURTON HOLMES, *Honorary President*   JAMES B. POND, *Executive Secretary*

The AMERICAN PLATFORM GUILD
Incorporated
2 WEST FORTY-FIFTH STREET
NEW YORK 19, N. Y.

Phone: Murray Hill 6-0908

February 25, 1946

Mr. Kenneth Strickfaden
853 26th Street
Santa Monica, California

Dear Mr. Strickfaden:

I have the pleasure to inform you that at the last meeting of the Board of Directors of the American Platform Guild, you were elected a member of this organization. Your membership card is enclosed.

We are delighted to have you one of us. We are most anxious to make this Guild a vital organization, working for the general good of the platform.

Sincerely yours,

Executive Secretary

JBP
Enc.

A notification of Ken Strickfaden's induction into the American Platform Guild. The Guild arranged engagements for speakers and lecturers. At the time, the Guild was under the leadership of the well-known and highly respected Lowell Thomas.

Appendix D.
Film and Television Chronology

When Kenneth Strickfaden was asked to provide a figure representing the total number of films to which he had contributed, the man confessed to having stopped counting at around the sixtieth. But there is the good news that Ken kept a chronological record of his work in the entertainment industry. The bad news is that Strickfaden's records are not only incomplete, but also contain numerous illegible inscriptions. Kenny was a generous man in regards to supporting worthy charities, but quite stingy with his use of notebook paper. The man's timeline covering some 60 years in the industry is crowded onto only two sheets of paper! Although there is the comforting news that he had someone make up a neatly typewritten list, the revised statistics contain only the decipherable titles. Consequently, the task of assembling this chronology turned out to be not only time-consuming but an exercise in frustration.

In addition to the problem of deciphering illegible notes, many of Ken's intelligible titles continue to remain unconfirmed. *Zombie People*, for example, is listed among Ken's films of 1928. Two difficulties are encountered here. First is the fact that film references do not list this title. Secondly, "zombie" was not used as a screen title until 1932 (*White Zombie*). Strickfaden's notes for 1928 also document such credits as *The Clutching Hand* (1936) and *Buck Rogers* (1939). Although both serials have been confirmed as Strickfaden films, there appears to be no explanation as to why they were so incorrectly dated. Another notebook entry which continues to remain a mystery is *War Monster*. He dated this title as a film of 1938. Not any of the film references examined list this title.

Mr. Electric claimed *The Perils of Pauline* as one of his credits for 1975. Heretofore, the only sound films displaying *The Perils of Pauline* banner were released in 1933 (serial), 1947 and 1967. The latter production, starring Pat Boone, originated as a television pilot but remained unsold until augmented with additional footage for release to theaters. It is probably this version of *Pauline* to which Ken's notes refer. One possible explanation for the inaccuracies in Strickfaden's dates is the considerable amount of time that may have elapsed before documenting them in his records. One of the entries in Kenny's chronicles is comprised of a list of motion picture titles under the heading "films to be dated." The passage of time is known to short-circuit a person's memory.

A considerable amount of effort was given to tracking down "Man from Mars" only to discover that it was not a Hollywood film but an integral part of Kenny's lectures.

And last, but not the least of importance, is the fact that Strickfaden failed to keep track of numerous films with which he had a connection. Many of the titles included in this chronology were identified as Strickfaden films through the study of motion pictures on video tape. *Murder by Television* (1935) is but one example of the films verified by this method. A master electrical panel and a weird space beacon are two of several Strickfaden signatures appearing in this film. Another title determined to be a Strickfaden film is *The Chewing Gum Fan* (1939). This is a Paramount program filler in which a "nutty" professor sets a head-mounted fan into motion by gum-chewing jaw action. The professor's laboratory is decorated with numerous Kenstric devices. An identical laboratory was employed for a Paramount sequel in which the ubiquitous professor demonstrated a *Burned Toast Scraper* (1940).

While considerable effort was given to making this chronology as accurate as possible, moments arose when the decision to either include or omit a title evolved into a film detective's "nightmare." *Ace Drummond* (1936), for example, featured an elaborate high voltage laboratory but without a Strickfaden signature until the very last chapter. The scene was judged to be a clip from another production. The same can be said for *The Phantom Creeps* (1939). Here, too, the short duration of time in which Kenny's "Meg Senior" Tesla coil is seen raised suspicion that it may have been borrowed from *The Invisible Ray* (1936), *Son of Frankenstein*

Murder by Television (1935) was identified as a Strickfaden film through the study of the motion picture on video tape. A master electrical panel and a weird space beacon are but two of several Strickfaden signatures appearing in the film (courtesy of Jerry Ohlinger's Movie Material Store, Inc.).

(1939) or other films with similar storylines. On the other hand, *Night Key* (1937) was included in this chronology because of the appearance of a cone-shaped Tesla coil resembling a design used in earlier Strickfaden films.

Finally, the circumstances under which this chronology was assembled preclude any claim for it being either complete or free from error. Although this list does contain a few titles from my "gray" file, I would rather mistakenly provide Ken an undeserved credit than knowingly omit one to which he is entitled.

Feature and Short Subject Films

The Phantom of the Opera (1925)
Wings (1927)
Cockeyed World (1929)
Follies of 1929 (1929)
The Ghost Talks (1929)
The Phantom of the Opera (1929) [The 1925 film with added soundtrack]

Pleasure Crazed (1929)
The Return of Sherlock Holmes (1929)
Romance of the Rio Grande (1929)
Showboat (1929)
Words & Music (1929)
Harmony at Home (1930)
Just Imagine (1930)
A Connecticut Yankee (1931)
Frankenstein (1931)
Behind the Mask (1932)
Chandu the Magician (1932)
Doctor X (1932)
The Mask of Fu Manchu (1932)
Murder at Dawn (1932)
Mystery Ranch (1932)
The Rainbow Trail (1932)
Sherlock Holmes (1932)
Six Hours to Live (1932)
White Zombie (1932)
Cavalcade (1933)
The Invisible Man (1933)
Marie Galante (1934)
Mystery Liner (1934)
Air Hawks (1935)
Bride of Frankenstein (1935)
Murder by Television (1935)
WereWolf of London (1935)
Ghost Patrol (1936)
The Invisible Ray (1936)
Revolt of the Zombies (1936)
Night Key (1937)
Bulldog Drummond's Peril (1938)
Arrest Bulldog Drummond (1939)
The Chewing Gum Fan (1939)
Ice Follies of 1939 (1939)
Son of Frankenstein (1939)
The Wizard of Oz (1939)
The Burned Toast Scraper (1940)
Dr Cyclops (1940)
Fantasia (1940)
Sky Bandits (1940)
The Devil Bat (1941) a.k.a. *Killer Bats*
Man Made Monster (1941) a.k.a. *Atomic Monster*
The Ghost of Frankenstein (1942)
The Man With Two Lives (1942)
The Strange Case of Doctor Rx (1942)
Frankenstein Meets the Wolf Man (1943)
Sherlock Holmes Faces Death (1943)
House of Frankenstein (1944)
House of Dracula (1945)
The Scarlet Clue (1945)
Devil Bat's Daughter (1946)
The Face of Marble (1946)
Abbott & Costello Meet Frankenstein (1948)
Master Minds (1949)
The War of the Worlds (1953)
The Amazing Transparent Man (1960)
Beyond the Time Barrier (1960)
The Time Machine (1960)
Monstrosity (1965) a.k.a. *The Atomic Brain*
Jesse James Meets Frankenstein's Daughter (1966)
Kaleidoscope (1967)
The Perils of Pauline (1967)
The Illustrated Man (1969)
Dracula vs Frankenstein (1971)
Blackenstein (1972)
The Clones (1973)
The Capable Computer (1974)
Death Race 2000 (1974)

Young Frankenstein (1974)
The Man Who Fell to Earth (1976)
Star Wars (1977)
Coma (1978)
The Manitou (1978)

Sgt. Pepper's Lonely Hearts Club Band (1978)
The Empire Strikes Back (1980)
Frankenstein Island (1981)
Raiders of the Lost Ark (1981)

Serials

Most of the chapterplays that made use of Strickfaden's devices were based on plots with a science fiction content. About fifty serials qualify for this category. Just how many of those fifty serials employed Ken's talents is difficult to tell. Through the study of old films available on video tape, I was able to identify a number of serials that were unrecorded in Strickfaden's notes.

The Vanishing Shadow (1934)
The Lost City (1935)
Phantom Empire (1935)
The Clutching Hand (1936)
Flash Gordon (1936)
Shadow of Chinatown (1936)
Undersea Kingdom (1936)
Blake of Scotland Yard (1937)
Fighting Devil Dogs (1938)
Flash Gordon's Trip to Mars (1938)

Buck Rogers (1939)
Flash Gordon Conquers the Universe (1940)
Mysterious Doctor Satan (1940)
The Shadow (1940)
Batman (1943)
Manhunt of Mystery Island (1945)
The Monster and the Ape (1945)
Hop Harrigan (1946)
Jack Armstrong (1947)

Television
(partial list)

1939 — Installation of a color camera chain system (NBC)
1948 — Installation of a color camera chain system (NBC)
1951 — Installation of a color camera chain system (NBC)
1953 — *Flash Gordon* (syndicated)
1954 — Special electrical effects, station KTTV
1959 — *The Steve Allen Show* (NBC)
1961 — *The Steve Allen Show* (ABC)
1965 — *Lost in Space* (CBS)
   The Munsters (CBS) "Just Another Pretty Face"
   Voyage to the Bottom of the Sea (ABC)
1966 — *The Munsters* (CBS)

"Shrimperstein" (special electrical effects)
Special electrical effects, station KHJTV
1967 — *The Monkees*: "I Was a Teenage Monster" (NBC)
Commercials: Dupont, Personna, Del Monte, etc.
1968 — Commercials: Union Carbide, Eveready, General Foods
1970 — Commercials and product promotionals
1971 — *Li'l Abner* (ABC 4/26)
1972 — *The Sixth Sense* (ABC)
1973 — Commercials: Magnavox, FBI, etc.
1974 — Commercials and product promotionals
"Frankenstruck" (parody)
Horror Hall of Fame (ABC 2/20)
1975 — Commercials & product promotionals
1976 — Kawasaki promotional
The Monster Squad (NBC)
1977 — *The Hardy Boys Mysteries* (ABC)
Man from Atlantis: "The Amazing Electrical Man" (NBC)
1978 — *The Bob Hope Show* (NBC)
Wonder Woman (CBS)
1979 — *The Bob Hope Show* (NBC)
Struck by lightning (CBS)
1980 — *Buck Rogers in the 25th Century* (NBC)
Commercials and product promotionals
"Franky" (spoof)
Dallas (CBS)
1983 — *On the Town* (syndicated variety)

The list that follows represents a sample of Ken's notes covering film and television productions which remain unconfirmed due to unresolved questions concerning dates, titles and unreadable records.

Demon Dracula	The Last Frontier (Las Vegas show?)
Games People Play	Nemo
Hello America (Las Vegas show?)	Out of This World (Cole Porter)
Hollywood Hall of Fame (Vincent Price)	Star Trek
	War Monster
Hoot Gibson western(s)	Wings of Doom
The Hunchback of Notre Dame (1923)	Young Edison (The Idea of Edison?)
	Zombie People

Selected Bibliography

If all of the books which profile Kenneth Strickfaden were to be listed, it would take several pages to register them. The topics covered, however, are generally limited to his work in Universal's *Frankenstein* series and similar productions. Very few, if any, provide substantial data on the man's personal life or his activities beyond Hollywood. Readers can find supplementary facts regarding Strickfaden's career in periodicals. But even then, the emphasis is on his work in the film industry.

Books

Atkins, Rick. *Let's Scare 'Em: Grand Interviews and a Filmography of Horrific Proportions, 1930–1961*. Jefferson, N.C.: McFarland, 1997. See Chapter 4, "The Electrifying Kenneth Strickfaden," pp. 61–67.

Kinnard, Roy. *Science Fiction Serials*. Jefferson, N.C.: McFarland, 1998, pp. 11, 14, 21, 30, 53, 84.

Maxford, Howard. *The A–Z of Horror Films*. Bloomington: Indiana University Press, 1997, p. 253.

Rickitt, Richard. *Special Effects: The History and Technique*. New York: Billboard Books, 2000, pp. 20, 251.

Schecter, Harold, and David Everitt. *Film Tricks: Special Effects in the Movies*. New York: Harlin Quist, 1980, pp. 88–91.

Turner, George E., ed. *The Cinema of Adventure, Romance, and Terror*. Hollywood: ASC Press, 1989, pp. 92, 208, 211, 214.

Weaver, Tom. *It Came from Weaver Five*. Jefferson, N.C.: McFarland, 1996, p. 304.

Books to Which Strickfaden Contributed

Ackerman, Forrest J. *Lon of 1000 Faces*. Beverly Hills: Morrison, Raven-Hill, 1983. "I Panicked the Paris House as Erik," by Kenneth Strickfaden, pp. 213–14.

Kyriazi, Gary. *The Great American Amusement Parks*. Secaucus, N.J.: Citadel Press, 1976. Photographs by Kenneth Strickfaden, pp. 63, 64, 98, 147–153.

Stanton, Jeffrey. *Venice California, Coney Island of the Pacific*. Los Angeles: Donohue Publishing, 1993. Photographs by Kenneth Strickfaden, pp. 120, 132, 154, 158, 161, 165, 167.

Periodical Articles

Branning, Don. "Praise for a Man Who Made Edison Look Like a Tinker." *Los Angeles Examiner*, July 12, 1981, pp. A3, A6.

Cox, Vic. "Strick Struck the Sparks of Monster Pix." *Los Angeles Times* Calendar, November 8, 1981, pp. 1, 6, 7.

"Electric Shocks ... Do They Really Kill?" *Popular Science*, July 1938, pp. 44–45, 101. Includes photograph of Strickfaden as a young man.

"The Electrical Wizard of the Motion Pictures." *IBEW Journal*, May 1972, pp. 8–9.

Funk, R.D. "Strickfaden Saw Beauty Everywhere." *Santa Monica Evening Outlook*, April 12, 1980, pp. 8D–9D.

Goldman, Harry. "Mr. Electric: The Kenneth Strickfaden Story." *Filmfax*, #48, January/February 1995, pp. 37–41.

Hanson, Eugene M. "High Voltage Magic." *Popular Mechanics*, September 1949, pp. 140–42.

"A Latter-Day Merlin Whips Up Magic in His Garage for *The Munsters*." *TV Guide*, July 23–29, 1966, pp. 12–14.

Ludington, William. "Mr. Electricity: The Multi-Volted Career of Kenneth Strickfaden." *American Classic Screen*, January/February, 1983, pp. 26–29.

_____. "The Return of 'Mr. Electricity,' Kenneth Strickfaden." *American Classic Screen*, May/June 1983, p. 34.

MacQueen, Scott. "Kenneth Strickfaden." *Gore Creatures* #24, October 1975, pp. 24–26.

"Man Made Lightning from Boulder Dam." *The New York Times*, November 1, 1936, RP4, p. 3. Includes photograph of Strickfaden and apparatus.

"The Master of Movie Thrills." *Popular Mechanics*, March 1935, pp. 348–352, 133A.

Scott, John. "Movie Edison, Diabolic Genius." Source undetermined, ca. 1932, pp. 13, 19.

Storrs, Les. "He Was Never 'Teacher's Pet.'" *Santa Monica Evening Outlook* (date undetermined), pp. 17–18.

Warga, Wayne. "The Birth of a Mirthful Monster." *Los Angeles Times Calendar* section, April 14, 1974, pp. 1, 67.

Selected Obituaries

Ackerman, Forrest J. "Kenneth Strickfaden 1897–1984." *Starlog*, #83, June 1984, p. 66.
Angell, Edward. "Kenneth Strickfaden 1896–1984." *TCBA News*, 1984, Vol. 3, #2, pp. 2–3.
Folkart, Burt A. "Designer of Ghoulish Film Gadgets Dies." *Los Angeles Times*, March 3, 1984, section IV, p. 7.
"Hollywood Lighting Expert Dies." *Santa Monica Evening Outlook*, March 2, 1984, p. A-5.

Additional References

"Charles Strickfaden Scrapbook, Thomas Delong Research Files 1908–1995." Archives and Special Collections, Williams College, Williamstown, MA 01267.
"Dedication: Kenneth Strickfaden." *TCBA News*, 1983, Vol. 2, #2, pp. 2–3.
"The Electrical Wizard of the Motion Pictures." *TCBA News*, 1992, Vol. 11, #2, p. 14 (reprint of *IBEW Journal*, May 1972).
"The Kenneth J. Strickfaden Notebook." *TCBA News*, 1994, Vol. 13, #3, pp. 10–11.
"The Kenneth J. Strickfaden Notebook." *TCBA News*, 1994, Vol. 13, #4, pp. 9–10.
"Kenneth Strickfaden 1896–1984." *TCBA News*, 1984, Vol. 3, #2, pp. 2–3 (obit).
"Kenneth Strickfaden 1897–1984." *TCBA News*, 1986, Vol. 5, #2, p. 3 (*Starlog* obit reprint).
"The Ken Strickfaden Notebook." *TCBA News*, 1995, Vol. 14, #1, pp. 12–13.
"The Ken Strickfaden Photo File." *TCBA News*, 1995, Vol. 14, #2, p. 18.
"The Ken Strickfaden Photo File." *TCBA News*, 1995, Vol. 14, #3, p. 18.
"The Ken Strickfaden Photo File." *TCBA News*, 1995, Vol. 14, #4, p. 18.

Index

Academy of Motion Picture Arts & Sciences 102, 103, 105, 106, 107, 108, 194
Ace Drummond (1936; serial) 200
Ackerman, Forrest J 45, 46, 52, 96, 97, 111, 140, 151
Adamson, Al 111
The Adventures of Buckaroo Banzai (1984) 151
Air Hawks (1935) 50, 145
Ali Baba Goes to Town (1938) 112
Allen, Evan 36, 37
Allen, Irwin 91
Allen, Steve 90
American Cinematographer (periodical) 94
American Platform Guild 198
American Red Cross 33, 102
Amusement centers: Coney Island 25–28; Ocean Park Pier 24, 28, 120; Pike amusement zone 120; Santa Monica Pier 24, 28, 134, 135, 136; Venice Pier 24, 28, 43, 136
Anaconda (MT) 13, 14
Anderson, Leland I. vii, 111
Angell, Edward vi, vii, 1, 4, 59, 82, 96, 97, 108, 138, 139, 140–141, 150, 151
Angell, Janice vii, 4, 108, 139
Arntzen, Gene 112–113
Aronson, Edward vii, 83
Ashland (OR) 14
Astaire, Fred 154
Atlantic City (1944) 126
Atwill, Lionel 86
Aurandt, Richard G. vi, 82, 96, 97, 105, 108

Bailey, Ken 111
Bailey, Mildred 19
Baker, "Curly" 135
Bara, Theda 60
Barcroft, Roy 87
Barthel, Alfred 124
Batman (1943) 85
Batman (1989) 138
Baxter, Warner 78
Beetle Juice (1988) 138
Behind the Mask (1932) 49
Beiderbecke, Bix 19
Belle of the Yukon (1944) 112
Bellerophon Society 59
Benenson, Bill 99
Berkeley, Busby 113
Berman, Sydney 126
The Black Box (1915; serial) 78
Blow Your Own Horn (1923) 78
Bogart, Humphrey 154
Boone, Pat 200
The Border Wireless (1918) 30
Bowhay, A.S. 72
Bowie, David 96
The Boy Electrician (book) see Morgan, Alfred P.
Boyle, Peter 93
Brabin, Charles 60
Bradley, Milton 96
Brainstorm (1983) 151
Bride of Frankenstein (1935) 54–55, 103, 152, 165, 183
Brisbane, Arthur 74
Brook, Clive 48

Brooks, Mel 93, 94, 95, 110, 111
Bruyere, Marion 20, 130, 131
Buck Rogers (1939; serial) 50, 55, 103, 106, 108, 199
The Burned Toast Scraper (1940) 200
Burton, Tim 138, 150

The Capable Computer (1974) 93
Carillo, Leo 132
Carillo, Ottie 132
Carson, Sam 132
Cavalcade (1933) 60
Chandu the Magician (1932) 49, 80, 130, 142–143
Chaney, Lon 45
Chaney, Lon, Jr. 86
Charles, Earl 135
Charles, Ray 135
Cheney, Margaret 99
Chevrolet, Gaston 134
The Chewing-Gum Fan (1939) 200
Clarke, Mae 52
Claws of the Hun (1918) 30
Cleopatra (1963) 45
The Clones (1973) 93
The Clutching Hand (1936; serial) 55, 80, 199
Cockeyed World (1929) 47
Col. Farley's Boys Ranch 102
Coma (1978) 98
A Connecticut Yankee (1931) 53
Corman, Roger 96, 111
Cox, Victor 108, 141
Creek, Nancy L. 13, 22, 129, 130
Crosby, Bing 19, 126

Daly, Marcus 13
A Daughter of Uncle Sam (1918; serial) 30
The Death Ray (1924) 48
DeCoursey, Slim 108
Delong, Thomas A. 17, 127
Devil Bat (1941) 85
Devil Bat's Daughter (1946) 86
Disney *see* Motion Picture Studios
Dr. Cyclops (1940) 85, 106, 108
Doctor X (1932) 53
Dorsey, Jimmy 19
Dorsey, Tommy 19
Douglas Aircraft Co. 45
Downey, Morton 19
Dracula vs. Frankenstein (1971) 91–92, 152, 167

Dunston, Clara 42, 44
Dvořák, Antonín 76

The Eagle's Eye (1918; serial) 30
Edison, Thomas A. 16, 27, 98, 109, 136
Edison Medal 74
Edward Scissorhands (1990) 138
Edwards, Douglas W. 108
Eisenberg, A. and H. 58
Electrical Experimenter (periodical) 34–35, 79
Electrician and Mechanic (periodical) 16
Electro Importing Co. 33
Elkins, Eddie 124
The Empire Strikes Back (1980) 99
Eshelman, Cliff 135
Evans, Bernard 136
Expositions 68–69, 70–71, 85

The Fabulous Dorseys (1947) 126
Famous Monsters (periodical) 52
Fantasia (1940) 85, 118
Fessenden, R. 24
Fighting Devil Dogs (1936; serial) 55, 146
Fischinger, Oskar 118
Fisher, Max 124
Flash Gordon (1936; serial) 50, 55, 108, 152
Flash Gordon Conquers the Universe (1940; serial) 55
Flash Gordon's Trip to Mars (1938; serial) 55
Flettner, Anton 70
Folkart, Burt 140
Follies of 1929 (1929) 47
Forrest Gump (1994) 154
Foster, Dee (Vandercook) viii, 96
Foster, JoAnne (Keller) vii, 96
Foster, John v, 82, 96, 104, 108, 138, 150, 151, 187
Foster, Lois vii, 96
Foster, Mary (Taylor) viii, 96
Frankenstein (1931): Academy show 103, 106, 108; author's childhood experience 7, 9, 11; the making of 50–52
Frankenstein Island (1981) 99
Frankenstein Meets the Wolfman (1943) 85
Frankenweenie (1984) 138, 150
Frazier, Paul 60
Fry's Electronic Store 81

Garr, Teri 94, 95
Gernsback, Hugo 33, 34

Ghost of Frankenstein (1940) 85
Gibson, Hoot 47
Glen Oaks Memorial Park 21
Goldman, Harry 1, 7, 156, 208
Gone with the Wind (1939) 151
Gore Creatures #24 (periodical) *see* MacQueen, Scott
The Grapes of Wrath (book) *see* Steinbeck, John
Graves, Frank 52
The Great Depression Era 52, 53, 61, 85
The Great Dictator (1940) 151
The Great Radium Mystery (1919; serial) 78
Gregory, Howard 112
Gridiron immortals 89
Griffith Observatory 81, 82
Gunther, "Wuzzy" 135
Gutenberg, J. 74

Hall, Danny 52
Hall, Richard 90
Hanks, Tom 154
Harmony at Home (1930) 47
Harrison, William H. 72
Harryhausen, Ray 153
Hart, William S. 30
Hedges, Ralph E. 115–116
Hidden Dangers (1920; serial) 78
Hirschfeld, Gerald 94
Hitler, Adolf 48, 109
Hoag, Harry 16, 135
Hollywood Magic Castle 197
Hollywood Museum (Los Angeles) 90
Hollywood USO *see* United Service Organization
Hope, Bob 98
House of Dracula (1945) 86, 161, 183
House of Frankenstein (1944) 86
How Green Was My Valley (1941) 45
How to Make Things Electrical (book) 16
The Hun Within (1919) 30
The Hunchback of Notre Dame (1923) 45, 47
Hymowitz, Victor 82

IBEW (labor organization) 46, 88, 92, 189
IBEW Journal (periodical) 92, 208
Ice Follies of 1939 (1939) 85
The Illustrated Man (1969) 91
I'm a Man (1918) 30

Inceville 136
Induction Coils (book) *see* Norrie, H.S.
The Invisible Ray (1936) 50, 103, 108, 200
Ithaca College 89
It's Alive! The True Story of Frankenstein (documentary) 109

Janssen, Werner 127, 128
Jessie James Meets Frankenstein's Daughter (1966) 148–149
Jordan, Miriam 49
Jurassic Park (1993) 154
Just Imagine (1930) 47, 103, 106, 108

Karkus, Steve 116–118
Karloff, Boris 56, 57, 58, 59, 69, 79, 117–118, 152
Keller, JoAnne *see* Foster, JoAnne (Keller)
King of Jazz (1930) 126
KISS (rock group) 97
Kyriazi, Gary 28, 208

Lady, Let's Dance (1944) 126
Laemmle, Carl, Jr. 50
Laemmle, Carl, Sr. 45
Lang, Eddie 19, 20
Lassie Come Home (1943) 45
Lazenby, Lawrence 136
Lee, Gypsy Rose 112
Lee, Peggy 88
Lesser, Sol 111
Lindsay, Raymond 52, 118
Lockhart, June 91
Lodge, Sir Oliver 75
Loring, "Bake" 134–135
Los Angeles Herald Examiner (periodical) 74
Los Angeles Times (periodical) 140, 141, 208, 209
Lost Chords (book) *see* Sudhalter, Richard M.
The Lost City (1935; serial) 55, 80
Loy, Myrna 53, 57, 60

MacQueen, Scott 47, 208
Magnus effect 70
Man Made Monster (1941; aka *The Atomic Monster*) 85, 86
The Man Who Fell to Earth (1976) 96
The Man with Two Lives (1942) 85

212 Index

Manhunt of Mystery Island (1945; serial) 55, 86
The Manitou (1978) 98
Marconi, Guglielmo 16, 75
The Mask of Fu Manchu (1932) 49, 53, 55–60, 79, 103, 106, 107, 108, 152, 165, 167, 183
Master Minds (1949) 148
Mathewson, E.P. 66
Matthews, Grindell H. 48
Maui (HI) 20, 131
Mayes, Thorn 110–111
McDowell, Roddy 45
Melodia *see* Willard, Charles; Willard, Laura
Mercer, Johnny 19
Metronome (periodical) 20, 126
Metropolis (1926) 78
Modern Electrics (periodical) 16
The Monster and the Ape (1945; serial) 146–148
Monsterscene (periodical) *see* Harrison, William H.
Montgomery, Irv 135
Moon, Irwin vi
Moreland, Mantan 87
Morgan, Alfred P. 16
Motion picture studios: Biograph 136; Bison 136; Burbank (Warner Bros.) 67, 93; Circle Productions 148; Columbia 55, 67, 145, 190–191; Criterion Pictures 145; Disney 47, 67, 88, 118; Fox 46, 52, 103, 142; Kalen 136; Lasky 46; Lloyd 54; Mascot 55; Metropolitan (MGM) 42, 67, 87, 103; Monarch 54; Monogram 54; Nassour Studios 87; New World Productions 96; Paramount 46, 91; Pathé 48; PRC 86; Republic 55, 86; Universal 45, 50, 54, 55, 86, 103, 144; Warner Bros. *see* Burbank Studios
Murder at Dawn (1932) 50
Murder by Television (1935) 167, 200
My Lucky Star (1939) 112
Mysterious Doctor Satan (1940; serial) 55
Mystery Liner (1934) 54
Mystery Ranch (1932) 54, 162

Nagle, Ann 86
National Recovery Act (NRA) 84, 85
Natural History Museum (L.A. County) 193

Neighbor, Jacob L. 72
New Magic (1984) 140, 151
New York Times (periodical) 68
New York World (periodical) 74
Night Key (1937) 201
Norrie, H.S. 16

Obersetzer 114–115
O'Brien, George 54
Oldfield, Barney 134
Orchestra World (periodical) 20, 126
O'Sullivan, Maureen 53
Ovington, Earle 81, 82

Parker, Cecilia 54
The Perils of Pauline (1967) 200
Persons, Liz 132
The Phantom Creeps (1939; serial) 200
The Phantom of the Opera (1925) 45, 46, 47
The Phantom of the Opera (1929; with sound) 47
Pleasure Crazed (1929) 47
Popular Electricity (periodical) 16
Porter, Cole 98, 205
Powder (1995) 151
The Power God (1926; serial) 78
Price, Vincent 93
The Prussian Cur (1918) 30

Raiders of the Lost Ark (1981) 99
The Rainbow Trail (1932) 54, 130, 162
Rathbone, Basil 80
Reithmiller, Leo 135
Remenyi, Edourd 76
The Return of Sherlock Holmes (1929) 47
Rhapsody in Blue (1945) 126
Richardson, Sally 20
Riley, Chester (radio personality) 90
Rogers, Mary 53, 132, 133
Rogers, Will 53, 132, 133
The Romance of Elaine (1915; serial) 78
Romance of the Rio Grande (1929) 47
Roosevelt, Franklin D. 84

Sands, Eddie 135
Santa Monica (CA) 22, 23, 35, 41, 44, 45, 61, 88, 132, 133, 134, 136, 140, 188
Saticoy (CA) 136
Saturday Evening Post (periodical) *see* Eisenberg, A. and H.
The Scarlet Clue (1945) 87

Index

Schwarzenegger, A. 151, 152
Scott, John 60
Seder, Rufus 99
Sgt. Pepper's Lonely Hearts Club Band (1978) 98
The Shadow (1936) 50
Shadow of Chinatown (1936; serial) 146
Shaffer, Jim 96, 97, 108
Shelley, Mary W. 50
Sherlock Holmes (1932) 48, 49
Sherlock Holmes Faces Death (1943) 85
Sherman, Sam 91, 92, 111
Shipstad, Eddie 111
Showboat (1929) 47
Six Hours to Live (1932) 53
Sky Bandits (1940) 85, 145
Son of Frankenstein (1939) 80, 81, 103, 107, 152, 159, 200
Spangenberger, Carl 22, 42, 136
Stagecoach (1939) 151
Stanton, Jeffrey 28, 208
Star Wars (1977) 99, 151
Starlog (periodical) 140, 209
Starrett, Charles 57, 58
Steiger, Rod 91
Steinbeck, John 61
Stevens, Onslow 55, 144
Stokowski, Leopold 128
Stone, Andrew 111
Stone, John S. 75
Storrs, Less 136, 208
The Strange Case of Doctor Rx (1942) 85
Strickfaden, Carolyn 46, 85, 104
Strickfaden, Charles G. 14, 16–20, 22, 41, 100, 121–131, 135
Strickfaden, Francis (Frank) J. 12–13, 42, 86
Strickfaden, Frank L. 14, 20–21, 22, 121
Strickfaden, George P. 12
Strickfaden, Gladys (Ward) 22, 44, 98
Strickfaden, Kenneth: art 184–187, 195, 196; birth 14; death 139; education 24, 110, 188; favorite foods 113; film acting career 58–60; film and television chronology 199–205; laboratory, first 15; lecture tours 3, 7, 63–73; marriage 44; military service 30–33; musical talent 23, 115; New York to California auto trip 36–41; obituaries 140–141, 209; religion 5, 44; "Re-Memories" (of Early Santa Monica) 132–137; special electric effects, first 47; site of burial 140; title, "Mr. Electric" 52; winning magazine article 34
Strickfaden, Marilyn *see* Throssel, Marilyn (Strickfaden)
Strickfaden, Nancy L. *see* Creek, Nancy L.
Strickfaden, Pamela viii, 20
Strickfaden, Sally *see* Richardson, Sally
Strike Up the Band (1940) 126
Strong, Frederick F. 81–82, 192
Sudhalter, Richard M. 19

Taylor, Mary *see* Foster, Mary (Taylor)
TCBA (organization) 1, 7
TCBA NEWS (periodical) 7, 9, 141, 209
Teagarden, Charlie 19
Teagarden, Jack 19
Temple of Music *see* Willard, Charles; Willard, Laura
The Terminator (1984) 151, 152
Tesla, Nikola 16, 48, 74, 81, 115
Tesla coil 21, 23, 25, 33, 34, 74–83, 86, 97
Tetzlaff, Teddy 134
Thanks a Million (1935) 126
Throssel, Marilyn (Strickfaden) vii, 46, 113, 119–120, 132, 163, 195
Titanic (1997) 154
Toronto Star Weekly (periodical) 70
Torrence, Ernst 49
Transtrom, Henry L. 76
Trevert, Edward 16
Trillingham, C.C. 72
Trimpi, Allen H. 91
Tron (1982) 150
Trumbauer, Frank 20
Trumbull, Douglas 140
Twining, H.L. 16

unconfirmed film and television titles 204–205
Undersea Kingdom (1936; serial) 55
United Service Organization (USO) 85

Vallee, Rudy 126
Vandercook, Dee *see* Foster, Dee (Vandercook)
The Vanishing Shadow (1934; serial) 55, 144, 165
Variety (periodical) 99
Venuti, Joe 20

Index

Wallach, Eli 109–110
Walter, Paul 22, 135, 164
The War of the Worlds (1953) 87
Ward, Gladys *see* Strickfaden, Gladys (Ward)
Wayne, John 151, 154
Weston, Tobias 36, 37
Whale, James 50
White, Pearl 78
White Zombie (1932) 53, 199
Whiteman, Paul 17, 18, 124, 126–127
Willard, Charles 24, 25, 26, 27, 47
Willard, Laura 24, 25, 26, 27, 47
Williams, Guy 91

Williams, L.J. 66
Wings (1927) 46
Wireless Telegraphy and High Frequency Electricity (book) *see* Twining, H.L.
Wishart, Frank 134
Wizard of Oz (1939) 3, 151, 152
Wolves of Kultur (1918; serial) 78
Words and Music (1929) 47
Wysock, William C. 81, 102

You Can't Have Everything (1937) 112
Young Frankenstein (1974) 93–95, 103, 110, 152